Men's Violence Against Women

Theory, Research, and Activism

Men's Violence Against Women

Theory, Research, and Activism

Christopher Kilmartin
University of Mary Washington

Julie Allison
Pittsburg State University

LEA LAWRENCE ERLBAUM ASSOCIATES, PUBLISHERS
2007 Mahwah, New Jersey   London

Senior Acquisitions Editor: Debra Riegert
Editorial Assistant: Rebecca Larsen
Cover Design: Tomai Maridou
Full-Service Compositor: MidAtlantic Books & Journals, Inc.

This book was typeset in 11/13 pt. Garamond Book, Italic, Bold, and Bold Italic with Zapf Humanist.

Copyright ©2007 by Lawrence Erlbaum Associates, Inc.

All rights reserved. No part of this book may be reproduced in any form, by photostat, microform, retrieval system, or any other means, without prior written permission of the publisher.

Lawrence Erlbaum Associates, Inc., Publishers
10 Industrial Avenue
Mahwah, New Jersey 07430
www.erlbaum.com

CIP information for this volume can be obtained by contacting the Library of Congress.

ISBN 978–0–8058–5770–2 — 0–8058–5770–2 (case)
ISBN 978–0–8058–5771–9 — 0–8058–5771–0 (paper)
ISBN 978–1–4106–1752–1 — 1–4106–1752–1 (e book)

Books published by Lawrence Erlbaum Associates are printed on acid-free paper, and their bindings are chosen for strength and durability.

Printed in the United States of America
10 9 8 7 6 5 4 3 2 1

*For all the courageous women and men
who work tirelessly to bring an end
to gender-based violence
And for those of you willing to join the efforts*

Contents

Preface xiii
   Acknowledgments xv
Introduction xvii
   About Language xx

PART I: THE PROBLEM, THE PERPETRATOR, THE VICTIM   1

1 Understanding Gender-Based Violence   3

   Gender-Based Violence   5
   Power   6
   Rape and Sexual Assault   9
   The Prevalence of Rape and Sexual Assault   10
   Intimate Partner Violence   11
   The Prevalence of Intimate Partner Violence   12
      Box 1.1: Joel Steinberg: A Violent Offender   13
   The Cycle of Violence   16
      Box 1.2: The Power and Control Wheel   18
   Sexual Harassment   23
   The Prevalence of Sexual Harassment   25
   Stalking   27

viii • CONTENTS

       The Definition of Stalking   28
       Stalking: Incidence and Prevalence Rates   28
       Cyberstalking   29
    Male Victims of Gender-Based Violence   30
    Homophobia and Gender-Based Violence   30
       Box 1.3: The Murder of Matthew Sheppard   31
    Summary   32
    Key Terms   34
    Critical Thinking Questions   35

2 Understanding the Offender   37

    A Model for Understanding Offenders   37
       Box 2.1: Perspectives on the Claim: "All Males
       are Potential Rapists"   39
    Component #1: Pathology of the Perpetrator   41
    Sexual Assault and Rape   41
       Box 2.2: The Role of Alcohol in
       Gender-based Violence   42
       Box 2.3: Interview with a Rapist   47
    Intimate Partner Violence   46
       Box 2.4: Letter from a Batterer   52
    Stalkers   53
       Simple Obsessional   54
       Erotomanic   54
       Love Obsessional   55
    Sexual Harassment   55
    Component #2: Decision to Act Violently   56
    Component #3: Means to Do Harm   57
    Component #4: Social Support for Violence   58
    Summary   61
    Key Terms   62
    Critical Thinking Questions   63

3 The Survivors: Consequences of Gender-Based Violence   65

    A Survivor's Story   65
    Who are the Survivors   67
    The Financial Costs of Victimizing   69
    Psychological Consequences of Victimizing   70
    Shattered Assumptions   70

Posttraumatic Stress Disorder   72
Consequences of Sexual Assault and Rape   72
   Box 3.1: Rape Trauma Syndrome   73
Consequences of Intimate Partner Violence   74
Consequences of Intimate Partner Violence and Stalking   75
Consequences of Sexual Harassment   75
   Box 3.2: "Battered Woman Syndrome"   76
Factors Related to PTSD Symptomology or Diagnosis   77
Characteristics of the Abuse   78
Sex of Victim   79
Revictimization   79
Depression   80
Recovering from Gendered Violence   81
Social Cognitions   82
Social Support   82
Summary   83
Key Terms   83
   Box 3.3: An Interview with Katie Koestner   84
Critical Thinking Questions   87

PART II: THEORY   89

4 Social Perspectives: Attitudinal Foundations of Gender-based Violence   91

Attitudes   92
   Box 4.1: Learning from Dad   93
Cognitively Based Attitudes   93
Behaviorally Based Attitudes   94
Affectively Based Attitudes   94
Classically conditioned attitudes   94
Operantly conditioned attitudes   94
Explicit versus implicit attitudes   96
   Box 4.2: Modern Sexism   96
Prejudice   96
Stereotypes   97
Levels of Processing: Automatic and Controlled   97
Gender Stereotypes   98
Masculinity   98

Box 4.3: On Girly Men   99
Femininity   100
    Box 4.4: Being Powerful vs. Feeling Powerful   101
Hypermasculinity   100
    Box 4.5: Of Stereotypes and Substereotypes   102
Hyperfemininity   103
    Box 4.6: Chivalry   105
Cognitive Dissonance Theory   108
Summary   110
Key Terms   111
Critical Thinking Questions   112

5   The Big Picture   113

The Historical Foundations of Gender Inequality   114
A History of Gender and Labor   114
    Box 5.1: Imagining the Self as a Person
        of the Other Sex   117
Culture and Violence   120
Toward Solutions   124
Summary   125
Key Terms   126
Critical Thinking Questions   126

PART III: INTERVENTION AND PREVENTION   127

6   Responding to Gender-Based Violence: Intervention   129

Intervention for Survivors   130
Personal Intervention   130
Public Intervention   136
    Box 6.1: Reducing the Risk of Rape
        and Sexual Assault   138
Intervention with Perpetrators   137
    Box 6.2: The Criminal Justice System   140
Criminal Justice Intervention   140
Reporting Gender-based Violence   141
From Arrest to Conviction   141

Box 6.3: Denying the Reality
of Gender-Based Crime   142
Box 6.4: Reporting Rates for Gender-Based
Violent Crime   143
Box 6.5: Police Response Advocacy Intervention
Programming   146
Treatment for Perpetrators   148
Box 6.6: Sex Offender Community Notification   149
Box 6.7: Recidivism Rates Among Sex
Offenders   151
Treating Offenders of Intimate Partner Violence   153
Effectiveness of Intimate Partner Violence Programs   154
Box 6.8: The Duluth Model Control Log   155
Summary   157
Key Terms   157
Critical Thinking Questions   158

7 Gender-based Violence: Towards Prevention   159

Box 7.1: On Blame and Responsibility   160
Moving Towards Violence Prevention   162
The Involvement of Men   162
Box 7.2: Resistance Awareness vs. Prevention   163
Box 7.3: An Interview with Don McPherson   165
Box 7.4: Safe Dates: A Dating Violence
Prevention Curriculum   172
Types of Gender-based Violence-Prevention
Programs   173
Men and Women Doing Prevention Work   174
Women as Active Participants in the Movement   175
Goals of Violence-Prevention Programming
for Men   175
Box 7.5: "The Box" of Masculinity   177
Box 7.6: Having Healthy Relationships   181
Box 7.7: On Privilege   182
Summary   183
Key Terms   184
Critical Thinking Questions   184

8 Model Prevention Programs   187

The Social Norms Approach   188

Box 8.1: An Interview with Alan Berkowitz   190
Mentors in Violence Prevention   199
   Box 8.2: 10 Things Men Can Do
      to Prevent Gender Violence   200
Men Can Stop Rape   201
The White Ribbon Campaign   202
One in Four   203
The Fraternity Violence Education Project   204
Use of Theatre   205
Community Efforts   207
Summary   208
Key Terms   209
Critical Thinking Questions   209

9   Developing Violence Prevention Programs   211

A Brief History   214
Program Structure   215
   Box 9.1: Start-up Suggestions   216
Theoretical Foundations   218
Obtaining Effective Members   219
   Box 9.2: Membership Commitment   221
Educational Programming for Men Interested
   in Violence Prevention   220
Discussions   223
Activities   224
Using Media   225
Experts in the Community   227
Providing Education   227
Raising Awareness   228
   Box 9.3: Protocol for Presenting to Schools   229
Summary   231
   Box 9.4: A Peer Educator Experience   232
Critical Thinking Questions   233
Epilogue: Final Thoughts   235
Testimonials from Women Activists   236
Testimonials from Men Activists   237

Glossary   239
References   247

Preface

It is an open secret around the world that men's violence against women is an all-too-frequent occurrence that takes many forms such as rape, intimate partner violence, stalking, and sexual harassment. Only in the past few decades have legislators, educators, activists, and researchers directed concerted efforts at ending this scourge of victimization that undermines women's quality of life. As we will also argue, it also has demonstrable negative effects on men, even when they are not victims or victimizers.

Men's Violence Against Women: Theory, Research, and Activism is an attempt to provide a snapshot-in-time of the state of the art in prevention of and intervention for this nearly ubiquitous social problem. We have tried throughout to offer a balance of theory, research, and first-person narratives that will help the reader understand the issues from multiple viewpoints. This book can be used as a primary text in college and university courses on gender-based violence from the perspectives of a wide variety of academic disciplines. It can also serve as a secondary text in courses such as psychology or sociology of women, men, or gender, similar courses taught in other traditional departments, or in interdisciplinary areas like women's, men's, or gender studies. In addition, it can be a valuable resource for professionals working in prevention of and intervention for men's violence against women.

Part I (chapters 1-3) is a basic description of the problem. In chapter 1, we describe the prevalence and patterns of men's violence against women in its many forms. We also include case studies and basic definitions of various types of men's violence against women. Clinical perspectives help us to understand the motivations of criminals, as well as the behavioral, emotional, and cognitive reactions of the victim/survivor. Chapter 2 is a focus on the offenders: their psychologies and the social influences that impel their crimes. Embedded within this chapter is a basic model for understanding the attacker's behavior. Chapter 3 describes the survivors: the psychological, interpersonal, and financial impact of victimization and the process of recovery.

The causes of gender-based violence go well beyond individual psychology. Part II (chapters 4 & 5) provides an overview of theoretical perspectives on gender-based violence from social psychological and macrosocietal perspectives. Perpetrators commit their crimes within a social context of many influences by other people. Chapter 4 is an examination of those influences and an application of classic social psychological theory and research as it relates to the problem. In Chapter 5, we expand the frame further to include a "big picture" analysis of how larger societal factors such as division of labor, the economic bases of a culture, and public social structures can contribute to men's violence against women. Since these factors are in flux, we also hint at what we can expect when they evolve in a direction that we consider quite predictable.

The overarching purpose of this book is to inspire others to do research and engage in prevention and intervention work. With an understanding of the foundations of the problem as described in Parts I and II, readers are in position to develop their own programs and strategies for engaging in social justice work in their everyday lives. In Part III (chapters 6-9), we tell the story of various attempts to solve the problem. Chapter 6 describes the two oldest approaches: methods for helping the survivors to heal, and measures for holding perpetrators accountable, as well as educating them to avoid relapse. Chapters 7 through 9 describe an important and newer addition: prevention, the attempt to cause something not to happen. Chapter 7 describes the basic approach to addressing men as allies in violence prevention and working together with the women who have done this work for so long. In chapter 8, we describe the state of the art in violence prevention programs, a sample of curricula, activist efforts, and organizations that have been developed by dedicated people over the past two decades. Finally, in chapter 9, we describe the process by which one community developed a program, in the hopes that it might inspire others who wish to make a similar contribution.

The pedagogical features of *Men's Violence Against Women: Theory, Research, and Activism* help to structure the journey. In each chapter, we have included an introduction to set the stage for the subject matter and a summary to reinforce the major message of the chapter. Key terms are highlighted and listed at the end of each chapter, and definitions of each term can be found in the glossary at the back of the book. Questions for critical thinking invite the reader to consider, discuss, and debate relevant topics. You will also find many text box features throughout in which we provide personal narratives, interviews, and in-depth examinations of various concepts and issues.

ACKNOWLEDGMENTS

We are very grateful to the experts who read earlier drafts of the manuscript and made so many useful comments and suggestions: Connie Kirkland (George Mason University), Robert Rando (Wright State University), Marie Laberge (University of Delaware), Jonathan Schwartz (University of Houston), James O'Neil (University of Connecticut), and Andrea Parrot (Cornell University). Our editor at Erlbaum, Debra Riegert, and her assistants have been a pleasure to work with. Rhawnie Praiswater and Ryan Massey helped in the preparation of the manuscript and Ian Thomson designed the front cover. Visionaries Don McPherson, Alan Berkowitz, Katie Koestner, and David Lisak were gracious in allowing us to use interview material that we have reproduced in their entirety. Our partners, Allyson Poska and Russell Green; Julie Allison's children, Allison, Amanda, and David; and many friends and colleagues have provided much sustenance along the way.

Introduction

These are exciting times. After nearly four decades of hard work on the issue of gender-based violence, we are seeing a convergence of ideas and hope for a solution. The work has included (a) the development of theory, (b) the conduct of research, (c) the implementation of educational programs, and (d) the accomplishment of strong personal and public advocacy work. Professionals from diverse disciplines and backgrounds are now addressing the issues surrounding this problem. More and more women-and men-are becoming involved in efforts ultimately aimed at eradicating violence. As Mahatma Gandhi said, "The future depends on what we do in the present."

Research directed toward understanding the dynamics underlying gender-based violence and advocacy work on the issue increasingly results in support for individuals who are both directly and indirectly involved in gender-based violence. There are more services than ever available for survivors and greater efforts to hold perpetrators accountable for their crimes. Many activists continue to fight against political infrastructures that undermine the social justice process. But there is a long way to go. Despite four decades of this work, gender-based violence continues to exist in epidemic proportions.

The purpose of this book is threefold. A primary goal is to provide an overview of the current state of research and knowledge on gender-based violence. Although this violence takes many forms, we will focus upon four: (a) sexual assault and rape, (b) partner violence, (c) sexual harassment, and (d) stalking. The first section of this book is intended to provide the reader with a broad understanding of the issue: its foundational structure, prevalence, and the personal and social consequences of its existence. As social scientists, we rely upon empirical data to shape such an understanding. Given that gender-based violence is such a personal matter, however, we offer a balance to this empirical understanding through the inclusion of the personal stories of survivors, and the personal stories of perpetrators give us insight into their motivations and practices.

A second purpose of this book is to provide an overview of theoretical perspectives that can help us to understand the assumptions that guide our work, and importantly, to provide a structure for future efforts. Thus, we offer theoretical perspectives surrounding the issue of gender-based violence from both clinical and social psychology.

Clinical psychology offers insights into the minds and behaviors of individuals. From this perspective, it is critical to understand how an individual becomes motivated to engage in behavior that is abusive, violent, and illegal. There is an attitudinal structure that operates to justify and support the existence of abusive and violent behavior, and we need to learn how it is shaped in order to prevent its formation and/or intervene after the fact. It is also vitally important to understand the psychology of the survivor—the typical reactions to victimization and the process of recovery from it.

Gender-based violence also occurs within a social context. Social psychological theory offers an additional perspective that goes beyond a focus on individuals. When a person decides to commit such an act, he or she is basing that decision on an entire lifetime of experiences that are strongly influenced by other people. Through social psychology, we come to understand the social foundations of gender-based violence. These bases involve both public social structures (e.g., the criminal justice system) and relational factors (e.g., interpersonal influence by individuals or groups), each of which may serve to either encourage or inhibit violence. Because we are social beings who influence one another, anyone can contribute to the problem. These violence-encouraging behaviors can be as substantial as contributing to the character assassination of a rape survivor who reports the perpetrator's assault, or as seemingly trivial as responding to a friend's sexist comments with silence. Also, because of individual and institutional influence, everyone has the potential to play a role in violence prevention, from funding extensive programming or effecting changes in the law to confronting someone who behaves in sexist ways. The bystander role is not neutral; it either supports or challenges the violence.

Through the first two parts of this book, we lay a foundation for its third purpose: to encourage the research and practice of prevention work. As renowned social psychologist Kurt Lewin once noted, "There is nothing so practical as a good theory." The theoretical groundwork provided in Part II offers insights into important components of prevention work that are most likely to be effective, and are discussed in the third part of this book. We highlight prevention programs that may serve as models for readers who are interested in developing their own programs. We also encourage the reader to identify behavioral strategies that can be used in one's everyday life to help further the cause of social justice. We believe that small behavioral changes in individuals can serve to assist in catalyzing social transformation.

As coauthors, we share a common interest in gender issues, yet it arises from the somewhat different experiences of being socialized and living in a society as a man and as a woman. We share a common interest in the science of psychology, but were trained from different perspectives: clinical and social. We have attempted to synthesize the theoretical insights from these two great traditions. In this book, we argue that men and women must work both separately and together, with open and respectful dialogue that results in somewhat different but ultimately equal contributions to the goal of ending violence. While writing this book, we sought to model these basic tenets, and hope that our final product serves to bring us closer to this goal. There is no first and second author to this book—we contributed equally.

The foundational assumption of this book is that gender-based violence is a human issue that has strongly negative effects on women and men, in that order. We believe that most perpetrators of gender-based violence are male because this abusive behavior results from an unequal balance of power between men and women in our social world. This reality necessitates that men take an active role in contributing to the solution.

It is also true that most men are not perpetrators of gender-based violence, and that men can also be survivors. We acknowledge male survivors of violence and the intensified emotional consequences that they may experience; however, to parallel the statistical reality of gender-based violence—that males perpetrate most gender-based violence upon females—our focus will usually be on female survivors.

ABOUT LANGUAGE

Finally, we have crafted the language of this book very purposefully to reflect the reality of gender-based violence. Perpetrators of these crimes are responsible and accountable for their actions, a fact that we want to emphasize linguistically; therefore, where we describe an incident of gender-based violence, we use the active voice. Too often we have seen statements such as, "In 2002, more than a thousand women were victims of murder in their own homes." The victim is the subject of the sentence, and in fact, the perpetrator is not to be found. We prefer to say, "In 2002, male husbands, ex-husbands, boyfriends, and ex-boyfriends murdered over 1000 female partners." Since the perpetrator is responsible for the crime, he or she should be the subject of the sentence, the doer of the action. Because we consider it subtle victim blaming, we have taken care not to refer to violence as something that takes place "between" people, as nobody would say that a robbery, burglary, or fraud has this interactive quality. We are also careful to never refer to a perpetrator attacking "his" victim, as "his" implies male ownership of a woman, a truly sexist notion that supports gender inequality.

Saying that rape is an act of sexuality is like saying that hitting someone over the head with a frying pan is cooking; therefore, when we write about sexual assault or rape, we use nonsexual language in order to illustrate the horrors and consequences of the act. For example, instead of saying, "He held her down and had sex with her against her will," we say, "He held her down and forced his penis into her vagina." It is important to acknowledge that, during a rape, a victim is definitely not "having sex." As you will find throughout this book, one could also argue that the perpetrator is not either.

In many cases, we have allowed ourselves the language of "he" and "she" when speaking about perpetrators and victims, respectively. Although we take care to note that males are sometimes victims and females perpetrators, it is men who commit the vast majority of violations. Our perspective is that this kind of violence is a gendered issue, centered in the cultural meanings attached to being male or female in a sexist society, and we wanted our language to communicate that this is anything but a gender-neutral phenomenon. At the same time, we want to acknowledge that the vast majority of men are not violent in any way, and that there are clear differences between perpetrators and normal, healthier men.

Another linguistic distinction we have adopted is when we refer to those whom these criminals attack, we use the term "victim" to refer to people in the present and the immediate aftermath of the crime, and "survivor," a more empowering term, to refer to people in any later stage of recovery. We understand that to identify a person as "victim" or "survivor" has significant implications, and ultimately, of course, it is the person going through the recovery process that gets to decide if and when one of these terms is appropriate. We maintain the term "victim-blaming" because the blaming is almost always in reference to actions (or nonactions) that are engaged in by a person who is attacked prior to, during, or immediately after the attack. We recognize that fear of victim-blaming in survivors may be long-lasting.

All of this meticulous attention to terms and grammar may occasionally result in unusual linguistic constructions that seem awkward to the reader. In fact, they seemed quite awkward to us in writing this book, especially at first. But we have proceeded in this fashion because we know that writers can smuggle in ideas that they do not want to communicate, even in an unwitting way, and we are committed to doing whatever we can to avoid doing so. There is more than enough victim blaming in gender-based violence for us to add to it in even the most miniscule way.

Finally, we have both been involved in this work for many years and have seen the devastation that this violence wreaks. We are passionate about this issue and do not want to write in so dry a fashion as to suggest that it is not an emotional matter for us. You will see that, in many cases, we communicate our passion in our writing. Our doing so is entirely intentional.

Men's Violence Against Women

Theory, Research, and Activism

PART I

The Problem, the Perpetrator, the Victim

Chapter 1

Understanding Gender-based Violence

On July 29, 1993, U.S. Marine Joseph Holguin raped fellow Marine Sally Fictum. They had been jogging together on the beach at Camp Schwab on the island of Okinawa when Holguin threw Fictum down onto the sand, pulled off her shorts, and forced his penis into her vagina.

That day, Fictum reported the rape to the military police. She later said that she was humiliated by her commanders, denied trauma counseling, and investigated for lying. She was so distraught that she attempted suicide by taking a large quantity of pills. Eventually, she was medically discharged from the Marines due to emotional trauma from the rape.

Holguin changed his story three times. First, he claimed that no penetration occurred. Then he acknowledged penetration, but argued that Fictum had consented to it. Finally, he sank to the floor, hugging his knees, and acknowledged that Fictum had said "no" and had asked him to stop (His actions, therefore, meeting the legal definition of the crime of rape.). Despite this admission, Holguin's commanding officer dropped the charge of rape against Holguin, who therefore never served a day in jail nor suffered any kind of official penalty for his violent crime (Moffeit & Herdy, 2003).

Sally Fictum is now a third-grade teacher and a rape survivor. We begin with her story not only to illustrate how rape changes lives forever, but also because Joseph Holguin's rape of her is representative of many of the realities of gender-based violence and its aftermath in our society:

- The crime involved penile penetration of the vagina, an act typically associated with sexuality.
- The perpetrator knew the victim.
- The victim was met with suspicion and doubt.
- The perpetrator was not held accountable for his behavior.
- An organizational structure (in this case, the U.S. Military) that is founded upon gender inequality supported the unconscionable treatment of the victim and the exoneration of the perpetrator.

There are also some atypical features of Joseph Holguin's rape of Sally Fictum:

- The crime was reported. Sally's roommate called the Military Police after noticing that she was distraught. Sally recounted the events to the authorities a very short time after Holguin's assault. Most survivors do not report their victimization at all, and even when they do, it usually does not happen so quickly.
- The perpetrator eventually admitted to his crime. Most perpetrators do not.

Fast-forward to ten years later: July 2003. Kobe Bryant, arguably the best National Basketball Association (NBA) player of his time, was charged with Level III Sexual Assault by the State of Colorado. According to the victim's testimony during a preliminary hearing, Bryant grabbed her by the neck, bent her over a chair, and attacked her at her workplace, a hotel in which he was staying ("Bryant preliminary," 2003).

On the first day of preliminary hearings in the case, the defense attorney spoke the alleged victim's name six times, despite the presence of laws prohibiting lawyers from doing so. At one point, the attorney suggested that her injuries "might be consistent with a person who has had sex with three different men in three days." ("Bryant preliminary," 2003). In the ensuing events of the case, the defense strategy of Kobe Bryant's lawyers was to question the alleged victim's mental state and sexual morality, focusing suspicion on her and away from the alleged perpetrator. Attorney Scott Robinson described this set of tactics as the "nutty, slutty defense" ("Bryant's attorneys," 2004).

The pressures exerted upon the alleged victim eventually succeeded. She became reluctant to testify, as so many survivors are, and the charges were dropped. The public will never hear trial testimony about what happened that fateful July day. However, Kobe Bryant made the following statement:

> I do not question the motives of this young woman.... Although I truly believe [his penetration of her] was consensual, I recognize now that she did not and does not view this incident the same way I did. (courttv.com, 2004)

We emphasize here that Kobe Bryant has not been convicted of any crime and that we cannot call him a rapist. For sexual assault experts, however, Bryant's statement contains contradictory elements that some might view as an admission of guilt. "Consensual" means "mutually agreed upon"; therefore, if one person thinks that the act is consensual and the other does not, it is not consensual. Yet like Joseph Holguin, Kobe Bryant will never be held to criminal penalties for his actions.

GENDER-BASED VIOLENCE

Gender-based violence is any attack directed against a (usually female) person due, at least in part, to a disadvantaged position within male-dominated social systems.

The context that serves to support the current epidemic of men's violence against women is embedded within a complicated web of ***privilege, toxic masculinity,*** and ***patriarchy.*** We will argue throughout this book that incidents of this violence involve the abuse of power that is granted to males in patriarchal societies.

Gender-based violence is a global phenomenon (Watts & Zimmerman, 2002). In addition to rape or sexual assault, it includes (a) intimate partner violence (IPV), (b) sexual harassment, (c) stalking, (d) trafficking, (e) forced prostitution, (f) exploitation of labor, (g) debt bondage of women and girls, (h) sex-selective abortion, (i) physical and sexual violence against prostitutes, (j) female infanticide, (k) the deliberate neglect of girls relative to boys, and (l) rape in war. In spite of nearly four decades of social awareness campaigns, strenuous efforts by feminists to change both attitudes and laws, gender-based violence remains both pervasive and horribly destructive (Watts & Zimmerman, 2002).

POWER

The concept of power can be ambiguous (Forsythe, 1999). To some, it can be used to describe the influences, either positive or negative, that people of authority or in leadership positions have on the lives of their students, employees, children, and so forth. (Shaw, 1981). For many, it may create personal inspiration to grow and develop as a human being. Others believe that the term power should be reserved for describing coercive forms of social influence (Bachrach & Baratz, 1963; Weber, 1947).

From this analysis, we find that power could potentially lead to extremely constructive outcomes, as when a supportive parent offers structured guidance in his or her child's life, or a teacher guides his or her students towards success and opportunity. The positive potential of power encourages hope and possibilities. Conversely, power can be tremendously destructive in nature, such as in the case where a person of greater size, strength, or status uses these circumstances to impose himself or herself onto another human being.

For the purposes of this book, descriptions of the coercive elements and consequences of power are necessary in order to understand the foundations of gendered violence. The work of sociologist Max Weber (1947), done in the 1940s, still applies here. He defined power as "the probability that one actor within a social relationship will be in a position to carry out his [or her] will despite resistance" (p. 27). Although the context of a social relationship may not allow a full understanding of all forms of gendered violence, it is this context that may encourage violent choices and create vulnerability for those afforded less power than others. Ultimately, power involves one person imposing his or her will upon another, causing unwanted and undesired actions and outcomes.

In 1959, French and Raven laid the foundation for our understanding of power by identifying five distinct yet related bases of power. The effects of these bases may be additive. Hence, having power from two or more bases functionally increases its total amount in the power holder. Following, we examine each type of power base, and the implications of such power for gendered violence.

Reward power refers to the power holder's control over the positive and negative reinforcements desired by the target person. In the context of close relationships, we find much potential for reward power. Intimate partners have the ability to share in the duties of the household, offer intimacy and pleasure, or provide financial support—all positive reinforcements. **Negative reinforcement** is also known as *escape conditioning* (contrary to the popular belief that negative reinforcement is punishment). In this case, the reward is an escape from discomfort by performing a behavior (e.g., taking a pebble out of one's shoe, taking an analgesic to relieve a headache, turning down the volume on a radio that is loud enough to be painful). In violent relationships, negative reinforcement can provide critical reprieves from the abuse and violence, such as the victim's apologizing to the abuser for not pleasing him/her so that the abuser will stop yelling or hitting.

Coercive power refers to the power holder's ability to threaten and punish the target person. With regard to close relationships, we may find a sex difference. Certainly both males and females have the ability to threaten or punish their partners; however, the intensity of threats or potential threats for most men, because of their (usually) greater physical size and strength, is an advantage in power. French and Raven (1959) noted that although coercive power tactics may lead to compliance, it is not likely to lead to any internalized acceptance of the "rule" or order. In other words, behavioral change is short-term and temporary. Hence, coercive power holders may need to engage in constant surveillance of those whom they are overpowering in order to ensure their cooperation.

Legitimate power is a unique form of power because it stems from the target person's belief that the power holder has a justifiable right to make requests or demands of another person. This would be the case, for example, when doctors instruct their patients to undress, when children are ordered to attend school, or when employees are required to arrive at work at a certain time.

When applied to gendered violence, an absurd derivative of gender inequality is revealed: patriarchal culture grants men some degree of legitimate power over women. Hence, it may not seem unacceptable for a man in a relationship to make demands of his partner, but at the same time, it is not viewed as acceptable for a woman to command her partner to act in particular ways. Of course, the current state of affairs is not reasonable or justifiable in a nation that constitutionally professes equal rights for all, but it exists within the vast majority of cultures that are founded on patriarchy.

Referent power stems from one's identification with, attraction to, or respect for another person. Generally speaking, we seek to model our own behaviors and attitudes after those whom we like and respect. The influence that these individuals or groups have on our behavior and attitudes gives them referent power. In the context of gendered violence, it is not uncommon for individuals to commit violence against those whom they are attracted to, like, or even love. When respect is present, and power is relatively equal, violence is less likely to exist. In one batterer education group, depicted in the documentary *To Have and to Hold* (Lipman, 1982), a reforming batterer remarks that it surprised him that he found it very difficult to refer to his wife by name in group discussions, rather than just calling her "my wife." He acknowledged that calling her by name granted her the status of a person—an elementary level of respect—and that when he called her "my wife," she had the status of a mere possession.

Expert power exists when someone believes that another person has specific knowledge or skills that are superior to his or her own. Such a level of expertise offers the power holder unique status. Those males who commit gendered violence often believe in men's general superiority over women, and in their own superiority over specific women. These offenders will assume a level of expert power over women, whether or not it exists in reality.

Joseph Holguin's power was based on his advantage over Sally Fictum in physical strength and his position as a male in a military culture that denigrates women. Kobe Bryant's power derived from a corresponding advantage in physical strength, and also from his considerable wealth, celebrity status, and the social support of a culture that lionizes men who excel in the athletic world.

This is not to say that men are not victims and women are not offenders. Researchers are beginning to look more closely at the dynamics of other kinds of gender-based violence: both female-on-male and the myriad forms of intra-gender violence of men and women. Although these forms of gender-based violence go beyond the scope of this book, it is important for us to be concerned about women's violence towards men, as it is important that *all* victims receive compassion and support (Kimmel, 2002). Ultimately, a more thorough understanding of women's violence allows us to better understand other forms of gendered violence, and serves to make us all safer.

For all types of violence, the commonality is a quest for power. Individual cases of gender-based violence both reflect and reinforce larger societal inequities in women's and men's power. The experience of the alleged victim in the Kobe Bryant case served notice to women everywhere: "Do not dare accuse a man of rape; you will pay a heavy price."

As previously mentioned, gender-based violence comes in many shapes and forms. We will concentrate on four: (a) rape and sexual assault, (b) intimate partner violence, (c) stalking, and (d) sexual harassment. These crimes are both cause and effect of an inequitable power structure between the sexes. Hence, men's violence against women and gender inequity have a mutual dependence upon each other. For example, a woman whose husband beats her thinks that she cannot leave him because of her economic dependence on him, or because she is afraid that he will injure or kill her if she leaves. The maltreatment of a survivor of gender-based violence by the legal system and/or the media, which are largely controlled by conventionally gendered men, is intimidating to other survivors, who may fear that they will be re-traumatized if they come forward.

RAPE AND SEXUAL ASSAULT

Rape is a legal term. Thus, strict definitions of the crime of rape will vary depending upon state or federal statutes. Traditionally, the concept of *nonconsent* has served as a primary definitional element for rape (Estrich, 1987). That is, when sexual penetration occurs, and one person has not consented, it is rape. Note that the determination of guilt here is dependent upon the alleged victim's behavior. Recent trends in rape statutes have begun to venture away from defining rape solely the behavior of the victim and towards the behavior of the perpetrator (Spohn and Horney, 1992). We will follow this trend and define rape as a nonconsensual, coerced, or forced act of genital penetration or envelopment. The very act of rape is violent in nature, but rape may also be accompanied by additional acts of force and violence perpetrated by the offender (e.g., holding the victim down, shoving, and/or hitting). Such additional acts are not necessary, however, for a rape to occur.

Sexual assault includes any form of nonconsensual, coerced, or forced touching of areas of the body that are typically associated with sexuality, such as when a person grabs another person and forces his/her lips against that person's lips, or holds someone down in order to touch his or her genitals. Sexual assault does not involve sexual penetration or envelopment.

THE PREVALENCE OF RAPE AND SEXUAL ASSAULT

The rate of rape and sexual assault in the United States is alarmingly high. Some of the earliest research was undertaken by Eugene J. Kanin (1957), who found that offenders had victimized 30% of women in rapes or attempted rapes while on a date. Twenty years later, slightly reduced yet disturbingly similar results have been found: 25% of the women in one sample reported that an attacker had caused them to suffer from attempted or completed rape—again, within the context of an acquaintance or a relationship (Kanin & Parcell, 1977).

In 1987, Mary Koss and her colleagues (Koss, Gidycz, & Wisniewski, 1987) began publishing the results of a massive research endeavor conducted two years prior to publication. They sent research assistants to 32 randomly selected higher-education institutions across the United States to administer the Sexual Experiences Survey (SES), an instrument designed to assess participants' experiences with both consensual and nonconsensual touching and penetration, to a large sample: 2,974 men and 3,187 women.

Researchers asked only about victimization since age 14 in an effort to exclude child molestation and incest from these statistics. Of the female college students questioned, 15.3% reported that a man had raped them and 11.8% said that offenders had attempted to rape them; 11.2% of women reported that an offender had attempted to coerce them into some form of sexual contact, and attackers had touched 14.5% against their will. Koss and her colleagues estimated that, on average, perpetrators rape one out of every eight and sexually assault one out of every four young women on college campuses. Reporting on a period of only one year in their college careers, these 3,187 women reported a total of 328 rapes, 534 attempted rapes, 837 episodes of sexual coercion (penetration obtained through pressure), and 2,024 experiences of unwanted sexual contact (fondling, kissing, or petting without consent), an average of more than one victimization per person.

Kanin (1957) had planted the seeds, but it was the research of Koss and her colleagues (1987) that uncovered the reality of rape. It was particularly shocking to the public that many of these acts of violence took place in college and university settings, long considered an enclave of relative safety for women. For so long, the stereotypical rapist was a madman lurking behind the bushes, waiting for his victim to present herself (Parrot & Bechofer, 1997; Vobejda,

1995; Allison & Wrightsman, 1993). Through the research of Koss and her colleagues, we came to understand that this crime takes place all too frequently, and also that the rapist is much more likely to be a neighbor, classmate, or date than a stranger. Fully, 84% of the attacks reported by the women in this research were in cases in which they knew the attacker. Of the women in this sample who reported that men had assaulted them, 42% also said that they never told anyone about the attacks.

Subsequent research has confirmed the findings of Kanin and Koss. In a 1992 publication, *Rape in America: A Report to the Nation* (Kilpatrick, Edmunds, & Seymour, 1992), 13% of females in the sample indicated that a man had raped them at least once. In these assaults, 78% knew their attacker. In 2001, Patricia Rozee and Mary Koss reported on the current state of rape in the United States. In spite of continuing efforts at education, risk-reduction, and prevention, rape rates remain consistent at about 15% of all women. In this paper, entitled *Rape: A Century of Resistance*, Rozee and Koss noted that, "Gender is still the most powerful predictor of rape" (p. 295). Do not be misled into thinking that because 15% of women are victims, 15% of men are offenders. Recent research indicates that a relatively small number of men offend, but that most do so repeatedly (Lisak & Miller, 2002).

According to the U.S. Bureau of Justice Statistics (BJS) (2003), there is some evidence of a trend towards decreased rates of rape. BJS reports that in 2002, there were 247,730 rapes reported by individuals above the age of 12. This number is lower than the 248,250 reported in 2001, and much lower than the number generated in 1993: 485,000. It is important to note that these are reported rapes only for individuals above the age of 12, and that no independent scientific study has been done to corroborate these findings. Additionally, to have nearly a quarter of a million sexual assaults and rapes in one year still suggests that the culture remains conducive to rape. Changes in reported rapes, however, offer hope that efforts to reduce the rate of sexual assaults and rape may be beginning to succeed.

INTIMATE PARTNER VIOLENCE

Intimate partner violence (IPV) refers to physical, sexual, and/or psychological/emotional harm committed by a current or former partner or spouse. According to Basile and Saltzman (2002), such harm may be actual or threatened. Tjaden and Thoennes (2000) extend the possible repertoire of possible harm in IPV to include stalking behavior. Hence, the perpetration of IPV may involve an arsenal of tools, all intended to overpower and control. IPV is likely to be part of a relationship dynamic that evolves into a predictable pattern of violence. And, like sexual assault and rape, IPV is founded upon a power differential that affords the offender dominance and control over his/her victim. For a classic and horrifying example of intimate violence, see Box 1.1.

THE PREVALENCE OF IPV

Beginning around 1971, sociologists Richard Gelles and Murray Straus began to systematically study the extent of violence within married couples. They developed the Conflict Tactics Scale (CTS), and then, over the next decade and beyond, conducted extensive studies of men's and women's experiences with violence within their relationships.

In 1980, Gelles, Strauss, and Steinmetz revealed their findings from interviews with 2,146 individual family members. Their results revealed the extent of intimate violence in married relationships:

- 28% reported violence within their marriage.
- 12% reported that something had been thrown at a spouse.
- 28% reported pushing or shoving.
- 23% reported slapping.
- 14% had involved kicking, biting, or hitting with a fist.
- 15.5% reported hitting with an object.
- 10% had involved spouse beating.
- 9% experienced threats with guns or knives.
- 9% involved the actual use of guns or knives.

Violence has occurred in about one out of every four married couples surveyed, and the most severe levels of violence (e.g., use of weapon, beating) had occurred in about 1 out of every 10. These data also imply that threats about the use of a weapon often results in its actual use.

Interestingly, Gelles, Straus, and Steinmetz (1980, 1988) did not find any sex differences in their data; partners reported that women had been violent as often as men. However, they found sex differences in the kinds of violence that was used: wives were more likely to throw things or to hit their spouses with an object, while husbands reported being more likely to push or slap their partners.

BOX 1.1
Joel Steinberg: A Violent Offender

On the evening of November 1, 1987, successful New York City lawyer Joel Steinberg had a business meeting. His wife, Hedda Nussbaum, a former editor for Random House Publishing Company in New York City, would be watching their daughter Lisa (who, it turns out, was illegally adopted). Six-year old Lisa had wanted to go with her daddy to the meeting, so she went into the bathroom to ask him if he would take her along. Steinberg emerged from the bathroom with Lisa lying limp and unconscious in his arms. According to Nussbaum, Steinberg explained, "I knocked her down and she didn't want to get up again. This staring business had gotten to be too much." Steinberg put Lisa on the bathroom floor and left, telling Nussbaum to "relax, go with her." Hedda Nussbaum watched her unconscious daughter lying still on the bathroom floor until early morning, when she called police. Lisa had gone into a coma by the time they arrived, and she died a few hours later.

The public response of shock and disbelief that followed landed both Steinberg and Nussbaum on the covers of national newspapers and magazines. Charges were leveled against both for the death of their child, until months of investigation led the prosecution to drop the charges against Nussbaum in exchange for her testimony against Steinberg. The prosecution explained that Steinberg was a violent offender who had been physically and emotionally abusive to Nussbaum for years, rendering her unable to harm Lisa or to come to her aid.

The dynamics of Joel Steinberg and Hedda Nussbaum's relationship is an example of a classic abusive relationship that escalated to heights nearly beyond imagination. It began in 1975 as so many abusive relationships do: like a normal romantic encounter, and absent any of the violence or abuse. Nussbaum fell in love quickly: "Basically, I worshipped him. He was the most wonderful man I had ever met." Steinberg encouraged Nussbaum to succeed in her job, to build her self-confidence, or so it seemed. Steinberg was also giving her mixed signals; while he was building her up, he was also tearing her down, injecting cruel, yet often veiled, criticisms of her on a regular basis.

It took three years for the verbal power and control tactics exacted by Joel Steinberg to escalate into horrific physical violence.

BOX 1.1 *(continued)*

He beat her so badly that her face was permanently disfigured, broke her knee and ribs, choked her, burned her with a propane torch, knocked her teeth out, pulled out her hair, and poked her eyes with his fingers. This physical violence was accompanied by severe psychological abuse. He would call her names, constantly criticize her, and isolate her from her friends, family, and co-workers. Steinberg only allowed her to use the telephone when he was present, and then only with a speaker feature so that he could monitor her conversations.

The power and control tactics reported by Nussbaum in the months following Lisa's death seemed almost incredulous, paralleling many abusive relationships. Friends and family members find it difficult to believe that the man they know could commit heinous acts against his most intimate partner. Most often, these crimes take place behind closed doors, and the perpetrator may appear completely normal in public and when he/she is in the company of associates, family, and friends. It is precisely this "unbelievable" component of abusive relationships that serves to maintain the silence of its victims. The common cultural belief that the wife is responsible for the quality of the marital relationship contributes to frequent blaming of the victim.

The severe brutality of Joel's Steinberg's abuse might encourage one to create a psychological distance between this case and the "average" perpetrator of IPV. Although the severity of Steinberg's violence transcends that of many abusers, the dynamics of his relationship with Hedda Nussbaum is quite representative of many abusive relationships. Thus, Joel Steinberg is not an exception to the rule; rather, he is an icon of the violent offender.

Joel Steinberg has been released on parole, and, at this writing, he was continuing his pattern of minimizations and denials. When journalist John Lombardi asks him about what happened that fateful night of November 1, Steinberg responds angrily, "How do I know what happened? I wasn't even there!" Later, when they returned to the subject, Steinberg, again angry, provides a justification for why it was impossible for him to hurt Lisa: "If a man my size, with a fist as big as mine, hit you in the forehead, you'd hit the floor and have a mark you'd remember, . . . How come nobody saw nothing?" (Lombardi, 2004)

We must be careful with our interpretation of this finding of no sex differences. Simplistic interpretations could lead us to conclude that women are abusing men just as often as men are abusing women. A closer look at the CTS reveals a lack of context for the various behaviors in question. According to Stucky Halley (2004), every action assessed on the CTS is different when performed by a male than by a female. Although these data tell us that married men and women are both engaging in violent behavior, it does not tell us why. Walker (1979) offers an explanation. Men's violent behavior in relationships is more likely to be part of a pattern of power and control, and violence is his tool to acquire or maintain this dominance. Women's violence is more likely to be a defensive reaction to a partner's attack (Kimmel, 2002).

This is not to say that women never perpetrate violence as a means of power and control, but only to suggest that gender is a central feature of violence between partners. It is well documented that men's violence has more severe negative consequences than women's violence. According to the Federal Bureau of Investigation's (FBI) *Uniform Crime Report* (2002), male partners murdered 1045 women (601 wives and 444 girlfriends) compared with women partners murdering 287 men (133 husbands and 154 boyfriends). Thus, in about 78% of cases, women were the victims. The Crime Report also lists 3,217 murders of acquaintances for that year but does not break down this group by sex. Males accounted for 89.2% of those arrested for all murders in 2002.

Other men's violence within relationships also results in more serious injuries than women's violence, accounting for one-half of 15–44 year old females' hospital emergency room visits, prompting former United States Surgeon General C. Everett Koop to describe domestic violence as the number one health problem for women in the country (Cromwell & Burgess, 1996).

Research from the National Violence Against Women (NVAW) survey support the conclusion that IPV is overwhelmingly violence committed by men against women (Tjaden & Thoennes, 1998, 2000). In this study of 8,000 men and 8,000 women, women were 7 to 14 times more likely than men to report that their partners beat up, choked, or attempted to drown them, and threatened or actually used a gun against them. 93% of women and 88% of men who reported that someone raped or physically assaulted them after the age of 18 were the victims of male attackers.

More recent research also supports the high prevalence of IPV committed by men and against women. Worldwide, at least one in three women reports that a male partner has beaten or abused her at some point in her life (Heise, Ellsberg, & Gottemoeller, 1999).

THE CYCLE OF VIOLENCE

In 1979, psychologist Lenore Walker published *The Battered Woman*. Before that time, most individuals had not even heard the term. Walker had interviewed over 400 women about their experiences with the violence of their male partners and identified a pattern in the dynamics of the relationship of about two-thirds of the interviewees. Although this pattern does not explain all violent relationships, it has become widely known and serves to help us understand the dynamics of many.

According to Walker (1979), a violent relationship may begin in similar fashion to a "normal" romantic relationship: fascination with and idealization of the other person—the feeling of "falling in love" or infatuation. Relationships that later become based on power and control often begin with the offender being charming and wildly romantic. The couple spends hours together, talking on the phone and writing love notes to each other. Recall that Hedda Nussbaum said of her feelings about Joel Steinberg shortly after they met, "He was the most wonderful man I had ever met." If the offender were to begin to exert dominance right away, it would most likely result in rejection by his (or her) potential partner. The goal of the offender is to establish a commitment from the partner during this ***"honeymoon" phase*** as a prelude to his eventual domination over her. Once the relationship has solidified and the offender begins his abuse and violence, the partner must rectify her (or his) positive feelings about the partner with the negative ones that arise from the abuse in order to end the relationship. This course of action is quite difficult to undertake for most, as is explained later in this chapter.

Men who abuse their female partners are more likely than normal and more healthy men to accept ideologies that define masculinity as dominant and aggressive (Gondolf, 1988). As one recovered batterer stated in the documentary film *Until the Violence Stops* (Epstein, 2003), "When I got to the dating age, I always looked forward to a time that I was going with a girl long enough that I could slap her, hit her, because that was not only cool, but showed ownership.... There was an incident when my two-year-old son had to protect his mother from me." They also exhibit high levels of power motivation and have a strong tendency to blame their partners for their own problems and even for their own violent behavior (Cromwell & Burgess, 1996).

Motivations differ among batterers. Some have antisocial personality disorders and their abuse is part of a general pattern of violence. Others exhibit forms of serious psychopathology, and their violence is a byproduct of their mental illness. The most common type of batterer is the power-and-control type, who is rarely violent outside the home (Holtzworth-Munroe & Stuart, 1994). It is this type of batterer who exhibits the cyclical pattern we are describing that begins with the honeymoon phase (see Box 1.2 for a discussion of the "Power and Control Wheel." We will save the discussion of the other types for Chapter 2.

The *tension phase* follows after the excitement of the honeymoon fades and the offender begins to engage in (usually) "mild" violent acts and other forms of intimidation. He may push or shove his partner, yell at her as he angrily smashes his fist into the wall, or throw objects across the room. Following these events, both spouses will rationalize his violence with excuses about being stressed or angry ("He's been working so hard lately.") and almost always, both will believe that the woman was at fault for the violence ("I shouldn't have asked for money then," and "She shouldn't have burned the dinner."). By making this attribution, they are erroneously holding her accountable for his violent behavior and responsible for preventing his violence in the future.

The *explosion phase* is an intense, acute episode of violence, often causing major destruction, serious injury, or even death. If the woman survives, the violent event can serve as a trigger for the woman to leave her partner (Walker, 1979). Left alone, the offender may feel threatened, vulnerable, and even remorseful following the explosion. He often apologizes profusely and promises that he will never hit her again. Hence, the honeymoon phase begins anew. The violent offender becomes charming and sweet, and he does whatever he has to do in order to achieve his goal of getting his partner to re-commit to the relationship. On the other hand, if the woman leaves, her partner may become enraged and the woman may thus be at increased risk for his killing her.

Walker's conception of the cycle of violence was groundbreaking, serving to provide an understanding of the dynamics of many violent relationships and a name to the experiences of thousands of women. It is important to remember, however, that not all—and

BOX 1.2
The Power and Control Wheel

A group of activists created The *Alternatives to Battering Program* (ATB) in Duluth, Minnesota in 1982. This educational intervention program for abusive partners, which came to be known as the "Duluth Model,", requires those who use violence in their relationships to take responsibility for their actions and strives to help them understand their behavior. Ultimately, the program helps participants identify healthy alternative behaviors to the power and control tactics that serve as the foundation for abuse and violence.

The widely used "Power and Control Wheel" is part of the educational curriculum of ATB, and it identifies the different kinds of abuse that those who use violence in their relationships carry out. Violence in relationships does not happen in a vacuum, but rather is part of a systematic pattern. This context includes

BOX 1.2 *(continued)*

Isolation. Isolation is frequently one of the first control tactics used by a violent person in a relationship. At first, isolating tactics may seem flattering, such as comments as "I just love you so much, I want to spend all of our time together." Later in the relationship, as offenders gain more power and control, they may refuse to allow their partners to see their friends or family members, or make the costs of these visits simply too painful.

Emotional abuse. These tactics include put-downs and name calling, or playing "mind games." One man related a story to one of the co-authors: He would regularly tell his wife that she could go "garage sale shopping," an activity she greatly enjoyed, on Saturday afternoons. Then he would decide on Saturday if she could go or not.

Economic abuse. A person who uses violence in a relationship may prevent his partner from working or keep careful control of the household money. He might require her to "hand over" her paychecks.

Sexual abuse. Very often, physical violence is accompanied by sexual violence (Walker, 1979), which may include sexually humiliating a partner by forcing unwanted sexual acts, or through sexual objectification.

Using children. The presence of children serves as a very powerful force for keeping a partner in an abusive relationship. This may also include using the children as a "mediator" of the relationship, or using visitation as a way to harass.

Issuing threats. This may include intimidations such as threatening to hurt the partner or the children, or threatening suicide.

Using male privilege. Those who engage in abusive behaviors very often subscribe to traditional gender roles, and assume superior status over their partners. Using male privilege includes assuming that one's partner has a subservient role in the relationship, and making the "big" decisions.

Intimidation. Very often, physical size alone can serve to intimidate. Leading up to an explosion may be other kinds of intimidating behavior, such as putting holes in walls, throwing objects, yelling, driving extremely fast, using aggressive looks, or destroying property.

perhaps even not most—IPV relationships do not follow this cyclical and escalating pattern (Johnson, 1995); however, most are developmental in nature, beginning with good times and positive feelings (Douglas, 1991; Frieze & Browne, 1989).

Whenever the issue of IPV emerges in the public eye, people begin to ask the question "Why does she stay?" This is an important question, but it is critical to understand that merely asking this question first reflects a belief that male violence is inevitable ("Boys will be boys.") and that the only solution is for women to avoid or escape from violent men. Making "Why does she stay?" the primary point of inquiry thus subtly holds women responsible for controlling the violence of men.

Donald McPherson, former National Football League (NFL) quarterback and advocate against gender-based violence, described the all too familiar linguistic pattern that warps how people tend to think about violence against a partner (personal communication, 2001):

> Jack beats Jill
> becomes...
> Jill was beaten by Jack
> which becomes...
> Jill was beaten
> and
> Jill is a battered woman

Note how the victim becomes the subject of the sentence when passive voice is used in the second statement, and then the perpetrator completely disappears from the conversation, shifting the responsibility and blame from Jack to Jill. In our experience, many of the materials that antiviolence groups publish fall victim to this same linguistic trap. They often contain passive voice statements like, "In the United States, on average, a woman is beaten every 15 seconds." As we stated in our introduction, we are committed to using active voice in every sentence that describes violence in order to put the perpetrator at the center of the discussion and to emphasize his (or sometimes her) responsibility and accountability for the wrongful behavior. At the same time, "Why does she stay?" is an important question, which we will take up after we address the question that we believe should be the point of entry into the discussion: "Why would a man hit a person whom he loves?"

One model of gender-based violence (Kilmartin & Berkowitz, 2005) describes the problem as a product of three components.

First, there is pathology on the part of the perpetrator. Several researchers have described personality, behavioral, and personal history differences between perpetrators and normal or healthy men (Dutton & Starzomski, 1993; Hamby & Sugarman, 1996). Second is the decision to act violently. Regardless of the reality of a person's traumatic childhood or mental health problems, he is nonetheless responsible for his actions, except in the rare circumstances where he is psychotic and literally out of control of his behavior. The third condition is social support. As we have already noted, gender-based violence takes place in a social context that supports male dominance. Some forms of this social support are peer groups that regularly denigrate women in their conversations, families that communicate that men are more important than women, and media that glorify a violent masculinity. All three components must be present for a violent action to take place. See chapter 2 for more details on this model and further inquiry into the psychology of the perpetrator.

To the second question, "Why does she stay?", Lenore Walker argued that battered women have developed a sense of **learned helplessness** through the course of the relationship. Before describing this phenomenon as it pertains to survivors of IPV, it is instructive to revisit the original experiments in which the concept was developed. Note that this is an animal model for the phenomenon; we present it as a parallel to a human process and do not intend in any way to associate animals with human victims.

In 1965, psychologists Martin Seligman and Steve Maier became interested in how learning processes might affect the development of major depressive disorders. They set up an animal experiment to test the effects of inescapable punishment, using a device called a "shuttle box." This large box contained two compartments, separated by a barrier that experimenters could open or close. They used two groups of dogs in their experiment: an experimental group and a control group. With the shuttle barrier closed, dogs in the experimental group were exposed to mild electric shocks that they could not escape. The control group received no treatment. The experimenters then opened the barrier to the shuttle box and tested the dogs one at a time. When the control group dogs were shocked, they quickly jumped over a small wall and through the opening of the shuttle to the other side of the box and thus escaped the shock. The experimental group reacted very differently, as Seligman (1990) described:

> "The dog that had found that nothing it did mattered made no effort to escape, even though it could easily see over the low barrier to the shockless zone of the shuttlebox. Pathetically, it soon gave up and lay down, though it was regularly shocked by the box. It never found out that the shock could be escaped merely by jumping to the other side." (p. 23)

Thus, those exposed to inescapable punishment develop a tendency to not take control of their own behavior, even when control is possible. The experience of having no control over their punishment causes them to think that no control will ever be possible. Seligman's (1990) contention is that this is what happens when people become depressed: they learn pessimism, the belief that bad things will always happen, and helplessness, the belief that they are not agents in their own lives, and therefore they do not try to make good things (or at least non-bad things) happen. And Seligman and Maier's experimental group dogs also exhibited evidence of a depression-like emotional state: while they were receiving the shocks, they whimpered.

Although we are not suggesting in any way that dogs and human victims are somehow comparable, IPV victims/survivors may undergo a similar process when they are subject to arbitrary punishments by their partners. They try hard to conform their behavior to the partner's standards, to no avail. Therefore, the punishments are inescapable, and often without realizing it, they resign themselves to what seems like their fate and do not attempt to escape the abuse. Slowly, the partner assumes control over the relationship, her behavior, and ultimately her life. Nedda Hussbaum serves as a keen example of a woman who was broken down to the point that she really believed that she had no choices.

Experts on IPV often use another animal analogy to illustrate the seemingly incomprehensible incapacity of the victim to leave the relationship. If one throws a frog into a pot of boiling water, it will immediately make attempts to jump out. But if one puts the frog into a pot of cold water and turns up the heat gradually until it boils, the frog will remain in the pot until it dies. Likewise, if a partner begins his abuse during the honeymoon phase, the relationship will likely end. Abusive people know this, and so they are on their best behavior at the beginning of the relationship. They then gradually "turn up the heat," beginning with milder forms of violence and other abuse that escalates as the relationship goes on.

One other aspect of the Seligman-Maier experiment is salient here. The experimenters were able to "cure" the "depressed," whimpering dogs by picking them up and dragging them across the barrier into the safe side of the shuttlebox. Eventually, the dogs began to make this movement on their own, and the new behavior was permanent for 100 percent of the dogs. Again, the parallel between animal and human victims is unfortunate, and we in no way intend to make anything more than an illustration of a psychological phenomenon. But this research offers the hope that women who survive IPV relationships are capable of learning that they can direct their own lives.

We have described the stories of Sally Fictum, the alleged victim of Kobe Bryant, and Hedda Nussbaum. Their lives were changed forever when Joseph Holguin (an admitted but not convicted rapist), Kobe Bryant (who was neither tried nor convicted), and Joel Steinberg (the only one of the three who suffered any legal penalty) entered their lives. Joseph Holguin now lives a quiet life in California. Kobe Bryant continues to play in the NBA and makes millions of dollars. Joel Steinberg is out on parole.

SEXUAL HARASSMENT

Clarence Thomas was nominated to the Supreme Court of the United States by President George H. W. Bush in 1991. He underwent confirmation hearings from a United States Senate committee in October of that year. The testimony included that of Anita Hill, a University of Oklahoma law professor, who claimed that Thomas, when he was her supervisor at the Equal Employment Opportunity Commission (EEOC) in the early 1980s, had pressured her for sexual favors and made frequent lewd comments in the workplace. Thomas was eventually confirmed by the all-male Senate Judiciary Committee and, at this writing, continues to sit on the Court, but Hill's highly publicized testimony raised public awareness of sexual harassment (Jaschik-Herman & Fisk, 1995; DeAngelis, 1992).

Sexual harassment is a workplace protection issue, and several other high-profile political and corporate sexual harassment suits have since emerged, including settlements in the tens of millions of dollars against the Mitsubishi Motor Company and the Ford Motor Company.

The Equal Employment Opportunity Commission (EEOC) (1980) defined sexual harassment as

> "Unwelcome sexual advances, requests for sexual favors and other verbal or physical conduct of a sexual nature when submission to such conduct is made either explicitly or implicitly a term or condition of an individual's employment; submission or rejection of such conduct by an individual is used as the basis for employment decisions affecting the individual; or such conduct has the purpose or effect of unreasonably

interfering with an individual's work performance or creating an intimidating, hostile, or offensive working environment." (p. 25024)

There are three basic criteria for sexual harassment. First, it must be sexual (e.g., repeated requests to discuss one's sexual behavior) or gendered (e.g., negative comments about men or women) in nature. Second, it must be unwanted. It is not illegal to flirt, tell sexual jokes, or view (most) sexually oriented material in the workplace if all concerned are willing to do so. It is only harassing if the person who is the target of the behavior finds it to be uncomfortable, offensive, or intimidating. Third, the conduct must take place in the workplace, broadly defined beyond the physical confines of the work environment. If someone is attending a house party and a coworker approaches him or her with unwanted sexual attention, the result may be that the person who is targeted by the behavior is negatively affected in the workplace.

The U.S. government defines two forms of sexual harassment. *Quid pro quo sexual harassment* is an attempt to coerce sexual cooperation through a proposed exchange. For instance, a supervisor might threaten an employee with being fired or demoted if he or she refuses to have sex with the supervisor (*sexual extortion*), or the supervisor might offer a reward for sexual cooperation (*sexual bribery*), such as a raise in salary or a promotion. Threats or offers for rewards can be explicit, where the nature of the proposed exchange is clearly stated, or implicit, where the threat or offer is strongly suggested. Many sexually harassing behaviors meet the criteria stated above (sexual, unwanted, within the workplace) but are not severe or frequent enough to warrant a charge under Federal law or organizational policy. A single incident of quid pro quo harassment, however, is chargeable.

In *hostile environment sexual harassment*, the offender engages in unwelcome and offensive, pervasive, and frequent sexually oriented behavior in the workplace, and as a result, unreasonably interferes with another employee(s) work environment. Frequent sexually oriented jokes and comments, repeated pressure for dates, staring at a person in a sexual way, displaying sexually oriented photographs, or asking about sexual experiences are examples of hostile environment harassment, provided that the sexual attention is unwelcome.

A single instance of hostile environment harassment is rarely chargeable under the law or organizational policies. Rather, it must be a pattern of behavior that, according to the EEOC, can be characterized as "severe," "persistent," "pervasive," or "sustained." Thus the occasional "slip" in which a person makes an inappropriate but isolated comment will not sustain a charge, although this comment meets the basic three criteria (Thus, the person making the comment would do well to apologize and resolve to be more careful in the future). To be chargeable, the sexual behavior must have the effect of negatively affecting the offended person's working life, hence the term *environment*.

Sexual harassment law is part of Title VII of the Civil Rights Act of 1964 that forbids discrimination in employment based on sex (as well as other characteristics such as race). In Title IX of the Education Amendments of 1972 (best known for increased opportunities for women in athletics), the U.S. Department of Education defined schools as students' workplaces and conferred the same basic protections. Thus, all students are entitled to an educational environment free from sexual harassment. Schools must take all reasonable steps to prevent and/or remedy harassing behavior from faculty, administrators, other school staff, vendors, visitors, other students, and anyone else who interferes with the learning environment through sexually oriented behavior. Moreover, the school environment is defined in similar terms to the Title VII definition of the workplace to extend beyond the physical confines of a campus. Thus, students are entitled to protection when traveling to and participating in athletic events, working as interns, or attending school-sponsored academic events off campus. Schools and employers face legal liability when they knew or should have known that sexual harassment was taking place, and yet took inadequate steps to deal with it. As with their employees, they must take all reasonable steps to prevent sexual harassment of their students and provide swift remedies when given notice of its occurrence.

THE PREVALENCE OF SEXUAL HARASSMENT

Sexual harassers victimize an estimated 40% to 60% of female employees (Swisher, 1995) and 15% of male employees (Pryor, 1987) at some point during victims' working lives. Offenders victimize women who work in jobs traditionally dominated by men at even higher rates (Sandler & Shoop, 1997). Approximately 50% of female college students report that a male professor or instructor has sexually harassed them (Fitzgerald, 1993), and in a 1991 study, the Government Accounting Office (GAO) estimated that harassers victimized an estimated 97% of female students at U.S. Military academies (Scarborough, 2006). As with all gender-based violence, most sexual harassers are male. Recent estimates put the figure at around 90%. The overwhelming majority of victims are women (Kilmartin, 2005; Magley, Waldo, Drawgow, & Fitzgerald, 1999). Louise Fitzgerald (1993) cited 19 studies demonstrating that the average man defines sexual harassment much more narrowly than the average woman. Hence, it is more likely that a man will cross the more narrow boundaries identified by women concerning what constitutes sexual harassment, and become a sexual harasser.

When men are victims of sexual harassment, other men are the most frequent harassers (Street, Stafford, & Bruce, 2003). As opposed to sexual attention or sexual coercion, men's experiences of harassment are more likely to be gender-based (Stockdale, Visio, & Batra, 1999). Stockdale and colleagues suggested that those men who may be more likely to be targeted for harassment are less likely to fit the offender's gender-role conceptions of masculinity, a notion consistent with the power-based structure of gender-based crime.

More than one out of six women and one out of 20 men report having resigned from a job because of unwanted sexual behavior (Kilmartin, 2007). Nearly all suffer emotionally, and most victims even develop physical symptoms from the stress caused by sexual harassment (Crull, 1982; see chapter 3 for a more in-depth discussion on the consequences of sexual harassment). In reaction to unwanted attention from male professors and instructors, many college women drop courses, change majors, or transfer to other colleges (Fitzgerald, 1992). In the workplace, sexual harassment results in increased use of health insurance, higher absenteeism, lowered morale and productivity, and greater turnover, costing an estimated $6.7 million to each Fortune 500 company (Wagner, 1992).

As with all types of gender-based violence, sexual harassment involves an abuse of power. Men are much more likely than women to offend because they are more likely to be in positions of organizational power, such as in the role of supervisor or manager. Moreover, the culture of masculinity influences men to (a) view women as subservient and as sexual objects, (b) to associate manliness with dominance, and (c) to view sexual activity as an enterprise in which they must persistently pressure women until they achieve a conquest (Kilmartin, 2007). The workplace provides daily opportunities of access to potential targets.

The personality characteristics of sexual harassers are quite similar to those of sexual assault perpetrators (see chapter 2). As with other forms of gender-based violence, sexual harassment is a product of men's social control of women (Fitzgerald, 1993), even though most men do not offend. Solutions to this pervasive problem are legal, educational, cultural, and individual.

STALKING

Robert Bardo grew up in a family of nine in Tucson, Arizona. When he was 16, he became a fan of "My Sister Sam," a popular television situation comedy. The character of "Patti," the younger of two sisters, played by Rebecca Schaeffer, particularly captivated him. Bardo's enthrallment would soon spiral into a deadly obsession.

Bardo's disturbing behavior began with letters. Rebecca responded, writing that the letter he wrote to her was "the most beautiful" that she had ever received. She signed it, "With love from Rebecca." She became his idealized fantasy, destined to disappoint the unrealistic image that Bardo had created of her in his mind. Bardo recounted, "She came into my life in the right moment. She was brilliant, pretty, outrageous; her innocence impressed me. She turned into a goddess for me, an idol. Since then, I turned an atheist, I only adored her."

He tried to visit her at the studio where "My Sister Sam" was produced. He carried a teddy bear and a bouquet of roses for Rebecca, but the guards turned him away. He returned a month later, this time with a knife, and was again denied access to the actress. Soon after, Bardo wrote in his journal, "I don't lose. Period." (Ramsland, 2005)

It was shortly after this second visit that Bardo saw Rebecca's new movie *Class Struggle in Beverly Hills,* in which there is a bedroom scene involving Rebecca and one of the male actors. Bardo became enraged and intent on punishing Rebecca for her loss of innocence. He prepared to murder her. He obtained her home address in Los Angeles from the Department of Motor Vehicles, and traveled there from Tucson on July 17, 1989.

Bardo visited Rebecca at her home twice the next morning. The first time, he introduced himself as her "biggest fan" and asked her for her autograph. She closed the door after she thanked him and politely asked him to leave. The second time Rebecca opened the door, Bardo shot her point blank in the chest. She was dead within 30 minutes. Rebecca Schaeffer's last words: "Why? Why?" Bardo offered an explanation, in a letter to his sister: "I have an obsession with the unattainable. I have to eliminate what I cannot attain." (Ramsland, 2005)

The Definition of Stalking.

Reid Meloy, a psychologist who specializes in criminal behavior, defines *stalking* as "the willful, malicious and repeated following and harassing of another person." (1998, p. 2). Many laws, however, restrict the definition of stalking to require that the targeted person is actually threatened with harm. This legal element is a dangerous requirement for many victims of stalking, who are left without legal recourse if they cannot demonstrate a threat.

In spite of the legal loopholes, experts are beginning to suggesting that it is critical to involve the criminal justice system whether or not actual threats of harm have been issued. According to the Stalking Resource Center of the National Center for Victims of Crime (NCVC), traditional advice for victims of stalking has been to simply ignore the stalking (e.g., disconnect your phone, stay off the computer, and he'll go away); however, the stalker is pursuing the victim for a reason, and being ignored is likely to escalate the stalking behavior—the stalker will find a different, more aggressive means of producing their desired reaction in the victim. The NCVC suggests that, rather than ignoring the behavior, a victim of stalking should seek help from law enforcement or other trained professionals so that a safety plan can be identified, and the stalker can be confronted.

The suggestion that victims of stalking should not ignore the stalker in no way means that victims should necessarily confront their stalker. The NCVC notes that only if a stalker does not understand that his behavior is unwelcome and frightening will confrontation work. If stalking is deliberate in nature, confrontation—especially by the victim—will only increase the stalker's sense of power and control, and hence the behavior is likely to escalate. This pattern again points to the importance of seeking professional help, so that the stalking can be thoroughly assessed and a plan of action and safety can be identified.

Stalking: Incidence and Prevalence Rates

Between February and May, 1997, the National Institute of Justice and the Bureau of Justice Statistics cosponsored and conducted the National College Women Sexual Victimization Study (NCWSV), a representative phone survey of 4,446 female students at 223 colleges and universities. Women were first asked a question that served as a screening tool: "Since school began in fall 1996, has anyone—from a stranger to an ex-boyfriend—repeatedly followed you, watched you, phoned, written, e-mailed, or communicated with you in other ways that seemed obsessive and made you afraid or concerned for your safety?" Those who responded affirmatively to this question were then asked to complete an incident report.

Thirteen percent of the college women surveyed reported that someone had stalked them at some point since the beginning of that academic year (Fisher, Cullen, & Turner, 2000). Of these women, 80.3% of the victims knew or had seen the stalker before. Thirty percent reported emotional or psychological injury from the stalking behavior. In 15.3% of the incidents, the victim reported that the stalker either threatened or attempted to harm them, and in 10.3% of the incidents, the victim reported that the stalker forced or attempted sexual contact.

Note that these incidence rates would change if the NCWSV were to alter their definition of stalking behavior to include "threatened harm" as a criterion. In fact, the rate would drop precipitously from 13% down to 1.96%. Therefore, the discrepancy between these two stalking rates precludes about 85% of victims from seeking assistance from the criminal justice system if stalking laws are narrowly defined.

In order to assess prevalence rates, the National Institute of Justice and the Centers for Disease Control and Prevention cosponsored a nationally representative phone survey of 8,000 women and 8,000 men. This National Violence Against Women (NVAW) project defined stalking as "a course of conduct directed at a specific person that involves repeated visual or physical proximity, nonconsensual communication, or verbal, written or implied threats or a combination thereof, that would cause a reasonable person to fear." Based on the results of this research, the authors concluded that stalkers will victimize 1 out of 12 women and 1 out of 45 men at some point during the victim's lifetime. Stalkers victimize 1,006,970 women and 370,990 men annually (Tjaden & Thoennes, 1998).

Cyberstalking

Recently, the relatively new phenomenon of **cyberstalking** has received attention. According to the NCVC, it is defined as threatening behavior or unwanted advances directed at another using the internet and other forms of online and computer communications. D'Ovidio & Doyle (2003), however, incorporate the offender's intentions into a definition, arguing that cyberstalking is "the repeated use of the internet, e-mail, or related digital electronic communication devices to annoy, alarm, or threaten a specific individual or group of individuals." In 2000, as part of the Violence Against Women Act (VAWA), cyberstalking became part of the federal interstate stalking statute. The majority of states, however, have not begun to legally address this crime.

According to the NCVC, cyberstalking can take many forms, but generally proliferates among chat rooms and in unwanted e-mails. Stalkers may go so far as to destroy the personal files of the victim, or steal his or her identity (D'Ovidio & Doyle, 2003). As is the case with many stalkers, those who cyberstalk may escalate their stalking behavior.

MALE VICTIMS OF GENDER-BASED VIOLENCE

The power dynamics of violence extend beyond that of male on female violence. According to the Bureau of Justice Statistics (BJS), in 2002, for every crime—except sexual assault and rape—perpetrators victimized males at higher rates than females. In 2001, males were 76% of murder victims. Fully, 90% of those who committed murder in 2001 were male. When the offense was sex-related, male perpetrators accounted for 93.4% of crimes.

The perpetration of violence is deeply connected to conceptions and practices of masculinity in our society. Recall that violence is gender-based when it is based upon unequal power relationships between men and women and supported by patriarchy. Although male on male violence is obviously a vital concern, most of it is beyond the scope of this book, as it is not usually gender-based. The major exception is crimes against gay men.

HOMOPHOBIA AND GENDER-BASED VIOLENCE

In the movie, *The Sandlot*, young boys from different "sides of the street," each with their own baseball team, square off, as boys sometimes do, and trade insults. The final insult, "Oh yea, you play like a girl!" resulted in a long moment of silence and results in a fight, as there is no worse insult for a boy than say that he is like a girl. Because masculinity is culturally defined as ***antifemininity***, boys learn at a very early age that they should never do or say anything that would cause people to think that they are feminine.

Christopher Kilmartin often refers to ***homophobia***, the irrational fear of and/or intolerance for homosexuality, as "antifemininity's vicious little brother," as loving a man is a quintessential feminine behavior. Homophobia and antifemininity serve as tools for enforcing gender stereotypical behavior (DeCecco, 1984) and hence maintaining the inequitable power structure that exists between the sexes, as males who behave in feminine ways risk social and even physical punishment. Arguably, homophobia functions to support gender-based violence.

In their review of 28 cases of random school shooting in the United States since 1982, Kimmel and Mahler, (2003) argue that the interface of adolescent masculinity and homophobia is a major factor in this violence. In almost every case, the boys who opened fire at their peers and teachers had been mercilessly bullied on a regular basis, and the specific content of this bullying was homophobic. Putdowns like, "You play like a girl!" and insinuations that a boy is gay are commonplace in male-on-male insults (Kilmartin, 2007). The effects of such berating can be devastating, even fatal. For another example of homophobia that resulted in murder, see Box 1.3.

BOX 1.3
The Murder of Matthew Sheppard

On October 6, 1998, Aaron McKinney and Russell Henderson lured Matthew Shepherd, a 21-year- old, 120- pound, gay college student at the University of Wyoming, from a bar into their truck by convincing him that they were also gay. Once in the truck, McKinney pulled out a revolver and demanded that Sheppard hand over his wallet. Sheppard refused, and McKinney proceeded to beat him with the revolver.

Henderson, the driver of the truck, witnessed the beating. McKinney told Henderson to stop the truck and tie Shepard to a fence. Henderson complied while McKinney continued to beat Sheppard. They took his shoes and wallet and left Sheppard tied to the fence. He was discovered the next day and taken to a local hospital, where he later died from his injuries. His skull had been crushed severely and his brainstem fatally damaged.

McKinney's and Henderson's murder of Matthew Shepard is a story about the power of homophobia. They used Sheppard's homosexuality to get him into the truck, and there was a sense of overkill in their violence. They could easily have overpowered and robbed him, but instead their deep hatred of Sheppard's sexual orientation drove them to commit a gruesome murder.

Homophobia serves as a basis for **hate crimes** that attackers perpetrate against gay men. Research indicates that male perpetrators, most of them heterosexually self-identified, sexually assault as many as one in eight men during the victim's lifetime (King, 1992). Data collected for the 2002 National Crime Victimization Survey conducted by the Bureau of Justice found that 31,640 men reported that someone had raped them. Because of the pressures to remain silent when one has been sexually victimized, this number is likely an underestimate.

In 1998, the American Psychological Association identified violence against gay men and lesbians as the most socially accepted form of hate crime today. It is also pervasive. Herek, Cogan, & Gillis (1997) surveyed nearly 2,000 gay and lesbian individuals and found that roughly one in five females and one in four males had reported that someone had committed a hate crime against them at some time after they were 16 years old. Within the most recent five years of the time of the survey, the reports were that offenders victimized one in eight women and one in six men.

In every other form of gender-based violence, women are the primary victims. But it is interesting to note that, in the case of homophobia-motivated crimes against gays and lesbians, offenders target men more often. There is apparently nothing more threatening to the fabric of our gendered world than a gay man, who represents a challenge to male sexual dominance.

SUMMARY

Throughout this chapter, we have tried to emphasize two basic considerations. First, gender-based violence is extremely prevalent and negatively affects everyone's lives, either directly or indirectly. Second, gender-based violence is supported by an unequal power structure that confers more social and economic power to men than to women.

Since the feminist movement began in the 1970s and took on the issue of gender-based violence as one of its causes, social science scholars have learned much about the characteristics and dynamics surrounding the issue. At the same time, community activists founded women's shelters and crisis centers to help keep women safe. They also exerted educational efforts to teach girls and women how to make it less likely that an attacker will victimize them (***risk reduction***) or techniques to thwart an attacker (***resistance awareness***). In 1970, there were virtually no community support options for victims of violence within the home. Today, over 2,000 shelter and service programs exist across the nation. The National Coalition Against Domestic Violence (NCADV), with the help of Soroptimist International, distributes over 65,000 information packets annually, in six different languages. Thousands of individuals, primarily women, have been involved in this work, and hundreds of thousands of women and children have been served and supported because of those who do this work. But these efforts have scarcely reduced the alarmingly high incidence rates of gender-based violence. Our society has done a better job of supporting victims who come forward; however, victim and survivor interventions are not addressing the heart of the problem: the perpetrator.

Risk reduction and resistance awareness, aimed primarily at changing women's behavior, are important components of this work. The prevention of violence, however, requires men to become involved. Because men are responsible for committing the majority of acts of gender-based violence, men must be primarily responsible for keeping it from happening in the first place (Corcoran, 1992; Berkowitz, 1994), and yet men seem apparently reluctant to become involved in this work.

Our plan for this book is to review the currently available theory, research, and practice in understanding, intervening, and preventing gender-based violence. In Part I, we explore the individual and cultural dynamics underlying gender-based violence. Here we will explore the prevalence of gendered violence, the consequences for the victims and survivors, and the dynamics of the offender.

In Part II, we will offer historical and theoretical perspectives on gender-based violence from both a clinical and social psychological perspective. We believe that examining gendered violence from multiple angles and perspectives will help provide a more thorough and extensive understanding of the problem and point us toward effective strategies for prevention.

Using the perspectives discussed in the second section, we review psychological concepts focused on prevention, including program development, in Part III. We offer practical insights on techniques for initiating and sustaining men's involvement in prevention programming. Additionally, we will discuss strategies for maintaining a strong feminist approach to violence prevention programming that involves men, yet is accountable to women.

Earlier, we mentioned that men seem reluctant to become involved in prevention work of gender-based violence. For many years, gender-based violence was viewed as a "women's issue." We believe that gendered violence is a human issue that belongs to both males and females. We know that when men's violence against women is decreased, men's violence against men is also decreased. Reducing gendered violence is good for all of us (Kimmel, 2002).

Although a small number of men have been involved in this work for some time (Kilmartin, 2007), we believe that the time is ripe for more men to get involved. Indeed, research is beginning to suggest that men are more interested in the issue of gender-based violence than previously thought. Like many women, once they are involved in this work, most find it interesting and rewarding and find that they benefit personally from this work (Allison, 2005).

KEY TERMS

Attitude

Coercive power

Cyberstalking

Cycle of violence

Decision to act violently

Depression

Economic abuse

Emotional abuse

Expert power

Explosion phase

Gender-based violence

Honeymoon phase

Hostile environment sexual harassment

Infanticide

Intimate partner violence (IPV)

Intimidation

Isolation

Issuing threats

Learned helplessness

Legitimate power

Masculinity

Negative reinforcement

Old-fashioned sexism

Patriarchy

Personality disorder
Positive reinforcement
Power
Privilege
Punishment
Quid pro quo sexual harassment
Rape
Referent power
Reward power
Sexual abuse
Sexual assault
Sexual bribery
Sexual extortion
Sexual harassment
Social psychology
Stalking
Survivor
Tension phase
Toxic masculinity
Using children
Using male privilege
Victim

CRITICAL THINKING QUESTIONS

1. How can we account for the high prevalence rates of gender-based violence?
2. In what ways can language influence perceptions of both survivors and perpetrators of gender-based violence?
3. How do privilege, toxic masculinity, and patriarchy contribute to gender-based violence?
4. Using concepts discussed in this chapter, provide an explanation for why someone might abuse and use violence against his or her partner.
5. The definitions of specific crimes guide both personal and legal judgments about both perpetrators and victims/survivors of those crimes. Describe the potential effects of 1) including *non-consent* as a criterion for determining the verdict in cases of sexual assault or rape, and 2) requiring that a targeted person is actually threatened with harm prior to making a determination of the presence of stalking.

6. How is sexual harassment unique from the other forms of gender-based crimes discussed in this chapter? How is it similar to these crimes?
7. What is the relationship between homophobia and gender-based violence?

Chapter 2

Understanding the Offender

To structure our discussion of perpetrators of gender-based violence, we begin by presenting a simple model. Theoretically, four conditions must be present in order for a violent incident to take place. The first is ***pathology of the perpetrator***. Most men are not violent, and there is some compelling research that those who commit these crimes differ in several dimensions from normal and healthy men. At the same time, we should acknowledge that, with regard to sexual assault, men are often socialized to employ what we might call a "normative level of coercion." As activist Rus Ervin Funk (in Kilmartin & Funk, 2004) has pointed out, we socialize the typical male to follow a sexual script in which he first tries to kiss a woman. If she is willing to kiss him, at some point he tries to touch her breasts. If she says "no" or pushes his hand away, he should not interpret this refusal as meaning "no," but rather "try again later." If she is willing to kiss him but not to have him touch her breasts and he does so without asking, he has committed a sexual assault. If he does not ask and obtain verbal consent, he has to guess at what the girl or woman wants, and commits an assault if he guesses wrong. If he tries to talk or otherwise pressure her into participating in a sexual behavior that she does not want, he is also exerting a measure of coercion. As one of our female students once remarked, "If I say no and you ask again, that's pressure." At the same time, most males would comply with a partner's "no," at least in the moment, and very few would use physical coercion to complete a rape. We can acknowledge a normative level of coercion (which we should try to de-normalize) while at the same time distinguishing between the insensitive male who tries to touch his date's breasts when she does not want him to do so, and the rapist. For purposes of this discussion, we are focusing on non-normative levels of coercion, such as rape and domestic partner violence. See Box 2.1 for a discussion of rape propensities in "normal" men. Box 2.2 is a discussion of the role of alcohol in gender-based violence.

A second component is the ***decision to act violently***. Regardless of the unfortunate events in a man's history, he makes a choice to commit the violent act, and he is responsible and accountable for his actions. We may propose an exception to responsibility in the rare instance of extreme psychosis where the person is hallucinating or deluded to the point where he has little or no control over his actions, but this is a situation that occurs in an infinitesimally small proportion of cases. There is no contradiction between understanding the forces that might impel a perpetrator's actions (the pathology) but at the same time holding him responsible for his behavior (the decision).

A third aspect of gender-based violence is the ***means to do harm***. Perpetrators' tactics of intimidation, physical strength, and/or access to weapons provide this part of the formula.

The fourth component is ***social support for violence***, which usually occurs at both the microsocial and macrosocial levels. At the microsocial level, peers and acquaintances (most of whom are males) exert negative influences on the perpetrator through, for instance, communicating hateful and disrespectful attitudes toward women. At the macrosocial level, structural inequalities between the sexes and cultural beliefs about violence and about women contribute to an atmosphere that condones and/or encourages perpetration.

In the remainder of this chapter, we take a look at each component and apply it to various forms of gender-based violence.

BOX 2.1
Perspectives on the Claim: "All Males Are Potential Rapists"

In 1975, Susan Brownmiller published the groundbreaking book Against Our Will: Men, Women, and Rape. The primary thesis of this work is that the crime of rape is a means by which men-as-a-group subjugate women-as-a-group. She noted,

> Man's structural capacity to rape and women's corresponding structural vulnerability are as basic as the primal act itself. Had it not been for this accident of biology, an accommodation requiring the locking together of two separate parts, penis into vagina, there would be neither copulation nor rape as we know it.... Man's discovery that his genitals could serve as a weapon to generate fear must rank as one of the most important discoveries of prehistoric times. (1975, pp. 4-5)

On the motivations behind men's proclivity to rape, she wrote, "It is nothing more or less than a conscious process of intimidation by which all men keep all women in a state of fear" (p. 5).

Other scholars have concurred with Brownmiller's arguments, and the implication that all men are potential rapists. Melani and Fodaski (1974) claim that "we live in a culture that, at best, condones and at worst, encourages women to be perennial victims, men to be continual predators, and sexual relations to be fundamentally aggressive" (p. 84). Sanday (1981, 1990, 1996) also linked violence against women to cultures based on patriarchy. Although her research would reduce the power of the argument to a statement such as "All men raised in patriarchal societies have the potential to rape," this still would leave enormous numbers of men with the potential for enacting this violence.

There are both biological and social explanations for the argument that "all men are potential rapists." Proponents of the biological explanation argue that men's genitalia provide the tools of rape and that the act of sexual intercourse itself creates vulnerability in women to be raped by men. The social explanation argues that we live in a culture that supports and encourages predatory behavior in men.

> **BOX 2.1** *(continued)*
>
> But data do not support this conclusion. As we have repeatedly noted, the vast majority of men do not rape, beat, sexually harass, or stalk women. In her extensive research (discussed more thoroughly in chapter 1), Mary Koss found that about 9% of men acknowledged committing sexual assault. Assuming that this statistic is fairly accurate, if the other 91% are potential rapists, there must be some social force that inhibits this "natural" capacity.
>
> To account for the discrepancy between potentials and actualities, we must look at the assumptions set forth in this context:
>
> *Assumption 1. Men's genitalia provide the tool for rape.* This assumption rests on the following logic: "All men have penises," "Rape involves penetration of the vagina by the penis," and, therefore, "All men may rape." These logically compatible statements offer nothing in the way of explanatory power on the reasons for rape. Nearly all humans have eyes, but they are not all voyeurs. Most humans have cooking utensils that could be used as assault weapons, but they do not all assault. Men are potential rapists in the same way that all of us are potential robbers or murderers. We have the physical wherewithal to commit the acts, but most of us would not ever consider doing so.
>
> *Assumption 2. The very act of sexual intercourse requires penetration of the vagina by the penis.* By definition, rape involves penetration. The act of sexual intercourse, however, does not require penetration. Perhaps the social construction that defines the act of sexual intercourse guides the perception of the act as penetrating. Yet the act itself, if consensual, involves both the entering of the penis into the vagina and envelopment of the penis by the vagina, at the same time. To perceive the male as actor and the female as object is a socially constructed perception and is not necessarily a physical reality, although some theorists argue that invasive and subjugating penetration, even within consensual intercourse, is a socially constructed reality (cf. Dworkin, 1990).
>
> *Assumption 3. Cultures founded upon patriarchy encourage all men in that society to subjugate women through rape.* Patriarchal cultures encourage males to be dominant, to be in control, and to assume power. Although violence against women, including rape, is one means of establishing such power and control, it is not the only means available. Indeed, many men and women are able to obtain masculine standards of high status through more socially acceptable mechanisms (e.g., education, community leadership, etc.) and do not commit violence against women.

> **BOX 2.1** (continued)
> Although our arguments dispute the claim that all men are potential rapists, a cautionary note is warranted. All individuals raised in a patriarchal society are vulnerable to its influences, including an ideology that at worst reinforces the perpetration of gender-based violence, and at best justifies the majority of its incidents through lack of offender accountability, victim-blaming, or simply silence. It is important that we all pause to consider the personal impact that patriarchy has on us as social human beings.
>
> Importantly, the claim that all men are potential rapists may have the effect of normalizing rape, animalizing men, and alienating men as potential allies in the effort to prevent sexual assault. We think it remarkably insensitive to suggest that all men are potential rapists, just as it would be insulting to suggest to someone that he or she is a potential murderer.

COMPONENT #1: PATHOLOGY OF THE PERPETRATOR

Researchers have demonstrated that perpetrators of gender-based violence differ in important ways from normal, healthy men. Before discussing the characteristics of these criminals, it is important to note that in using the term *pathology* we are not suggesting that these men have a diagnosable mental disorder as defined by the standard psychiatric scheme (although some undoubtedly do). Rather, we are suggesting that most violence (except self-defense and perhaps hurting someone in order to prevent him or her from doing harm to others) by definition reflects a disturbance in the psyche of the person who undertakes it. For example, men who commit gender-based violent crimes, rather than not conforming to cultural standards of masculinity, often show an over-conformity to these ideologies ("**hypermasculinity**"). Thus they are "normal" in the sense that they are somewhat typical as cultural natives, but we define them as pathological in that some aspects of their personalities, when combined with situational influences, lead them to hurt other human beings.

Sexual Assault and Rape

The stereotypical rapist is the sex-starved, faceless stranger who seems to jump out of nowhere and attack an unsuspecting woman

> **BOX 2.2**
> **The Role of Alcohol in Gender-Based Violence**
>
> For many years, scholars have been paying attention to the role of alcohol consumption in both perpetrators and victims of gender-based violence. In several studies, researchers have demonstrated a pattern. To cite only a few, Rodriguez, Lasch, Chandra, and Lee (2001) found that alcohol use was correlated with patterns of mutual violence in couples. In an investigation of dating couples, Hammock and O'Hearn (2002) found that males' alcohol consumption was associated with higher levels of psychological abuse. Men in one study were eight times more likely to commit acts of violence against their partners on days when they had been drinking (Fals-Stewart, 2003). Other researchers found that both perpetrator and victim had been drinking prior to the majority of acquaintance rapes (Norris & Cubbins, 1992; Larimer, Lydum, Anderson, & Turner, 1999).
>
> Abbey, Clinton, McAuslan, Zawacki, & Buck (2002) found a relationship between perpetrators' alcohol use and aggression, but also a curvilinear effect in the association between alcohol consumption and the level of violence in a rape. The most severe injuries took place when the rapist was either very drunk or completely sober. They surmised that sober rapists may be able to plan and execute their attacks in instrumental ways and that very drunk rapists were more out of control than those who had consumed more moderately.
>
> Students in introductory psychology courses are often taught to remember this phrase, almost as a kind of mantra: "Correlation does not imply causation." In other words, the fact that two things go together does not tell us how or why they go together. Undoubtedly, alcohol is present in many episodes of gender-based violence, but that does not mean that it is the cause of the violence. The most compelling evidence that alcohol does not cause violence is in the large numbers of people who have consumed it, even in large quantities, without ever hurting another person.
>
> There are several ways in which alcohol and violence may be related:
>
> 1. When people drink, they are more likely to overestimate threats to the self. For example, a drunken man might perceive that his date has hostile intent in talking to another man at a party, whereas he might be quite comfortable with this same behavior when he is sober. When someone believes that someone else is hostile, they are more likely to respond with hostility of their own (Hanson Frieze, 2005).

> **BOX 2.2** *(continued)*
>
> 2. Alcohol reduces inhibitions, so the person who is able to restrain the self when aggressive feelings arise may have more difficulty in doing so when intoxicated.
> 3. Alcohol may reduce one's self-awareness and fear of punishment, which are strong inhibitors of violence (Curtin, Patrick, Lang, Cacioppo, & Birbaumer, 2001; Ito, Miller, & Pollock, 1996).
> 4. Men who drink may become more motivated to be seen as strong and powerful and may become more susceptible to others' encouragement to act aggressively (Quigley, Corbett, & Tedeschi, 2002). A misogynistic male peer group might provide this kind of influence.
> 5. People are more likely to misperceive sexual intent in others when they are drinking (Zawacki, Abbey, Buck, McAuslan, & Clinton-Sherrod, 2003).
> 6. Sexual assault attackers often drink with their victims as a strategy for reducing victims' ability to resist the attack.
>
> In a potentially violent situation, alcohol may well be like throwing gasoline on to a fire. If there is no fire, the gasoline will not cause damage. Men who do not have the propensity to commit violence will not become more aggressive when they drink. Therefore, we cannot say that alcohol causes violence, although the evidence is rather clear that it can exacerbate violent tendencies when they are already present. People who behave badly in all sorts of ways when they are drunk often use their alcohol consumption as a rationalization, but people who hit their partners after they have been drinking are as responsible and accountable for their behavior as a drunk who gets behind the wheel of a car and causes an accident.

in some public place (Allison & Wrightsman, 1993). Obviously, these kinds of perpetrators exist, but in more than 75% of rapes, the victim knows the attacker (Parrot and Bechofer, 1991; Vobejda, 1995). Sexual assault is especially evident on the college campus; Koss (1990) estimated that attackers attempt and/or complete raping 5% of female college students every year, and in most cases, the attacker is known to the victim.

How is it that the picture of the stereotypical rapist does not match that of the typical rapist? The ***availability heuristic*** is likely responsible for the discrepancy. This cognitive distortion is the tendency to make judgments on the basis of the ease in which specific kinds of information can be accessed in thought (Baron, Byrne, & Branscombe, 2006). For instance, most people are more anxious on an airplane than in an automobile despite the fact that, statistically, cars are more dangerous than planes. Although many more people die in traffic accidents than plane crashes, a plane crash always makes the national news; a car accident rarely does unless it involves something unusual, like a celebrity victim. Therefore, airplane disasters are more easily brought to mind than car crashes, e.g., they are more available to people's thoughts, and thus there is a tendency to overestimate their occurrence. Likewise, a stranger rape is more likely to meet with publicity than an acquaintance rape and so it contributes to the formation of an inaccurate stereotype. Victims of stranger rapes are also more likely to report the attack, further contributing to a skewed estimation of their occurrence.

Studies of rape perpetrators are quite rare for several reasons. First, the U.S. criminal justice system does not succeed in incarcerating an estimated 99% of rapists (Lisak & Miller, 2002), and so it is difficult to identify members of that population. Second, not surprisingly, rapists are not very willing participants in research studies. However, there are two researchers, Nicholas Groth and David Lisak, who have succeeded in conducting interesting studies of rapists. Groth's research is on incarcerated perpetrators; Lisak's is on rapists whom the criminal justice system has not held accountable for their crimes.

Groth (1979) interviewed over 500 men who were serving prison sentences for rape at the time of the research. Based on these interviews, he identified three primary motivations for rapists, including power, anger, and, less frequently, sadism. Groth notes that, although each of these motives may be present to some extent in most rapists, they may be classified according to the most powerful motivation.

Most (55%) of the convicted rapists in Groth's sample were identified as **_power rapists_**, those who attack their victims in order to compensate for feelings of inadequacy by dominating and controlling another human being. The power-motivated rapist perceives the act of rape as a conquest, a way of demonstrating his ultimate masculinity. This type of perpetrator typically uses only as much force as is necessary to achieve this conquest.

Groth described 40% of convicted perpetrators as **_anger rapists_**. These men perceived themselves as having been harmed by women and seek to avenge these "offenses" by hurting them. It is typical for an anger rapist to use a weapon, exert more force than necessary to subdue a victim, and include verbal abuse in his attack. The goal of the anger rapist is to hurt and humiliate the victim. As one anger rapist put it, "I wanted to knock the woman off her pedestal, and I felt rape was the worst thing I could do to her" (Groth, 1979, p. 14).

Much less common (5%) are **sadistic rapists** who are sexually aroused by violence and domination. The sadistic rapist fuses sexuality and aggression, and obtains narcissistic pleasure from observing the suffering of his victim.

As we noted at the outset of this section, the stereotype of the rapist is that he is sex-starved. There is ample evidence from Groth's study that this is not the case. Both power and anger rapists, who make up the vast majority (95%) of incarcerated perpetrators, tend to plan their attacks meticulously and are not sexually aroused at either the onset or the duration of the crime. Often they obtain erections by masturbating or forcing their victims to stimulate them. Many anger rapists do not ejaculate during the rape or do not even remember whether or not they experienced orgasms. Sadistic rapists eroticize violence, and so their attacks are more sexualized, but it is obviously a perverted sexuality. As one rapist told Groth (1979), "I wanted pleasure, but I had to prove something, that I could dominate a woman. I felt exhilarated during the rape. It was so intense that it took away from the sex itself. The sex part wasn't very good at all." (p. 95).

David Lisak and his colleagues have undertaken several studies involving surveys of large groups of men, mainly in university settings, about their histories of using sexual coercion. The surveys do not use the term "rape" because rapists tend not to define their attacks as such. However, descriptions in the survey questions meet the legal definition of rape or attempted rape, e.g., "Have you had sexual intercourse with an adult when she didn't want to because you used or threatened to use physical force (twisting her arm, holding her down, etc.) if she didn't cooperate?" (These questions were modified from Koss & Oros, 1982.) When a participant answers any of these questions in the affirmative, researchers attempt to have him agree to an extensive interview. There was no involvement in the criminal justice system for these crimes, thus this research involves descriptions of unincarcerated rapists.

In a recent study (Lisak & Miller, 2002), 6.4% (120 out of 1882) of research participants met the criteria for committing rape or attempted rape. Within this group of admitted criminals, 63% had committed more than one rape, averaging 5.8, and many had committed other crimes as well. All told, the 120 rapists in the study admitted responsibility for 1225 acts of interpersonal violence, including child physical and sexual abuse. The authors reported that this pattern of criminal behavior is similar to that of incarcerated sex offenders.

In Lisak and Roth's (1988) study, the researchers compared sexually aggressive men with matched control-group participants. Compared with the men in the control group, attackers tended to say that women had hurt or manipulated them in some way. In a later study with similar methodology (Lisak, 1991), rapists showed high levels of hostility, as well as anger and power as motivations for their behavior. Thus, they seem quite similar to the incarcerated rapists in Groth's (1979) study.

Lisak and colleagues have provided additional insights in their descriptions of sexual assault perpetrators. One unsurprising finding is that these men score quite high on indices of hypermasculinity (Lisak, 1991). They also tend to uncritically accept the hegemonic cultural definition of masculinity, which includes hostility toward women (e.g., misogyny).

A straightforward interpretation of psychoanalytic theory might include the supposition that men who rape women harbor resentment toward their mothers. However, Lisak (1991) found that these men's feelings about their mothers were widely variable. On the other hand, rapists and attempted rapists were invariably bitter toward and disappointed with their fathers, whom they described as emotionally unavailable, abusive, and sometimes physically violent towards them. Lacking affirmation and love from this all-important male figure in their lives and accepting the woman-hating core of toxic masculinity, these men project their anger onto women and use an "I'm just having sex" rationale to attack them. See Box 2.3 for an actual interview with a rapist.

Intimate Partner Violence

Research describing partner-violence perpetrators reveals a variety of personality characteristics, histories, and behavioral patterns. In general, male batterers adhere strongly to masculine ideologies (Schwartz, Waldo, & Daniel, 2005; Jacupak, Lisak, & Roemer, 2002), and to the beliefs that violence is a justifiable means for problem solving and that men should control their female partners (Gondolf, 1988). They are often survivors of some form of childhood abuse and often witnessed violence between their parents when

BOX 2.3
Interview with a Rapist

The following transcript is from Dr. David Lisak's interview with a rapist. A videotape dramatization of the interview, "The Undetected Rapist," is available from the National Judicial Education Program (njep@nowldef.org).

Frank: We had parties almost every weekend. My fraternity was known for that. We would invite a bunch of girls and lay out the kegs or whatever we were drinking that night and everyone would get plastered. We would invite girls, all of us in the fraternity. We'd be on the lookout for good-looking girls, especially freshmen, the real young ones. They were the easiest, it's like we knew they wouldn't know the ropes kind of, it's like they were easy prey. They wouldn't know anything about drinking, about how much alcohol they could manage, and they wouldn't know anything about our techniques.

Interviewer: What were those techniques?

Frank: We'd invite them to the party and we'd make it seem like it was a real honor, like we didn't just invite any girl, which I guess is true [laughs]. And we'd get them drinking right away. We'd have a bunch of kegs but we almost always had some kind of punch also, it was almost like our own home brew. We'd make it real sweet, you know, we'd use some kind of sweet juice and then we'd just throw in all kinds of alcohol. It was powerful stuff. And these girls wouldn't know what hit them. They'd all be just guzzling the stuff because it was just juice, right? And they were so nervous being there because they were just freshmen anyway.

Interviewer: When you say it was just juice, you mean the girls wouldn't know it was spiked with alcohol?

Frank: They would know; they knew that. At least the smart ones did. I mean, this was a party, not some kind of social tea, so I think they must have known, or most of them did anyway. The ones that didn't had to be real naïve.

Interviewer: Did you count on them being naïve?

Frank: Yeah, I guess in a way we did. The real young and naïve ones were the easiest. They'd be plastered in minutes and they'd be our real targets.

Interviewer: What do you mean by "targets"?

Frank: That's when one of us would make a move. By then each girl would be kind of staked out, meaning one of the guys would be working on her, getting her drinks, keeping the juices flowing, so to speak. And you had to kind of pick your moment to make your move, you know, you basically had to have an instinct for it.

BOX 2.3 *(continued)*

Interviewer: Can you describe what happened on the specific occasion you referred to in your questionnaire?

Frank: Yeah, sure. I had this girl staked out. I had picked her out in one of my classes and worked on her and she was all prepped. I was watching for her and as soon as she walked out the door at the party I was on her. She was a good-looking girl, too. We started drinking together and I could tell she was real nervous because she was drinking that stuff so fast.

Interviewer: What was she drinking?

Frank: It was some kind of punch we had made, the usual thing.

Interviewer: Did she know it was spiked with alcohol?

Frank: I don't really know, although she must have after awhile. She had to know because she was plastered in minutes, and I started making moves on her. You know, I kind of leaned in close, got my arm around her, then at the right moment I kissed her and then moved in closer. You know, the usual kind of stuff. It was no surprise to her, I'm sure she'd done it a thousand times before. After a while I asked her to come up to my room to get away from all the noise and she came right away. Well, actually it wasn't my room. We always had several rooms designated before the party that were prepared for this.

Interviewer: Designated rooms?

Frank: Yeah, we'd set aside a few rooms to bring these girls up to once they were ready.

Interviewer: What happened when you got to the designated room?

Frank: She was real woozy by this time and I brought up another drink for her and sat her on one of the beds and I sat next to her and pretty soon I just made my move. I don't remember exactly what happened first. I probably leaned her down onto the bed and started working on her clothes, feeling her up.

Interviewer: How did she respond?

Frank: I don't remember. I started working her blouse off and I think she might have said something, but I don't remember. I didn't expect her to get into it right away.

Interviewer: Did she say anything?

BOX 2.3 (continued)

Frank: Yeah, at one point she started saying like she didn't want to do this right away or something like that. I just kept working on her clothes. And she started squirming but that actually helped because her blouse came off easier. Then I kind of leaned over her more and kept feeling her up to get her into it more, and then she tried to push me off of her with her hands and I pushed her down.

Interviewer: Were you angry?

Frank: Naw, but it did piss me off that she played along the whole way and then decided to squirm out of it like that in the end. I mean she was so plastered I don't really think she knew what was going on anyway, and maybe that's why she started pushing me. I just leaned on her and kept pulling off her clothes and at some point she stopped squirming. Maybe she passed out. Her eyes were closed.

Interviewer: What happened?

Frank: I fucked her.

Interviewer: Did you have to lean on her, hold her down when you did it?

Frank: Yeah, I had my arm across the top of her chest like this [demonstrates]. And that's how I did it.

Interviewer: Was she squirming?

Frank: Yeah, she was squirming, but not that much anymore.

Interviewer: What happened afterwards?

Frank: I got dressed and went back to the party.

Interviewer: What did she do?

Frank: She left.

Dr. Lisak Comments:

There are many things I think we can learn from this very disturbing interview. Most notably are some of Frank's terms—the language he uses. He uses terms like "prey," "targets," "staked out." These are all words that serve to dehumanize his victim, and they're the common language amongst criminals. It's also notable that Frank exhibits no empathy for his victim. At a time when she's experiencing extreme terror, his reaction is one of anger, not empathy, for her state. He also minimizes his violence and sanitizes it. If you remember in that reenactment, he demonstrates—he says—that he put his arm across the top of her chest. What he really shows is his arm across the woman's windpipe, which is probably blocking off her breathing and undoubtedly causing her immense terror.

they were young (Grusznski & Bankovics, 1990). They have a strong tendency to blame their partners and/or external circumstances for their violence (Cromwell & Burgess, 1996). Therefore, they blame the victim and abdicate responsibility for their own behavior. When a person sees the source of his or her problems as outside of the self, behavioral change is quite difficult. A batterer's belief that he hit his partner because she behaved badly results in the belief that the only means for him to stop being violent would be a modification in his partner's behavior. As we have already seen, many victims go to extreme lengths to adapt their behavior to their attackers' wishes, usually to no avail, as the source of the violence does not lie in the behavior of the victim.

The perception of one's own problems as originating outside of the self is one of the hallmarks of ***personality disorder***, an enduring pattern of behavior and inner experience that results in interpersonal inflexibility and disturbed relationships (American Psychiatric Association, 2000), and indeed, as many as 84% of abusive men show significant personality disturbances. In addition, most have alcohol abuse and anger control problems, and many have significant psychopathologies such as depression, anxiety, or thought disorders (Segal, Stewart, Peck, & Coolidge, 2000; Gondolf, 1995).

Holtzworth-Munroe & Stuart (1994) described three subtypes of abusers. The first is the highly dominant and narcissistic aggressor. This person's violence is in the service of controlling his partner in order to bolster his fragile sense of self-esteem. A second type is the jealous and dependent man who uses violence to control his partner because he is fearful that she will leave him. (Note the self-defeating aspect of this pattern. Jealous and dependent people tend to alienate their partners, resulting in the dissolution of the relationship.) The third category is the antisocial aggressor, who tends to engage in violence and/or other criminality outside of the home. For this group, interpersonal violence is part of a general pattern of violating others' rights. Recently, Holtzworth-Munroe and her colleagues, (Holtzworth-Munroe 2000; Holtzworth-Munroe, Meehan, Herron, Rehman, & Stuart, 2001) have suggested the inclusion of a fourth category to account for the heterogeneity found in partner violence: a low-level (subclinical) antisocial personality.

One other important dimension of batterers is the extent to which they are proactive or reactive. ***Proactive batterers***, sometimes referred to as "control freaks," are calculating in their violence, use it in the service of extreme domination of others, and are probably most similar to the narcissistic aggressor and antisocial types. Indeed, the heart-rate of some batterers actually slows down during an attack, supporting the view that their violence is not a reaction to rage, which would elevate the heart rate (Jacobson, 1993). One of the authors (JA) remembers a statement made by one particular batterer during a batterer's group: "I would decide when I stepped on the front porch whether we would have a good night, or a bad night."

Reactive batterers are more emotionally volatile. They can be described as men who "experience a constellation of feelings involving rage and jealousy. They find ways of misinterpreting and blaming their partners, holding them responsible for their own feelings of despondency, making impossible demands on them, and punishing them for inevitably failing" (Dutton & Golant, 1995, p. 34) (See Box 2.4 for a compelling example of a batterer). Narcissistic/dominant and jealous/dependent men are probably most appropriate for typical batterer education, which tends to emphasize power and control issues as well as anger management. Antisocial men are difficult to rehabilitate, and therefore prevention of future violence is best concentrated on criminal justice sanctions.

Lynch & Kilmartin (1999) describe the highly conflicted inner life of the jealous/dependent man, who has severe problems in resolving mixed feelings about attachment/separation and intimacy with his partner. The authors describe this conflict as the masculine dilemma: "not too close, not too far away." The relationship begins as most do, with a "honeymoon" phase in which there is little conflict and both partners are comfortable with being close. But after a time, his partner's intimacy feels intrusive and eventually overwhelms the man with anxiety. The battering incident is an extreme strategy for creating psychological distance from his partner. After the battering incident, however, he is flooded with his dependency needs and experiences his partner as too far away, so he responds by apologizing, promising to never hit her again, and trying to win her back with more "honeymoon" behaviors, as the cycle starts over again. Dutton & Golant (1995) exemplified a batterer's extreme ambivalence: "He would tell her to get out, and when she packed her bags, he would beg her to stay" (p. 37).

Everyone has ambivalence about intimacy and couples are always negotiating psychological space. However, batterers differ from normal, healthy people in that they lack both the insight and the skills to undertake this negotiation in nonviolent ways. Part of the conflict is centered in masculine socialization, as boys are told from an early age that being like a girl or spending time with girls makes

BOX 2.4
Letter from a Batterer

The following letter was written by a batterer to his wife and was sent to her while she was in shelter. It is entitled, "My Dearest," and vividly demonstrates the batterer's feelings of interpersonal superiority over his partner, demands for control in the relationship, minimization of his own abusive behavior, and sexual jealousy.

My Dearest:
You have been, and are being, a fool. No man before, now, or ever, has, and will love you like I. No man would ever put up with the things that I have.

This is not a plea for you to come back, so don't take it as one. Of course I want you back, but only if you agree to the following five terms.

1. *We will stop drinking—period—end of discussion.*

2. *I am cutting back smoking—when I get below you, you too will cut back with the goal being to quit soon.*

3. *I have learned the value of walking and exercise. You will try to walk with me everyday. I would not expect you to go as far or as fast, but I do expect you to make some effort.*

4. *I will have a vehicle at work. If you must take me to and from home, so be it. I have learned to deal with that.*

5. *You will not leave home anymore. People tell me you do that, because you're screwing around.*

I don't believe that.
Here are my goals with and with out you:
MYSELF- To stop drinking forever
To stop smoking forever
To keep up my walking
To get the shop rolling real good
To enjoy life
To get back to helping on old buildings
TOGETHER- All of the above
Get the house completed and ready to sell
Move to the country

> **BOX 2.4** *(continued)*
>
> *Take care of each other*
>
> *This is my last ditch effort to get us on track and living the life we both deserve. Yes, I was quite short with you Monday morning, but it was very upsetting to be left for three nights.*
>
> *Well there you have it, my hopes my goals, and my demands. Take 'em or leave 'em. It's high time we both got our acts together, and you know it.*
>
> *The bottom line is this.*
>
> *Do I love You? Yes without a doubt.*
>
> *Will I be a good husband? Yes*
>
> *Will I be intimidated and bullied by you? No*
>
> *We have had many good times, and should have many more. That's up to you. If you plan to answer do it now. I have waited for you too many times, too long. I will not wait anymore.*
>
> *This will be the last you hear from me.*
>
> *No matter what you decide, know this. I have, do, and will always love you. Do, at least, take my advice on drinking, smoking, and exercise.*
>
> *Love,*

a boy less masculine, as males are supposed to be independent. If he is heterosexual and does not resolve these feelings of ***antifemininity*** and ***hyperindependence***, he is at risk for using violence in order to deal with the anxiety that arises when he becomes close to a woman and experiences an emotional dependence on her.

STALKERS

According to the National Violence Against Women (NVAW) study, males are 87% of all stalkers, 94% of those who stalk women, and 60% of those who stalk men (Tjaden & Thoennes, 1998). This statistic is consistent with the distinct pattern found in other kinds of gender-based violence, an overwhelmingly male pattern of perpetration, especially against women.

The majority of those who stalk target someone they know (77% for female victims and 64% for male victims). An intimate partner stalked 59% percent of the women and 30% of the men, and these intimate cases were the most dangerous. Stalkers physically assaulted 81% and sexually assaulted 31% of the women in the sample.

Stalking can last months or even years. The NVAW study found that the average duration was 1.8 years. However, if a previously intimate relationship had existed between stalker and victim, the duration increases to an average of 2.2 years (Tjaden & Thoennes, 1998). Additional research suggests that stalkers lack relationship and social skills. Mullen, Pathe, Purcell, & Stuart (1999) found, for example, that in over half (52%) of the 145 stalking cases they reviewed, the stalker never had a girlfriend.

Stalkers have a variety of rationales and motivations for their behavior. Zona, Sharma, & Lane (1993) reviewed the cases of 74 stalkers identified by the Threat Management Unit of the Los Angeles Police Department. Based on their analysis of these cases, they identified three distinct types of stalkers:

The simple obsessional stalker: In this case, a previous relationship has existed between stalker and victim. The nature of the relationship may vary, from neighbor to lover, but nearly always, something has gone "wrong" in the relationship and the stalker believes that he has been mistreated. The stalking is an attempt to bring "justice" to the situation by punishing the victim. Thirty-five of the 74 cases were identified as simple obsessional in nature.

Erotomanic: Seven of the 74 cases involved erotomania, a diagnosable mental illness (American Psychiatric Association, 2000). In these cases, the stalker is deluded about the nature of his relationship with the victim. He believes that the victim is his romantic love and his "perfect match."

Love obsessional: Thirty-two of the 74 cases involved love obsession with a well-known or famous person. These stalkers may be deluded about the feelings that this person has for them, or they may understand that this person is not in love with them. They nearly always conduct a campaign in order to gain the attention of their target, often going to great lengths. Recall John Hinckley's efforts to attract the attention of Jodie Foster by attempting to assassinate President Ronald Reagan. John Hinckley suffers from schizophrenia, a severe psychological disorder. Zona et al. (1993) found that it was not uncommon for love obsessional stalkers to have a primary psychiatric diagnosis, and Meloy (1995) reported that many have personality disorders.

Mullen, Pathe, Purcell, and Stuart (1999) suggested an alternative typology of stalkers, based on motivations and context. The *rejected stalker* most closely parallels Zona et al.'s (1993) simple obsessional type who has been rejected and is motivated by a combination of retribution and reconciliation. The *intimacy seeker* parallels the love obsessional type, having a delusion of love and intimacy and an intense desire to have a relationship with his target. The *incompetent stalker* lacks the ability to form a lasting and mature relationship. Although there is not an infatuation with the target, there is attraction and a belief that the stalker deserves the love of the desired partner. The *resentful stalker* feels a strong sense of injustice and desires revenge through terrorizing his target. Finally, for the *predatory stalker*, stalking is a big game, and the power and control gained from his stalking behavior is pleasurable. He may fantasize about stalking and plan his activities well ahead of time. Not surprisingly, the predatory stalker is more likely than the other types to be a sex offender and/or to have been diagnosed as a paraphiliac (a person with deviant sexual practices that are not necessarily illegal).

A typology of stalkers can be helpful not only in aiding our understanding of the motivations behind their actions, but also in assessing the degree of threat that they pose and devising intervention and prevention strategies to maximize the safety of victims. As with other forms of gender-based violence, stalking involves a lack of empathy for the victim, poor insight into and perspective about one's own psychology and mental illness, and a willingness to abuse one's power.

Sexual Harassment

Foote and Goodman-Delahunty (2004) describe three cognitive patterns of sexual harassers. The least problematic of the three is the ***misperceiving harasser***, a man who misinterprets the dress and behavior of women as a display of sexual interest and views the workplace as an appropriate venue for seeking sexual relationships. This pattern is a part of a general trend in men to mistake friendliness in women as sexual interest and to interpret sexual harassment in narrower terms than women. One could characterize the misperceiving harasser more as naïve or insensitive than malevolent, and he may respond well to sanctions or other interventions designed to curtail his harassing behavior.

The ***exploitive harasser*** uses his position of power to attempt to sexually coerce women. Not surprisingly, he is quite similar to a typical acquaintance rapist in personality and attitude in that he tends to hold adversarial sexual beliefs, endorse hypermasculine ideologies, connect sexuality to social dominance, adhere to rape myths, and hold hostile sexist attitudes. His sexual harassment is part of a wider pattern of authoritarianism and dominance motivation.

The *misogynistic harasser* expresses hatred for women by engaging in behavior that makes the workplace hostile to them. This animosity may take the form of pornographic displays, offensive comments about women's abilities, derogatory humor directed at women, or other forms of sexism.

Foote and Goodman-Delahunty (2004) state that it is important to identify the type of harasser when an incident takes place, as each has his own distinctive pattern of cognitive distortions about women, sexuality, and the self. In primary prevention (attempts to address the entire population), trainers should address all types of attitudes that underlie sexual harassment. In secondary prevention (attempts to address at-risk workers), personnel should identify harassment-supportive attitudinal displays and act to educate the person who exhibits the risky behavior. In tertiary prevention (relapse prevention), the specialist should assess the type of cognitive style of the harasser and tailor interventions to correct his misperceptions.

COMPONENT #2: DECISION TO ACT VIOLENTLY

A decision is an act in which a person makes up his or her mind to engage in a behavior. As noted, perpetrators are responsible and accountable for their decisions unless they are psychotic or legally insane. Two cognitive factors may influence the decision to commit an act of gender-based violence. First, the attacker may not define his behavior in criminal terms. When a surveyor asks, "Have you had sexual intercourse with an adult when she didn't want to because you used or threatened to use physical force (twisting her arm, holding her down, etc.) if she didn't cooperate?", many more men answer in the affirmative than if the survey asks, "Have you ever raped someone?", despite the fact that these two questions are identical in content. Sexual assault perpetrators may think that they are "just having sex" or "working out a 'yes'" when their behavior meets the legal definition of rape. Stalkers may think that they are engaging in courtship behaviors rather than criminal activity. Batterers may justify their actions by believing that their role as heads of households makes their behavior acceptable. And sexual harassment perpetrators may think that they are merely being flirtatious. As sexual harassment prevention trainer Barry Shapiro (2000) noted, "Very few people get up in the morning and say to themselves, 'I'm going to go to work and sexually harass someone today.' They don't see themselves as offensive, annoying, obnoxious, and illegal. They see themselves as cute, witty, charming, and sexy." Regardless of the level of self-delusion, the law is clear. The impact, not the intent, of the person's violence is the main consideration.

A second cognitive factor influencing the attacker's decision is his beliefs about the amount of control he has over his behavior. A sexual assault perpetrator may believe that he cannot control himself once he has become sexually aroused. A batterer may believe that he cannot restrain himself because he is in a rage. A stalker may think that he is too love-struck to regulate his impulses. Many batterer-education programs attempt to undercut this rationalization by pointing out all of the decision points along the way to a violent incident. For example, the batterer chose to hit the wall instead of the victim, or to use an open hand instead of a fist or a weapon, or to hit the victim on her legs or back so that she would sustain injuries that would not be visible in public.

COMPONENT #3: MEANS TO DO HARM

Those who commit gender-based violence have a variety of tools to aid them in the commission of their crimes. Physical ones are the most obvious. Most men have greater upper-body strength than most women and can use it as a means to do harm. Obviously, the possession of a weapon and the willingness to use it are a means to both instill terror and to inflict serious injury or death.

It is the less-obvious tools that are the most insidious. Attackers may use alcohol and/or other predatory drugs to subdue their victims. Many perpetrators of gender-based violence use threats and other forms of intimidation to harm and humiliate their victims. Such threats are especially likely within the context of an intimate relationship, in which both partners are likely to know personal information about each other. For example, one of the authors (JA), worked with a batterer who would "lovingly" and (passive aggressively) refer to his wife as "Taco" in front of her friends and family. They were completely unaware of the latent purposes behind this apparent gesture of adoration: to intimidate her by reminding her of an episode at the dinner table when they were eating tacos and he was violent and seriously hurt her. Tools of violence are also readily available for those who are in positions of institutional and coercive power, such as those of supervisor or police officer. And stalkers can use many forms of technology to commit their crimes, including cell phones and electronic mail. Knoll (2004) reported an incident in which a stalker actually installed a Global Positioning System (GPS) in the victim's car without her knowledge! Thus, he was able to go to her location any time she used her car.

COMPONENT #4: SOCIAL SUPPORT FOR VIOLENCE

Most gender-based violence perpetrators hold hostile sexist attitudes toward women and these attitudes provide both the impetus and the rationalization for the violence. Societies support the prejudice of sexism through social/structural inequalities between men and women, sexism in language, and the leading metaphors of the culture (Lerner, 1986) (for example, the casting of monotheistic gods as male), to name only a few. Individuals support sexism through comments, language, and behavior, and also have the ability to work against sexism if they choose to do so.

At the microsocial level of social groups of men, sexism is often manifested through language in the sexual objectification of women, derogatory jokes, and labeling of women with, for instance, animal names or the names of women's genitals. In our experience, many college students, both male and female, seem quite comfortable calling female students "girls" even though they would never refer to an adult male as a "boy"; thus they routinely refer to adult women with a word that describes a child.

Men generally behave in sexist ways to win the approval of other men. For example, public harassment of women, such as with whistling or catcalls, is not about sexuality at all. In fact, one cannot imagine a man's public sexualization of a woman resulting in her agreeing to go on a date with him. Generally, this kind of offensive behavior is performed in dyads or small groups of men. The harassment serves several functions. First, it announces the man's heterosexuality to the other men and anyone else who happens to be present. Second, it is a way of bonding with other men through the mistreatment of a member of a group that is seen as the enemy. And most importantly, it announces to the victim that men are in control

2. UNDERSTANDING THE OFFENDER • 59

of her social and physical space, with an implicit threat of punishment if she does not conform to their demands and expectations.

Men behave in sexist ways because they believe that their male peers are sexist individuals who enjoy and value these displays. However, there is emerging evidence that this may not be the case. In a study by Kilmartin, Green, Heinzen, Kuchler, and Smith (2004), researchers gave groups of college men anonymous surveys measuring sexism, rape-supportive attitudes, and level of comfort with other men's sexist behavior. Then they completed the same surveys a second time to indicate their estimation of the attitudes of "the average man in the room." Their responses to the first set of surveys, taken together and averaged, are the *actual* average attitudes; responses to the second surveys are the *perceived* average attitudes. The perceived averages were significantly higher in sexism, rape-supportive attitudes, and comfort with other men's sexist behavior than the actual attitudes. In other words, men overestimate other men's hostility towards women.

The basis of this misperception is in the comparison of an individual's inner experience with other men's social appearances. To illustrate: if someone tells a joke that a listener does not think is funny, he or she may laugh nonetheless because others are laughing. In observing this person's laughing, another person in the group who does not think the joke is funny, but who is also laughing, would of course assume that the other listener enjoyed the joke. One would not know that the first person found the joke unfunny unless he or she revealed the opinion.

One way to conceptualize sexist behavior in men's groups is as a performance based on the belief that other men are sexist and will thus approve of the offensive display. When men compare their inner experience with other men's social appearances, they tend to keep their objections to themselves for fear of social disapproval from other men. Although masculinity is thought to include a strong element of independence, there is tremendous conformity in many men's groups.

Social psychologist Solomon Asch (1965) was a pioneer in the study of conformity, and his classic experiments illustrate both the power of group pressure and the solutions to negative conformity in groups. He brought groups of people into his laboratory and told them that they were participating in a visual-perception experiment. He showed them a vertical line (the "standard line") and then three comparison lines. The task was to judge which of the comparison lines was closest in length to the standard line. The first member of the group gives an answer that is obviously wrong. The next person gives the same wrong answer, as does everyone else in the group. In actuality, all members of the group except for one are confederates—actors hired to pose as research participants. The goal of the research is to measure the conditions under which group pressure influences a person to conform to an opinion that is clearly wrong.

In a control condition in which participants judged the length of the lines without experiencing any group pressure, they produced the correct answer nearly 100% of the time. When the group's wrong judgment is unanimous, that percentage drops dramatically, sometimes dipping below 50%. But, interestingly, if just one of the confederates gives the correct answer, the participants' percentage of correct answers rises sharply, into the 80–90% range, despite the fact that the participant and the correct confederate are vastly outnumbered.

Asch's research illustrated two important social-psychological principles. First, social pressure is very powerful and can often get people to do things they really do not want to do. Second, the perception of an ally is also powerful in creating the condition for independent action.

Combining Asch's research with that of Kilmartin et al. (2004), we see that men's sexist behavior may often be based on a misperception of other men's sexism, and that if men do not speak up about their discomfort, other men might perceive them as comfortable. If everyone is laughing at the joke and those who do not like the joke think they are the only ones, they do not believe that they have an ally in the group and therefore they are powerfully influenced by group conformity. Although most men never commit gender-based violence, they contribute to its attitudinal underpinnings by being passive bystanders despite their discomfort. If one man in the group is prone towards this violence, he may perceive that he has more social support than he actually has. (See chapter 8 for a discussion of ways to reduce conformity to sexism in men's groups.)

At the macrosocial level, social/structural inequalities and cultural belief systems contribute to gender-based violence. Anthropologist Peggy Sanday (1981; 1990; 1996) is a pioneer in the study of the social conditions that give rise to rape. A large effect of social/structural inequalities is the social separation of the sexes. For example, Sanday found high rates of rape in societies where men's residences are apart from women and where the sexes do very little work together. It is not surprising, then, that the homosocial atmosphere of fraternities and men's athletic teams creates a risk factor for sexual assault (keeping in mind that the vast majority of fraternity men and athletes are not rapists). Not surprisingly, power distinctions between the sexes are also related to rape-proneness. In U.S. society, men hold a largely disproportionate share of wealth and political power. Scott Coltrane's (1998) research supports Sanday's findings and adds that rape and other forms of gender-based violence are also negatively correlated with men's involvement in child-care activities. Structurally, the refusal of men to do "women's work," with its underlying belief that women are subordinate to men, is associated with conditions in which men dehumanize women and feel entitled to attack them.

Another critical factor is the response of the society to the problem. As we have already seen, legal, political, and other social systems are often insensitive to the scourge of gender-based violence. To illustrate: within a few years of the horrific September 11, 2001 attacks on the World Trade Centers and the Pentagon, male partners or ex-partners murdered as many women as the number of people who died on that day (calculated from Federal Bureau of Investigation (FBI) Uniform Crime Reports, 2002, 2003, 2004). One can view violence against women as a sort of incremental terrorism, and yet it does not seem to be foremost in the consciousness of political leaders or the public. There may be the perception that victims of this sort of violence somehow contributed to their own victimization. In a typical major newspaper, a stranger murder such as a drive-by shooting will be on the front page or will be a lead article in the local section. But unless there is something strikingly different from the usual about it, the murder of a partner will be at the bottom of page three in a much shorter article, thus contributing to the perception that the life of a spouse is somehow less valuable than someone whose violent death seems more random.

SUMMARY

Gender-based violence is only partly centered in the individual psychology—the beliefs, decisions, and personality characteristics—of the attacker. It is also woven into the cultural fabric of a society that grants disproportionate power to men. Toxic masculinity provides justifications and rationalizations for men's subordination of women, and this set of cultural beliefs is both created and maintained by individuals, groups, institutions, and the society at large. Within these cultural conditions, violence-prone men feel entitled to wield that power irresponsibly, and social systems often fail to hold them accountable for their violence.

KEY TERMS

Anger rapist
Decision to act violently
Exploitive harasser
Hypermasculinity
Intimidation
Love obsessional stalker
Means to do harm
Misogynistic harasser
Misperceiving harasser
Normative level of coercion
Pathology of the perpetrator 37
Patriarchy
Personality disorder
Power rapist
Primary prevention
Proactive batterer
Reactive batterer
Sadistic rapist
Secondary prevention
Simple obsessional stalker
Social support for violence

CRITICAL THINKING QUESTIONS

1. What is meant by *normative level of coercion*? Use this concept to distinguish between men who might engage in this type of coercion and perpetrators of gender-based violence.

2. It is important to distinguish between understanding the perpetration of gender-based violence and excusing such violence. Explain why each of these is important, and the differences between these concepts.

3. Potential perpetrators of gender-based violence must have the *means to do harm*. In our society, do men have a larger repertoire of such means to commit gender-based violence than women? Explain your response.
4. In order for gender-based violence to be pervasive, the authors argue that there must be *social support for violence*. Use this concept to explain how the majority of individuals who do not commit such violence may still contribute to their incidents.
5. Describe the relationship between alcohol and gender-based violence.
6. Explain why men who are uncomfortable with sexist behaviors may also reinforce the sexist behaviors of their peers, or even engage in such behaviors. What are the social consequences of such paradoxical behavior?

Chapter 3

The Survivors: Consequences of Gender-based Violence

A SURVIVOR'S STORY

When I was 19 years old, I went to visit my sister. We were going to go to a huge concert with a bunch of her friends. After the concert, the plan was to camp out at a nearby lake. During the concert, we were all drinking. My sister ended up getting sick and passing out in our camper early in the afternoon. My sister, being nine years older than me, is very protective of me. Before she left to go sleep it off in the camper, she told me to stay with her friend Kevin. She told me that he was a great guy, she trusted him completely, and that he would take care of me. It comforted me to know that there was someone who would be there for me while I partied at the concert.

I was drunk, but not so drunk that I couldn't enjoy the concert. It was a great concert. As soon as it got dark, though, the tone of the whole day changed. It became obvious to me that Kevin wasn't the "nice guy" that my sister and I thought. It was also obvious what he wanted: to have sex with me. He kept taking me to isolated areas where it was just he and I. I kept trying to go back to the concert, but Kevin wouldn't go. Over and over again, he asked if I would go to his truck with him. I told him repeatedly that I had no intention of having sex with him. I told him that I was committed to my boyfriend and had no intention of being unfaithful. I told him this over and over again.

Kevin did not listen. He became even more persistent. He told me that my boyfriend was probably out with another woman since I was out of town. He told me that I "needed" him. He wouldn't take no for an answer. I knew I was not about to have sex with Kevin that night. I had absolutely no desire. I did not know that Kevin would rape me that night.

All evening long, I endured Kevin's obnoxious behavior. All evening long, I rejected his requests to go to his car and to have sex with him. It was the last thing on my mind as I was puking my guts out and it was the last thing on my mind before I passed out next to my sister in our trailer. The night was finally over. Or so I thought.

"Mr. Nice Guy" returned when I got sick. He had been by my side while I got sick, over and over again. He helped me to the makeshift bed in the trailer, where I prepared to pass out right beside my sister. I remember him preparing to go to bed, too, right beside my sister and I. I felt relieved that Kevin had finally gotten it through his head that we would not be having sex that night. I passed out, thankful that the night was over.

When I awoke, my pants were off, and Kevin was about to penetrate me. I said to him very loudly, "What the fuck do you think you are doing? I told you I didn't want to have sex!" His reply was incredulous: "Oh, come on, Sheila, yes you do. Now you'd better shut up because your sister is going to be pissed off at you if she finds out. She'll also be mad at me, now do you want that?" He put his hand over my mouth, hard, so I couldn't scream.

I was pushing on his chest, trying to get free from the weight of his body that was on top of me. The harder I pushed, the more force he used and the rougher he got. I was powerless. I just turned my head and cried, praying that it would be over soon. It felt like forever, as he penetrated me, over and over again.

Finally, he was done. After he stopped raping me, he reiterated that I could never tell my sister. Before he put his pants back on and left, he told me "You were great, thanks." I never saw him again.

For three years, I didn't tell anyone what happened to me the night of the concert. I didn't tell my sister, my parents, any of my friends, or my boyfriend. It felt like "my secret." I was completely alone.

Recently, I have been able to face this with full force and I am healing. I began to share my story, with my friends, my boyfriend, and my parents. Today, with their support, and with counseling, I am not only doing well, I am thriving. I am a strong and successful woman. I have a great family, a loving fiancé, a college education, and a professional career that I enjoy tremendously. I am happy (anonymous personal communication).

In a matter of a few hours, this survivor's life was changed forever. The physical pain was clearly excruciating, but to her, it paled in comparison to the intensity and the duration of the emotional scars. Notice, as well, that with the support of her family and professional treatment, she is now doing well. She is not a rape victim, but rather a survivor.

The purpose of this chapter is to discuss the consequences of gender-based violence for victims and survivors. (We use the term ***victim*** to describe the immediate aftermath of the assault and ***survivor*** to describe the long term recovery process.) A survivor of gender-based violence will never be the same person as he or she was prior to the experience. However, it is important to remember that survivors can regain their physical and emotional health and well being.

WHO ARE THE SURVIVORS?

Although it is true that anyone may be a target of violence, sex and sexual orientation directly affect the likelihood of being targeted by a perpetrator. Attackers are more likely to assault girls and women through rape, sexual assault, acts of IPV, sexual harassment, stalking, trafficking, and forced prostitution than boys or men. Abusers are more likely to neglect females as children, to use them as tools of war, and to systematically rape them. ***Feticide*** and ***infanticide*** perpetrators victimize females more often than males.

Yet, perpetrators of violence also assault boys and men. Not counting prison sexual attacks, when a perpetrator rapes a boy or man, the attacker is usually either a stranger or an authority figure from church, athletics, or some other community organization (Whealin, 2004). Therefore, as with nearly all incidents of gender-based violence, the attack is an abuse of power. In this case, the abuse is legitimated by the differential power between the authority figure and the victim.

Like assaults against women, men's rape against men is motivated by a need to exert power and dominance over another. Pro-feminist activist Rus Ervin Funk (1997) describes a horrific account of three men who violently attacked him both physically and sexually after he had presented a "Rape and Racism" workshop. Their abusive comments during the assault clearly indicate that these men were feeling threatened by a man who was stepping outside of the boundaries of culturally-defined masculinity. According to Funk, these men chose violent physical assault and rape as a way to punish him for doing so.

The National Crime Victimization Survey (NCVS) (Rennison & Rand, 2003) contains a breakdown of data on criminal victimization, including the crimes of rape and sexual assault, and the characteristics of victims. These characteristics include race, age, sex, household income, marital status, U.S. region, and type of residence.

Race

According to the NCVS, Blacks report higher levels of rape and sexual assault than Whites and people of other races. Indeed, Blacks reported significantly higher levels of victimization in overall violence and aggravated assault compared to other races.

Age and Sex

Although the NCVS does not collect data from individuals under the age of twelve, there is a clear pattern that identifies the age of highest vulnerability for becoming a target of rape or sexual assault for those older than twelve. By far, those between the ages of 16 and 19 report the highest rates of victimization, with 10.4 assaults reported per 1,000 females. The age group is followed by those between the ages of 20 and 24 (5.4 females/1,000) and 12–15 (4.3 females/1,000). Ruling out young children whom attackers victimize, girls and young women are clearly more likely to be targets of rape and sexual assault than boys and men.

Household Income

People who reported making between $7,500 and $14,999 report the highest incidence of rape and sexual assault (3.2/1000). However, according to Rennison & Rand (2003), individuals from households making less than $50,000 report higher rates of rape and sexual assault than those making more.

Region

The NCVS found that residents from the western United States were more likely to report that an attacker raped or sexually assaulted them than individuals from the Northeast. This phenomenon was part of a trend for violent crime in general; residents from the West and Midwest report more victimization than residents in the South and Northeast.

Residence

In comparing those from rural, suburban, and urban areas, we find that sexual assault and rape rates are consistent with residence effects for other kinds of violent crime. Those from urban populations are more likely to report that someone sexually assaulted or raped them than those from either rural or suburban areas. Many of these variables have a direct relationship with social power imbalances. It is not a coincidence that women, Blacks, youth, and those with lower incomes report the higher rates of rape and sexual assault.

However, these statistics are meaningless for survivors. What may be most significant is being able to share their story with someone who will listen to them, believe them, and support them. The empowering process of healing—of becoming a survivor in the true sense of the word—takes time. Understanding what they are going through in the midst of their confusion is an important part of the process. Below, we will identify possible effects of gender-based violence, the commonalities among various types of victimization, and the unique consequences of each. But first, we look at the financial impact of violence.

THE FINANCIAL COSTS OF VICTIMIZING

Although most of this chapter is concerned with the psychological consequences of victimization, it is important to understand that such acts also have a significant economic impact. It is difficult to calculate these costs, as they are multifaceted and include both tangible and intangible losses. Violence has a profoundly negative financial effect on individuals, families, communities, and society.

Tangible Costs

According to Miller, Cohen, and Weirsema (1996), the tangible financial costs of violence are substantial. They may include property damage and loss, productivity loss (e.g., loss of wages, lost productivity at work, related costs to employers of survivors), and the price of medical care, mental health treatment, and other victim services. The financial fallout is a domino effect, as the economic impact of one individual's victimization creates financial problems for other individuals, families, and communities. Ultimately, the entire society pays.

Intangible Costs

Miller et al. (1996) argue that there is also an indirect negative economic impact of victimization. These intangible costs occur as a result of loss of life or pain and suffering in the victim. The authors calculated financial loss for victims who die based on their life expectancy and consequent lost wages. For nonfatal injuries, they estimated average jury awards for various crimes based on pain, suffering, and decreased quality of life.

The researchers applied these estimates to incidence rates of crime based on figures from the National Crime Victimization Survey, Uniform Crime Reports, Vital Statistics, National Incidence and Prevalence Survey of Child Abuse and Neglect, National Family Violence Surveys, and the National Women's Study. They estimated the following intangible costs:

Rape (excluding child sexual abuse)	$127 billion/year
Assault	$ 93 billion/year
Murder (excluding arson and drunk driving deaths)	$ 71 billion/year
Drunk driving	$ 61 billion/year
Child abuse	$ 56 billion/year
Total annual costs of victimizing:	***$408 billion/year***

PSYCHOLOGICAL CONSEQUENCES OF VICTIMIZING

When an individual commits an act of gendered violence, the survivor is changed forever, in every sense of the word. Janoff-Bulman (1998) reports that, in her 20 years of studying the reactions of trauma survivors, the phrase she most often heard was "I never thought it could happen to me" (p. 99).

Shattered Assumptions

Reactions to victimization vary depending upon the person, situation, and type of crime. However, there is an underlying common thread in the stress reactions of traumatized people—one's views and assumptions about people and the world change radically (Janoff-Bulman, 1985a, 1985b, Janoff-Bulman & Frieze, 1983). These ***shattered assumptions*** take three general forms.

The Assumption of Invulnerability. Despite the fact that we are all aware that disasters occur, often unexpectedly, in all parts of the world, most of us have a belief in the benevolence of our personal, interpersonal, and social lives, and in the benevolence of those with whom we interact. Even though chance plays a powerful role in our lives (Janoff-Bulman, 1998; Krantz, 1998), human motivation may cause us to underestimate the role of random events and overestimate the degree of personal control that we have over these events. This cognitive proclivity is self-protective. It helps us to feel safe and secure as we go about our daily activities (Janoff-Bulman, 1992). It would be very difficult to live with a belief that the world is malevolent, unpredictable, and uncontrollable.

The benevolence of the world comes into serious doubt for survivors of violence, especially for those who believed that their lives were in danger during the assault (Kilpatrick, Saunders, Amick-McMullan, Best, Veronen, & Resnick, 1989; Resnick & Kilpatrick, 1994). In one study, 80% of survivors of attacks in which the perpetrator completed a rape, physically injured the victim, and threatened his or her life exhibited signs of post-traumatic stress disorder (PTSD, to be discussed later in this chapter) (Kilpatrick et al., 1989).

The Assumption That the World Is Fair. Most people prefer to believe that the world is fair and just (Lerner, 1970) and a fundamental philosophy in mainstream U.S. society is that it is a meritocracy—that people get what they deserve. The **belief in a just world** allows us the safe assumption that if we work hard, take care of ourselves, and are kind to others, then good things will come to us. The logical converse of this belief is that people who suffer negative outcomes also deserve them, and this belief is commonly held by those from Western cultures (Bard & Sangrey, 1979; Janoff-Bulman, 1998).

Because of this just world phenomenon, survivors have two choices. They can blame themselves for the event, believing that they deserved what they got, or they can change their belief that the world is fair and safe. Many survivors engage in *self-blame* by rationalizing that they must have directly or indirectly participated in their own victimization. If the world is fair, a survivor might believe that future safety can be insured by making wiser choices and being a better person. However, this process may cause the survivor to sacrifice self-esteem because of the self-loathing that accompanies self-blame (Harvey & Herman, 1992; Janoff-Bulman, 1998; Koss & Harvey, 1989).

Positive Self-Perceptions

Survivors who sacrifice their self-worth for their safety live in a confusing world. Not only do they feel radically different from the people they were before the attack, but they feel radically different from other people. Survivors also question themselves, their behavior surrounding the event, and their character. Their sense of being fundamentally different from others can also lead to extreme feelings of loneliness (Warshaw, 1988). One woman recounts, "I felt as if my whole world had been kicked out from under me and I had been left to drift all alone in the darkness. I had horrible nightmares in which I relived the rape and others which were even worse. I was terrified of being with people and terrified of being alone" (Warshaw, 1988, p. 54).

POSTTRAUMATIC STRESS DISORDER

Posttraumatic Stress Disorder (PTSD) is a psychiatric diagnosis included in the ***Diagnostic and Statistical Manual of Mental Disorders*** (DSM-IV) (American Psychiatric Association, 2000). Several criteria must be met for one to be diagnosed with this disorder. Foremost is the experience of an intensely negative emotional response to a traumatic event. The trauma can be a natural disaster or accident, but PTSD is usually more severe and long-lasting when it is of human design, and DSM-IV cites rape as an example (American Psychiatric Association, 2000).

CONSEQUENCES OF SEXUAL ASSAULT AND RAPE

The experience of fear, helplessness, or horror is nearly universal in those who have experienced rape. In one study, victims of rape who presented to a hospital were asked to complete a symptom checklist two to three hours after the assault (Veronen, Kilpatrick, & Resick, 1979). (See Box 3.1 for a discussion of Rape Trauma Syndrome.) The results indicated that the majority of victims were experiencing emotional and visceral reactions to their experiences:

- 96% reported that they were afraid.
- 96% reported that they were worried.
- 92% reported that they were terrified and confused.
- 80% reported having racing thoughts.
- 96% were shaking or trembling.
- 80% reported that their hearts were racing.
- 72% were in physical pain.
- 68% reported tense muscles.
- 64% reported rapid breathing.
- 60% reported numbness.

> **BOX 3.1**
> **Rape Trauma Syndrome**
>
> Psychiatric nurse Ann Burgess and sociologist Lynda Holmstrom coined the term ***Rape Trauma Syndrome*** (RTS) in 1974 to describe two phases of physical, psychological, social, and sexual reactions to victimization.
>
> In the acute phase, the most frequent response is fear and anxiety (Gidycz & Koss, 1991; Veronen, Kilpatrick, & Resick, 1979). Others include
>
> 1. *Denial, shock, and disbelief.* The tendency toward denial is nearly universal, with victims thinking "this can't be happening."
> 2. *Confusion and disruption of personality.* Victims often appear dazed. Some may shake, tremble, or go numb.
> 3. *Guilt, hostility, and blame.* Janoff-Bulman (1979) contends that next to fear and terror, self-blame is the second most common response to being raped. It is quite easy for a victim to revisit pre-assault behaviors or choices and erroneously identify them as causally related to the crime. A victim may say, "If only I would have stayed home," "If only I hadn't drunk so much," or any variety of cognitions that imply victim responsibility for the assault.
> 4. *Regression to a state of helplessness or dependency.* Survivors of rape have lost control of their lives and often feel personally incompetent. They may begin to rely on others in an attempt to feel safe again.
> 5. *Distorted perceptions.* Feelings of distrust or paranoia may occur. In one study, 41% of rape victims believed they would be raped again (Koss, 1988).
>
> During the second phase of RTS, which may last for months or even years, survivors face long-term consequences. They may develop phobias—intense fears of specific object or situations—as a rape event serves as a classical conditioning stimulus (Kilpatrick, Resick, & Veronen, 1981). The phobia may be specifically associated with the rape, such as a weapon or location, or more generalized, such as a fear of men, of being alone, or of going out at night.
>
> Changes in lifestyle are common during the long-term phase of RTS. Young college students may drop out of school, and survivors may move to another home or even another state. Some may begin abusing food, abusing drugs, abusing alcohol, or sleeping all of the time, while others may stop eating or sleeping.

> **BOX 3.1** *(continued)*
>
> Finally, rape survivors have the distinct task of dealing with the fact that the perpetrator has also attacked their sexuality. Sexual satisfaction with intimate partners is often strongly and negatively affected (Feldman-Summers, Gordon, & Meagher, 1979), as is the survivor's desire to engage in sexual activity (Becker, Skinner, Abel, Axelrod, & Treacy, 1984).
>
> The symptomology of RTS is consistent with the criterion-based diagnosis of PTSD. Because PTSD is recognized by the American Psychiatric Association, it seems the more useful diagnosis for rape victims who may be having intense reactions to the assault. However, the conceptualizers of RTS deserve credit for bringing the reality of the consequences of rape for survivors, and for serving as validation for survivors as they find their way through mass confusion.

The second criterion for PTSD is the re-experiencing of the traumatic event, which can take several forms: intrusive thoughts; repeated nightmares; or, less commonly, flashbacks in which the event seems as though it is actually happening again. Survivors may also respond intensely and viscerally to people or things psychologically associated with the assault.

The third criterion is emotional, psychological, and behavioral change, such as avoidance of people or things associated with the trauma; decreased interest in previously enjoyed hobbies; or feelings of numbness, loss, or detachment.

The fourth criterion involves increased levels of physiological arousal or anxiety, including two of the following: difficulty falling or staying asleep, irritability or outbursts of anger, difficulty concentrating, hypervigilance, or exaggerated startle response. Finally, the symptoms described above must be present more than one month following the trauma (symptoms at less than one month are diagnosed as Acute Stress Disorder) and must cause impairment in the survivor's daily functioning.

CONSEQUENCES OF INTIMATE PARTNER VIOLENCE

Arias and Pope (1999) interviewed 68 victims of partner abuse at a women's emergency shelter. Fully 88% of them had PTSD symptom scores at or above clinical levels. Most of the other 12% were not diagnosable because it had been less than one month post-trauma, so the duration criterion was not met. Psychological abuse was highly predictive of PTSD even after controlling for the effects of physical abuse. Importantly, women with lower PTSD scores also reported more resolve to leave the relationship than those with higher scores (Veronen et al., 1979). Not surprisingly, higher scores were also positively and significantly correlated with having experienced more severe relationship violence (Koss, Bailey, Yuan, Hererra, & Lichter, 2003) and may indicate higher levels of terror regarding the consequences of ending the relationship. See Box 3.2 for a discussion on "Battered Woman Syndrome."

CONSEQUENCES OF INTIMATE PARTNER VIOLENCE AND STALKING

To add stalking to partner violence compounds the symptoms associated with PTSD. Researchers have investigated the experiences of women who were targets of violent partners and attempted to describe the further effect on women whose partners also stalked them (Mechanic, Uhlmansiek, Weaver, & Resick, 2000, 2002). These abusers were likely to use extremely high levels of concurrent emotional abuse, sexual assault, and physical violence, sometimes to the point of rendering their victims unconscious. The result of such systematic violence is not surprising: these women were highly likely to evidence higher levels of psychological distress and symptoms of PTSD and depression.

Mechanic et al. (2002) investigated women victimized in violent relationships that later involved stalking and found higher levels of both violence in the relationship and PTSD in those stalked compared to women in violent relationships who were not stalked. Case studies document that stalking can lead to depression, anxiety, guilt, shame, helplessness, humiliation, PTSD (Abrams & Robinson, 2002), and substance abuse (Mechanic, 2003).

CONSEQUENCES OF SEXUAL HARASSMENT

In recent research, investigators have also begun to explore the relationship between PTSD and sexual harassment, although data are still quite scarce (Street, Stafford, & Bruce, 2003). Avina and O'Donohue (2002) note that even less severe examples of sexual harassment meet the first criterion of PTSD: the nature of the event is traumatic. Such incidents threaten the financial well-being,

> **BOX 3.2**
> **Battered Woman Syndrome**
>
> As mentioned in chapter 1, Lenore Walker published The Battered Woman in 1979, describing how IPV develops in some relationships, as well as the defensive cognitive coping strategies that a survivor routinely uses to make her world seem more understandable and safe. She may deny the abusive behaviors and her emotional responses to them, minimize the extent of the violence, and rationalize the partner's behavior. Justifications, such as "Well, the dinner was late" or "He's been under so much stress lately, I really shouldn't have asked for the money then," serve to diminish the gravity of the situation. Certainly the violent partner contributes to these justifications, minimizations, and denials in attempts to hold the victim responsible for his violent behavior.
>
> Additionally, Walker used the concept of *learned helplessness* (described in chapter 1) to provide a more thorough understanding of a victim's commitment to her relationship. Although there may be episodes when she is able to forestall or mitigate an attack, eventually she comes to understand that she is powerless to prevent it or to influence the batterer. Victims often come to accept the degrading comments of their partners, which destroys their self-esteem. They also come to believe that there is nothing they can do to extricate themselves from the abusive situation. Walker notes, "The very fact of being a woman, more specifically a married woman, automatically creates a situation of powerlessness. This is one of the detrimental effects of [gender]-role stereotyping" (1979, p. 51).
>
> IPV survivors, educators, and advocates welcomed the concept of "Battered Woman Syndrome." There was a sense of relief that these violent relationships were finally getting the attention they desperately needed and that an understanding of the dynamics of violent relationships was beginning to take shape. Walker's feminist explanation for the existence of violent relationships—inequities in the power structure between men and women—also channeled a new direction for addressing the issue.
>
> However, the term *battered woman* is regrettable. It directs the focus of these relationships onto the victim as if she were the one who needs to be explained. Rothenberg (2003) argues that this term is a cultural compromise that emphasizes women's weaknesses rather than their resourcefulness and that creates the possibility for a self-fulfilling prophecy, which could serve to inhibit the victim from making any attempt to leave the violent relationship. To be a

> **BOX 3.2** *(continued)*
> battered woman is to be a woman without choices or self-control. It also provides a curious sense of status which risks offering a false sense of power from adopting a victim role and thus gaining sympathy from others. In spite of the important and positive contributions of Walker's work, we believe the term battered woman has outlived its usefulness.

personal boundaries, and sense of control in their workplace for the victims.

According to the National Women's Study (Dansky & Kilpatrick, 1997), there is a relationship between PTSD and sexual harassment, even after controlling for the effects of other physical and sexual assault victimization. Fontana and Rosenheck (1998) studied the impact of both duty-related stress and sexual harassment stress for female military veterans who sought treatment for PTSD. They found that although both types of stressors contributed to the development of symptoms, sexual harassment in the workplace was nearly four times more influential than work stress. Richman, Rospenda, Flaherty, and Freels (2001) also found a relationship between sexual harassment and an increase in levels of depression, anxiety and hostility, and alcohol abuse for both women and men.

FACTORS RELATED TO PTSD SYMPTOMOLOGY OR DIAGNOSIS

A critical issue with regard to diagnosis of those traumatically assaulted is the length of time that the survivor remains symptomatic. Rothbaum, Foa, Riggs, Murdock, and Walsh (1992) assessed the presence of PTSD symptoms in 95 rape survivors, beginning about two weeks following the assault and continuing weekly for three months. They found that at assessment one, 94% had some symptoms of PTSD, decreasing to 65% at assessment 4 and to 47% at assessment 12. In The National Women's Study, researchers found a 31% prevalence rate for PTSD and reported that, compared to those who have not been victimized by crime, survivors of rape are 6.2 times more likely to develop PTSD at some point in their lives (Kilpatrick et al., 1992). They were also 4.1 times more likely than non-crime victims to have contemplated suicide, and 13 times more likely to have attempted suicide.

The prevalence of PTSD among rape survivors may depend upon a number of factors. Resnick and Schnicke (1993) found a lifetime prevalence rate of 24% for those who had been exposed to civilian trauma and a 25% PTSD prevalence among crime victims in general. For survivors of rape, levels of PTSD varied with specific factors related to the assault. Thirty-two percent of survivors of completed rape met the diagnostic criteria, rising to 50% for crimes that include fear of death or injury, comparable to the aforementioned 47% rate found by Rothbaum et al. (1992). And, as mentioned earlier, when completed rapes were combined with threats to life and injury, the prevalence rate increases to 80% (Kilpatrick et al., 1989).

Not all individuals who experience trauma develop PTSD, which is an important point for two reasons. First, although it is possible for a survivor to not develop these symptoms, is not possible for a survivor to avoid all negative outcomes. It is important to understand the relationship between assault and the eventual development of PTSD, but one must be careful not to trivialize the consequences for survivors who are able to stave off PTSD. Second, a comparison of those who experience trauma and develop PTSD with those who do not gives us prognostic power and may offer insights into more effective techniques for supporting and treating survivors.

Many factors are important to the eventual diagnosis of PTSD in survivors of gender-based violence. Characteristics related to the trauma itself and individual risk factors are both important, and interact in their predictive utility of the eventual development of the disorder (Halligan & Yehuda, 2000). Currently, several risk factors have been identified as important to the diagnosis of PTSD in general.

Characteristics of the Abuse

The intensity and frequency of the violence play an important role in the likelihood of symptom. For sexual assault, the use of escalated physical force or weapons, the fear of death, and the presence of injury are all significant predictors of negative psychological impact (Acierno, Resnick, Kilpatrick, Saunders, & Best, 1999).

Greater and longer psychological distress has also been found in those for whom the attacker was someone they knew (Harvey & Herman, 1992; Katz, 1991; Koss, Gidycz & Wisniewski, 1987). This finding may seem paradoxical, but, as Katz (1991) explains, violence committed by someone you know can destroy your sense of personal judgment concerning whom you can trust. And not surprisingly, more severe and longer-lasting abuse is related to a poorer sense of well-being and more florid PTSD symptoms (Koss et al., 2003).

Sex of Victim

Even when controlling for type of trauma, females are consistently almost twice as likely as men to develop PTSD. This sex difference is especially prominent in avoidance behaviors and feelings of numbness. Several researchers attribute this difference to a greater likelihood for females to be at continuing risk (Breslau, Chilcoat, Kessler, Peterson, & Lucia, 1999). Predictably, there is one important exception: male rape victims. Although the likelihood that an attacker will rape a man is considerably lower, PTSD symptoms for male rape survivors are higher than for female survivors. When the trauma is a life-threatening accident, a natural disaster, the threat of a weapon, or a physical attack, females report higher rates of PTSD. When the trauma is rape, men have a higher risk of developing PTSD (65%) than women (45.9%) (Ballenger, Davidson, Lecruiber, & Nutt (2000).

In light of the standards of masculinity in our society and the corresponding expectation that men maintain strength, power, and control, it is not surprising that male rape survivors show greater risk of developing PTSD. Chances are also likely that even fewer men reveal the attack to another person, thus complicating their recovery, and there may also be fewer services available to male victims.

Revictimization

Once a person has suffered an attack, he or she is at greater risk of being targeted by a perpetrator in the future (Nishith, Mechanic, & Resick, 2000; Resnick & Kilpatrick, 1994). Not surprisingly, repeated victimization is related to the diagnosis and severity level of PTSD. In a study conducted over a nine-month period, Christine Gidycz and her colleagues (Gidycz, Hanson, & Layman, 1995) found that females whom attackers had sexually assaulted during the first three months of the study were three times more likely to suffer a revictimization within the next three months compared with others. A sexual assault during the second three-month period was associated with a 20-fold increase in the likelihood of another victimization occurring in the following three months.

There is a strong relationship between experiencing multiple traumatic events and experiencing PTSD symptoms (Resnick & Kilpatrick, 1994). Moreover, the effect of trauma on symptoms is cumulative: more and different types of assaults were associated with more intense symptoms (Gruy, W. Dickinson, & Candib, 1999; Follette, Polusny, Bechtle, & Naugle, 1996). However, it is not yet known if the effects are additive or multiplicative (Koss et al., 2003). Resnick & Kilpatrick (1994) note that repeated exposure to trauma is associated with greatly increased risk of developing PTSD, and although most research on repeated victimization has been conducted with survivors of sexual assault and rape, it is important to remember that violent relationships, stalking, and sexual harassment are almost always repeated assaults. Prior assault also increases the likelihood of PTSD symptoms following subsequent victimizations (Resnick, Yehuda, Pitman, & Foy, 1995).

DEPRESSION

Depression is a mood disorder characterized by sadness, despair, feelings of worthlessness, and low self-esteem. Not surprisingly, it has been found to be a frequent effect of gendered violence (Koss et al., 2003). For survivors of rape, the research is clear: they are at high risk for both acute and chronic depressive symptoms. In one study, 54% of survivors were experiencing depression one month post-rape (Frank & Stewart, 1984). Forty-three percent within the same sample had severe enough symptoms to be classified as major depression, according to DSM-III (American Psychiatric Association, 1980). Dickinson et al. (1999) studied female medical workers who were assault survivors. Compared to those not experiencing sexual assault, these women were three times more likely to experience major depression in their lifetime and two and a half times more likely to report recent depression.

Depression is also widespread among women IPV survivors (Koss et al., 2003; McCauley, Kern, Kolodner, Dill, Schroeder, DeChant, et al., 1995). According to Koss and her colleagues (2003), rates of depression range from 39% (Beach, Jouriles, & O'Leary, 1985) to 83% (R. Campbell, C. M. Sullivan, & Davidson, 1995), with a mean prevalence rate of 48% (Golding, 1999).

Like PTSD, there is a sex difference in rates of depression. Women are significantly more likely than men to experience these symptoms. Koss et al. (2003) suggest that further investigating the relationship between gender inequities, including gendered violence, could be enlightening. But there is another possibility that there is a distinctly masculine form of depression that is more likely to result in symptoms that are outside of the current diagnostic criteria. For instance, men may be more likely than women to respond to emotional conflict by abusing substances, acting out violently, becoming over-involved in work or sports, or engaging in extramarital affairs as a strategy for dealing with depressive states (Lynch & Kilmartin, 1999).

Koss et al. (2003), however, question the utility of official diagnoses. Simply put, they argue that there is no common sense in applying a psychiatric label to a victim or survivor of gendered violence, particularly if the woman is in an ongoing violent situation. They offer the death of a loved one and its relationship to depression as an analogy. When a person loses a loved one, and he or she is depressed, an official diagnosis of depression is not necessary to understand the psychological well-being of the survivor. Koss et al. (2003) believe that to pathologize the psychological state of a survivor via mental diagnosis instead of recognizing that her feelings are natural emotional and psychological consequences to human trauma, is "galling" to victims (p. 136). The researchers point out that when individuals are traumatized by catastrophic events, their symptoms of PTSD are recognized as natural.

However, Koss and colleagues are only responding to the stigma of being labeled as mentally ill, an unfortunate byproduct of diagnosis. The major purpose of any diagnosis is to describe a problem that merits attention, as PTSD surely does. And as a practical matter, most health insurance providers refuse to finance psychological services in the absence of a diagnosis. Therefore, a refusal to affix a diagnostic label may effectively prevent a survivor from getting the treatment she needs. Moreover, diagnosis provides a structure for research and efficient information retrieval, which can help all survivors by identifying patterns in the course of a disorder and its treatments. Still, the stigma of mental illness remains, and so diagnoses should be made when they are warranted and helpful, and psychotherapists can take precautions to protect their clients against the harmful effects of stigma as well as the possibility that it could lead to self-blame by explaining the purposes of diagnosis and making it clear that the survivor's reactions represent normal responses to trauma.

RECOVERING FROM GENDERED VIOLENCE

The process of recovery for a survivor takes a good deal of time. But it is possible for them to move on and lead full and successful lives with friends and family who love and support them.

For survivors of sexual assault, the intensity of the immediate aftermath usually subsides within two to three months (Neville & Heppner, 1999). Many of the differences found between survivors and non-victims abate significantly after three months (Atkeson, Calhoun, Resick, & Ellis, 1982). Eighteen months post-rape, approximately 75% of survivors report no serious negative effects.

When violence is ongoing, emotional and psychological consequences for survivors, especially depressive symptoms, are likely to endure (Koss et al., 2003; J. C. Campbell & Soeken, 1999). Therefore, the patterns of violence that exist in IPV, stalking, and some cases of sexual harassment often prolong the recovery process. Once the violence stops and the survivor trusts that it has ended for good, the healing may begin. However, recovery from gendered violence does not always take place in a predictable way. Just when a survivor thinks that she is "over it," symptoms may return.

SOCIAL COGNITIONS

Perhaps the most critical factor contributing to the physical, social, and psychological well-being of a survivor is her level of self-blame and the character of her core set of beliefs (Koss & Burkhart, 1989; Koss et al., 2003). A survivor's understanding of and explanation for the violence can lead to either self-loathing or self-empowerment. It is vitally important that the survivor understand that the responsibility and blame for the attack lies with the perpetrator.

Recall during the discussion of Rape Trauma Syndrome that self-blame and guilt are common among survivors and may serve to minimize the collapse of their assumptions about the predictability and safety of their world. Ultimately, however, self-blame is destructive to the psyche of survivors, who later in their recoveries must find a way to reconcile their victimization with the positive worldviews that they held prior to it (Janoff-Bulman, 1998). The process is one of coming to accept that the world is predictable most of the time; that it is mostly, but not always, a good place; and that good things usually happen to good people, although sometimes they do not.

SOCIAL SUPPORT

One of the most important factors related to recovery for survivors is social support. Survivors of rape who are able to talk freely about the assault with nonjudgmental listeners are likely to show fewer symptoms of psychological distress (Routbort, 1998) and greater levels of psychological well-being (C. M.Sullivan & Bybee, 1999). Specifically, survivors who were supported by an advocate available to help them obtain the services they needed, as opposed to simply finding refuge in a shelter, have significantly lower PTSD scores. (See Box 3.3 for more information.)

SUMMARY

The recovery process for survivors of gender-based violence is intense and difficult, and it can be an emotional roller-coaster. Most will experience some symptoms of PTSD and/or depression. Many will be diagnosed with these or other disorders. There is no "one size fits all" recipe for going through the recovery process and there is no predictable timeline. What may be most important to remember is that victims can recover and move on to live fulfilling and satisfying lives with healthy and secure relationships. Strong social support from nonjudgmental others is of critical importance to the recovery process.

For those who are fortunate enough to not have to go through the process of recovery, it may be difficult to come to a true understanding of the seriousness of the psychological, physical, sexual, and emotional consequences of gender-based violence for survivors. It is much easier and much less threatening for the outside observer to trivialize the event and its aftermath, or to find fault with the victim. As we mentioned in our introduction, the bystander role is not neutral; it either supports or challenges the violence. Those who take this "easier" route (perhaps unwittingly) support the violence. Acknowledging the realities of gender-based violence is the first step towards challenging it.

KEY TERMS

Depression
Diagnostic and Statistical Manual of Mental Disorders
Emotional abuse
Learned helplessness
Masculinity
Posttraumatic Stress Disorder

> **BOX 3.3**
> **An Interview with Katie Koestner**
>
> Katie Koestner appeared on the cover of TIME magazine at the age of 18 in her quest for justice after being raped while on a date by a fellow student at the College of William and Mary. Since that time, she has lectured at over one thousand colleges, universities, and high schools across the country, coauthored two textbooks on sexual assault, and founded Campus Outreach Services, a national educational partner for schools on student risk and wellness issues. Katie serves as an inspiration to others who have experienced gender-based violence. She has been dedicated and effective in her work aimed at ending rape and violence. Following is a personal interview with Katie where she shares her insights into the issue, how we can help victims and survivors of sexual assault and rape, and what she hopes for the future.
>
> **JA:** Katie, Your story is a very powerful one, and has led to changes in protocol at schools, colleges, and universities regarding incidents of sexual assault all across the nation. What do you see as the most significant changes with regard to such protocol?
>
> **Katie:** *I've been analyzing policies and protocols since 1990 when I went through the process myself. When I first reported my assault to my residence hall assistant, he did the right thing by taking me to the health center. But at the time, there was no formal protocol for responding to sexual assault cases on campus. Most schools did not have protocol or policies for handling sexual assault or rape cases at the time. I went to the school health center and was sent home with sleeping pills. It was an extremely frustrating experience. Determined to make sure that the process would work better for those who came after me, I researched the problem and then wrote a protocol manual. I began traveling to other schools to share both my story and my advice on school policy and protocol from the perspective of someone who had gone through the system first hand.*
>
> *Since the early 90's, most colleges have added written policies and protocols to their handbooks. I'm not sure if any school has incorporated every idea I've recommended, but of course there are new permutations of this problem and newer technologies to help us respond each year. I am also encouraged by how many colleges also have sexual assault response coordinators. Schools often have a trifold brochure that outlines rights and options for survivors. A few schools have gone one step beyond that with rights and options of those accused of assault. A big change for the better has been the*

BOX 3.3 *(continued)*

shift away from looking at what the victim did to resist the assault and toward the responsibility of the perpetrator for committing the assault. When victims are blamed for their actions we lose focus that this is a crime perpetrated by those who are ignoring the unwillingness of their victim or are using coercion, physical force, threats, intimidation, or a power imbalance to create vulnerability.

JA: Where do you see the gaps of intervention work (e.g., university policy and protocol) today? In other words, what are your hopes for the future with regard to how sexual assault cases are handled by educational administrations?

Katie: *There are still a lot of gaps. I think a lot of universities have pockets of extremely well trained, well intentioned, and well versed individuals. But having these individuals in place is not the status quo, especially at some of our smaller colleges. The average faculty or staff member is not trained on response, and their ability to provide the proper support is therefore inconsistent. Schools should look toward adopting electronically or internet based protocols for all staff to follow when they receive a sexual assault report. This will provide a more unified response from an institution to victims and reports. There are a lot of students out there who are not women's studies majors who get assaulted. Certain groups of students, like student athletes or students of color, who are assaulted may not know where to go or feel comfortable with the designed office or point-person. Oftentimes, male survivors do not have good access to support on campuses as well.*

JA: Recent data suggest that the incidence rates of sexual assault are trending downward, and that reporting rates are increasing. What is your response to these trends?

Katie: *Hopefully, this means we're doing something right. I believe that the incidents may be moving from the college to high schools. One thing we may need to address is that a higher proportion of students entering college may have already been assaulted. I hear a tremendous number of stories from high school students when I'm working with that age group. I also hear from middle school girls about the casualness of giving oral sex to high school boys. This age and power difference from such a young age should not be overlooked as having a tremendous impact on future relationships. Universities may need to consider that these are the kinds of experiences that their future students will be bringing with them to college. Some women still see themselves as sexual objects, and learn to use their*

BOX 3.3 *(continued)*

sexual power to control male sexuality. In my opinion, this will always be a limitation for women achieving real equality.

I'd like to hope that by sharing my story over last 15 years, some good has been done. This is not a crime of complete silence, and I hope that by breaking this silence, even though I am a white woman of socio-economic privilege and don't well represent all victims, reports have increased. While I don't have quantitative data to support this, I do have qualitative data in the form of thousands of e-mails received from students who have heard me speak and tell of the impact that hearing my story had on their lives and choices.

JA: There is growing attention toward doing prevention work in the area of sexual assault and other forms of gender-based violence. What do you see as the relationship between intervention and prevention work?

Katie: *When our colleges are responding effectively to sexual assault reports, prevention should follow. Meaning, the more visibility consequences for committing sexual assault have, potential offenders will think twice about whether they can get away with crossing the line. The prevention work that I've been trying to do is cultivating a masculinity that doesn't involve violence against women, like the "strength is not for hurting" campaign that the Men Can Stop Rape organization has marketed.*

JA: Where do you intend to focus your energies in the future?

Katie: *I want to continue to inspire others to take a stand against sexual violence through my story and activism. I would like to continue to work with varying populations of teenagers and young adults. I try to be involved in lots of communities, not just traditional institutions of higher education. I have worked with rural schools, urban schools, communities of color, immigrant communities, and community colleges from coast to coast. Another population often missed are faith-based schools, who may be uncomfortable with feminist messages. It's critical that we look everywhere, in every nook and cranny, because sexual assault knows no boundaries. For example, women who are raped in prison are often ignored. Individuals from every community deserve to be treated with dignity and have the right to be respected.*

Power
Rape Trauma Syndrome
Self-blame
Shattered assumptions
Survivor
Victim

CRITICAL THINKING QUESTIONS

1. Distinguish between the terms ***victim*** and ***survivor***.
2. In what ways do victims of gender-based violence differ? What do many of them have in common?
3. How do individual incidents of gender-based violence hurt all individuals within a society?
4. As noted in the DSM-IV, symptoms of ***post-traumatic stress disorder*** may be more severe and longer-lasting when the trauma is caused by humans than when caused by a natural disaster. Why this might be the case?
5. If our society were truly egalitarian, how might the effects of trauma caused by gender-based violence be different for victims and survivors?
6. What can be done on a societal level to increase support for victims and survivors of gender-based violence?
7. What factors might aid the process of recovering from victimization?

PART II
THEORY

Chapter 4

Social Perspectives: Attitudinal Foundations of Gender-based Violence

It doesn't make any sense. In such a great and powerful country that values individual freedoms, legislates the protection of civil rights, and pledges "liberty and justice for all," patriarchy and its ensuing sexism prevail. Men make significantly more money than women and dominate over them in the political realm. In the United States of America, in spite of laws that define rape, sexual assault, and physical assault as criminal behaviors that will not be tolerated, and specify criminal penalties for these acts, men commit violence against women in epidemic proportion. Male attackers put women in danger at home, at work, and in the community on a daily basis.

It makes perfect sense. In such a great and powerful country that values rugged strength, power, and control, violence against those in weaker positions simply becomes a natural extension of those values. Most or all of the ideals professed to be important to American ideology are *relative* values. That is, in order for them to be expressed, a second party must be involved. Although personal power, control, and strength can certainly be advantageous, it is the interpersonal, social, and international power, control, dominance, and strength that are honored and rewarded in our society. In addition to being relative, these values are strongly defined as culturally masculine.

Our love of power and control, together with our disdain for violent crime create a contradiction. How is it possible to detest rapists, "wife beaters," sexual harassers, and stalkers, yet admire the masculine qualities that serve to support their violent crimes? How is it possible to abhor the crimes of gender—rape, partner violence, sexual harassment, and stalking—yet derogate and silence the survivors? Perspectives from the field of *social psychology* may help provide some insights to explain these apparent contradictions.

Social psychology is the study of the social influences of situations, especially the people in those situations (Myers, 2005). At the heart of social psychology is the understanding of the ways in which people view and affect one another. Social psychology researchers have convincingly demonstrated that situations, especially when they involve the presence of others, can have a powerful impact on the thoughts, feelings, and behaviors of other individuals (see Box 4.1 for a chilling example).

Social psychology can offer specific insights into these contradictions through the application of two theoretical traditions. First, an examination of the research on attitudes in general, and stereotypes specifically, will help provide an understanding of how we think about concepts relevant to gender-based violence on both a social and an individual level. Second, an awareness of research on cognitive dissonance will help us to gain insight into how individuals manage attitudinal contradictions that may exist when confronted with specific episodes of men's violence against women.

ATTITUDES

Attitudes refer to favorable or unfavorable evaluations of particular people, objects, events, or ideas (Eagly & Chaiken, 1998; Petty & Wegener, 1998). They are comprised of three components, often referred to as the "ABC model": affective, behavioral, and cognitive (Crites, Fabrigar, & Petty, 1994; Myers, 2005; Zanna & Rempel, 1988). The *affective component* is the emotional responses to various objects, the *behavioral component* is the way that actions are affected, and the *cognitive component* includes thoughts or beliefs regarding the object. However, it is not the case that each of these components contribute equally to any given attitude. Indeed, attitudes may be primarily based on any of the three (Zanna & Rempel, 1988).

> **BOX 4.1**
> **Learning from Dad**
>
> *The following letter was written by a 10-year-old boy to the Sparks Municipal Court Judge Andy Cray of Nevada (Curran, 1989).*
>
> **JUST LIKE DAD**
>
> *My mom couldn't iron my Cub Scout shirt today 'cuz her arm is in a sling. She made a stupid mistake and messed up the checkbook, so after all it was her own fault. I wish she'd learn to do things right so Dad wouldn't have to teach her a lesson.*
>
> *My Dad's a really neat guy. He coaches pee-wee football and takes me to the hockey games. He even came to see me in my school play, but mom couldn't come. Dad said if people saw her black eye, they might not understand it's for her own good. The way Dad explains it, it really does make sense. After all, he works all day and pays the bills while she just sits at home. He deserves the best. After all, he's the MAN of the house, the king of the castle. She should know better than to burn the roast or leave the house without him. 'Cuz dad says "A woman's place is in the home, taking care of us". I hope that when I get married, my wife is a perfect cook and beautiful and smart and never make mistakes, so I won't have to hurt her too bad.*
>
> Clearly this young boy was strongly affected by observing his father's abusive behavior toward his mother. From this letter, we can deduce that both his thoughts, such as "Mom deserves it when dad hurts her" and "A mom's role is to be a perfect housewife," and his feelings, such as admiration of his father and disrespect for his mother, have been repeatedly reinforced by his dad. The final passages of his letter imply his behavioral intent to carry on the abusive patterns into his own future relationships.

Cognitively Based Attitudes

Cognitively based attitudes are founded on beliefs, perceptions, and information—generally judged to be factual—that one has about an object, such as the beliefs that men should not be emotional or women should not be administrators. Individuals may form these attitudes from observation or seek out information in order to develop these attitudes. For example, before deciding to go on a date with a particular person, someone may ask mutual acquaintances about the potential date and assume that information to be true.

Behaviorally Based Attitudes

A behaviorally based attitude is one that is inferred from recent or past behavior, either with regard to the self or others. Consistent with the social psychological theory of self-perception (Bem, 1972), a person can develop an opinion by observing the self. Hence, a young man may ascertain that gender equality is important to him after he confronts his friend, who has just shared a sexist joke, regarding the inappropriate nature of the joke.

Affectively Based Attitudes

One's feelings and values can also serve as the catalyst for formation of the attitude. Such feelings may be positive (e.g., liking, admiring, respecting) or negative (e.g., fearing, disdaining, resenting). The function of such values is not necessarily to be factually correct (although most of us believe we are), but to support and validate a basic value system.

Cognitive, affective, and behavioral components are not always congruent. For example, a person may hold the belief that gay and lesbian people deserve respect and equal treatment (cognitive component), yet he or she may be uncomfortable around gay or lesbian individuals (affective component) and therefore avoids them (behavioral component). Attitudes, particularly affectively based attitudes, may also result from either classical or operant conditioning.

Classically conditioned attitudes. Classical conditioning takes place when a stimulus that naturally elicits an emotional response is paired with a neutral stimulus. Through the association of the stimuli, the neutral stimulus by itself may produce the response (Olson & Fazio, 2001; Pavlov, 1927). For example, while a man is in the process of kicking or hitting his partner, a specific song may be playing on the radio in the background. Through the process of pairing the song with the pain and terror of the violent behavior, the victim may develop an aversion to the song. Note that the attitudinal response to the stimuli is most likely an affective response.

Operantly conditioned attitudes. The frequency of specific behaviors may increase or decrease as a result of the consequences of those behaviors (Skinner, 1938). When we are rewarded for a particular act (through positive or negative reinforcement), we are likely to engage in that act again in the future. For example, if an adolescent boy tells his friends a sexist joke, and his peers laugh, he is quite likely to tell that joke again in the future. Conversely, if we are punished for a particular act, we are less likely to engage in that action again, at least in that particular situation. If the same boy tells the same joke to his mother and she responds with a discussion about sexism against women, the consequences of such sexism, and the inappropriateness of sexist jokes, he may not repeat the joke, at least not to his mother or others he perceives to be like her.

This process of operant conditioning naturally applies to the development of attitudes, as verbal or physical demonstrations of attitudes are directly reinforced or punished (Cacioppo, Marshall-Goodell, Tassinary, & Petty, 1992). Attitudes that are reinforced will likely be strengthened and expressed more frequently.

Explicit vs. implicit attitudes. Once an attitude has been established, it may exist on one of two levels. When an attitude exists on an explicit level, it is in full consciousness and can be easily identified and retrieved (Fazio & Olson, 2003). Implicit attitudes are less accessible to the conscious mind and are therefore less controllable than explicit attitudes. That is, their activation can be automatic and beyond our realm of awareness (Fazio & Olson, 2003). A person's explicit and implicit attitudes toward the same object may be inconsistent.

Consider, for example, attitudes toward gender roles and relationships between the sexes. One may care deeply about treating men and women equally and express this attitude frequently and explicitly. But the same person may experience discomfort in the presence of a man who is crying or a woman who is issuing orders as she supervises a team of workers, reflecting an implicit attitude more consistent with societal traditions: the beliefs that men should not be emotional and women should not be in charge.

It is also possible, of course, that one's explicit attitude is inconsistent with his or her expressed attitude. This situation could result if the explicit attitude is socially unacceptable or "politically incorrect" (e.g., embracing a sexist attitude). If this is the case, then the attitude may be easily brought to consciousness, but it is likely to be expressed in more subtle ways, or not at all. Explicitly sexist attitudes that are not expressed directly are referred to as ***modern sexism*** (See Box 4.2).

> **BOX 4.2**
> **Modern Sexism**
>
> In modern society, there are strong normative pressures to be fair and to treat individuals equally and respectfully. Mandates of political correctness leave no room for the outward expression of prejudicial attitudes or behavior. Therefore, those who adhere to sexist or racist beliefs may appear egalitarian on the surface but still maintain negative attitudes toward specific groups of people. In essence, the prejudice is hidden from view.
>
> Swim, Aiken, Hall, & Hunter (1995) borrowed from research on racism (Dovidio, Mann, & Gaertner, 1989; Gaertner & Dovidio, 1986; McConahay, 1986; Sears, 1988) to distinguish between *old-fashioned sexism* and *modern sexism*. Old-fashioned sexism is clearly sexist. It supports traditional gender roles, promotes unequal treatment of women, and justifies its existence through stereotypical notions of men's superiority. The more subtle modern sexism is less obviously prejudicial. It reflects a denial of sexist discrimination, animosity towards women's demands, and a reluctance to support issues relevant to women.
>
> Although it is not inappropriate that normative pressures toward egalitarianism exist, the resulting form of modern sexism renders it more difficult to identify and to combat. Although it is more subtle, modern sexism is not less damaging to women. For example, Swim et al. (1995) found that people who endorse modern sexism were also more likely to endorse male political candidates who were judged to be insensitive to women's issues.

Prejudice

Prejudice is a hostile or negative attitude toward a distinguishable group of people, based solely on their membership in that group (Aronson, Wilson, & Akert, 2005). Each of the ABC components of attitudes may be affected by prejudice. A prejudiced person might dislike members of the group (affect), may believe that members of the group are characteristically inferior to their own group (cognitive), and may behave in a discriminatory way towards them (behavioral).

Perhaps one of the most harmful aspects of prejudice is its consequential ignorance of the diversity within groups of human beings. How often have we heard the phrases "Men, they're all alike!" or "Girls, they're all alike!" (we note the pejorative term "girl" in this context to reflect societal reluctance to refer to sexually mature females as women)? This **out-group homogeneity bias** precludes us from discovering another's individuality: his or her talents, gifts, and idiosyncrasies (Linville, Fischer, & Salovey, 1989; Quattrone, 1986).

Stereotypes

The affectively based attitude of prejudice is supported by the cognitively based attitude of *stereotypes,* which are overgeneralizations about individuals, based on group membership. As renowned psychologist Gordon Allport (1954) once stated, "Given a thimbleful of facts we rush to make generalizations as large as a tub."

Stereotyping is a natural cognitive process that allows us to process information through the data-reductive process of simplifying our reality and our understanding of the world (Aronson, Wilson, & Akert, 2005). The process of stereotyping is wholly human and not inherently malevolent. Certainly, however, stereotyping can have negative consequences.

Levels of Processing: Automatic and Controlled

Stereotypes may be activated easily and without effort. Patricia Devine and her colleagues refer to this phenomenon as **automatic processing** (Devine, 1989; Zuwerink, Montieth, Devine, & Cook, 1996). Hence, when we see a woman, our stereotype of a woman may be automatically activated. This is potentially troubling, as even those who adhere to egalitarian values are likely familiar with the traditional stereotypes of men and women that will be activated. The automaticity of stereotype activation creates vulnerability for prejudiced and non-prejudiced individuals alike to interact with others using the stereotype as a perceptual guide in interactions.

In order to prevent stereotypes from creeping into perceptions of or interactions with others, non-prejudiced people undergo a two-step cognitive process. The first step is the automatic activation of the stereotype. If we are busy, overwhelmed, distracted, or indifferent, chances are we will go no further, and interactions based on the stereotype will take place. However, we choose to control the impact of the activated stereotype by acknowledging and consciously ignoring it, or by refuting its accuracy. Doing so reduces the negative impact of stereotypes but also takes time, attention, and effort on the part of the perceiver.

To take the second step and go beyond automatic activation, one must be aware of his or her potential for stereotyping and consciously choose not to engage in it. The implications of this process are huge; in order to not be sexist, one must consciously confront one's potential to be sexist, based on an awareness of gender stereotypes. And although automatic stereotype activation is normal for everyone, people who are trained in non-prejudicial thinking decrease their stereotype activation over time (Kawakami, Dovidio, Moll, Hermsen, & Russin, 2000).

Gender Stereotypes

The stereotypes most relevant to gender-based violence relate, of course, to beliefs about men's and women's places within the social order. These stereotypes are organized around the concepts of masculinity and femininity.

Masculinity. The traditional concept of U.S. masculinity revolves around four themes: antifemininity, status-achievement, inexpressiveness-independence, and adventurousness-aggressiveness (Brannon, 1985) See Box 4.3 for a prime example of stereotypical masculinity. Each of these themes serves as a set of behavioral prescriptions for boys and men regarding how they should feel, think, and behave. Ultimately, they create risks of violence.

Antifemininity ("No sissy stuff.") Males learn from an early age that there may be serious and negative consequences if they exhibit feminine mannerisms or express an interest in feminine activities or toys. In essence, boys and men are socialized in part by being taught how not to be, act, or feel. Most boys are taught that they must not express feelings (other than anger), be emotionally vulnerable, have emotional or sexual feelings for other males, or choose a profession associated with femininity (e.g., secretary, elementary school teacher).

Status and achievement ("The Big Wheel.") Stereotypically, men gain status through what they do, especially in sports and work, as opposed to who they are. Being successful in these arenas affords men power and commands respect from other men. Central to this value is the accumulation of wealth and possessions. As the adage goes, "He who dies with the most toys wins."

Inexpressiveness and independence ("The Sturdy Oak," or "The Male Machine.") This dimension dictates that men should be emotionally composed and task-oriented at all times, prepared to immediately fix any problem that comes their way.

> **BOX 4.3**
> **On Girly Men**
>
> On July 17, 2004, California Governor Arnold Schwarzenegger was frustrated by a legislative stalemate over his proposed budget. In a rally before hundreds of supporters, he called upon voters to terminate the legislators at the polls in November if they did not pass his budget, and he pugnaciously resorted to name-calling. Because the legislators could not come to an agreement on the issue of a budget, they were "girly men." The audience reinforced Schwarzenegger's mockery, responding with resounding applause (Nicholas, 2004).
>
> The messages embedded in Schwarzenegger's speech support the patriarchal values that provide a foundation for men's violence against women. First is the masculine belief that it is appropriate to respond to emotional frustration by blaming others and attacking the perceived source of frustration. Second is a reinforcement of sexist gender stereotypes. Even for a grown man representing an entire state of people, apparently the worst insult he could inflict upon a group of mostly male legislators was to refer to them as females. Finally, by virtually ignoring the female legislators involved in the budget debates, Schwarzenegger reveals the sexist privilege of powerful men that offers them the option of including women, or not, in their business matters.
>
> Arguably, Schwarzenegger is the epitome of masculine standards in our society. His evolution from body builder to actor to husband of Maria Shriver, a member of one of the most powerful families in the United States, to Governor of one of the largest states in the nation is not just a testament to his charisma and work ethic. More significantly, Schwarzenegger's success is also an example of how positively reinforcing it can be to display hypermasculinity.

Adventurousness and aggressiveness ("Give 'Em Hell.") Men are expected to be prepared to take physical risks at any time. Indeed, it is expected that they even enjoy physical risks like driving fast or playing a contact sport, and that they display an attitude of contempt toward danger. This dimension also demands that men be prepared to be violent and aggressive when deemed necessary.

As noted in previous chapters, standards of traditional masculinity are deeply connected to power and, ultimately, to gender-based violence. See Box 4.4 for a discussion of the relationship between real and perceived power among men.

Femininity. Cultural femininity is described as warm, expressive, and nurturing. Susan Basow (1995) notes that stereotypes of females generally divide into three sub-stereotypes: the housewife (traditional woman), the professional woman (independent, ambitious, self-confident), and the Playboy bunny (sex object).

Kay Deaux and her colleagues (Deaux, Winton, Crowley & Lewis, 1985) asked participants to list attributes for various sub-stereotypes of females, including the generic woman, housewife, athletic woman, and sexy woman. They also collected data on the stereotype and sub-stereotypes of males: the general man, blue-collar working man, athletic man, macho man, and businessman (see Box 4.5 for the specific characteristics identified for each).

Based on their data, Deaux et al. (1985) drew three conclusions regarding gender stereotypes. First, sub-stereotypes of women and men are just as strong as stereotypes of men and women in general. Second, stereotypes about women are more strongly differentiated than stereotypes about men. Third, perceptions about the sexes appear to be conceived in terms of opposites, for both male and female perceivers. Indeed, women and men appear to be remarkably similar in terms of the extent to which they see the sexes as different.

General attitudes towards males, females, masculinity, and femininity serve to support patriarchal ideology, and the consequential gender roles serve to reinforce this power differential. Although these general attitudes are important to our understanding of the social fabric that supports men's violence against women, a comprehensive understanding of all of its attitudinal foundations requires that we also explore more extreme and specific attitudes related to masculinity, femininity, sexism, and men's violence against women.

Hypermasculinity. The concept of hypermasculinity was developed to describe the extreme "macho" man (Mosher & Sirkin, 1984). It consists of three related components. First, hypermasculine men have sexually calloused attitudes toward women, equating heterosexual intercourse with male power and female submissiveness, and perceiving the sex as an "achievement" rather than a means of intimacy. Second is the belief that violence is an acceptable and often preferred means of expressing power, dominance, and manliness. Third is the view that danger is exciting and enjoyable.

> **BOX 4.4**
> **Being Powerful vs. Feeling Powerful**
>
> As a facilitator of a men's group a few years ago, Julie Allison vividly recalls a short but important conversation with a group member who had been using violence in his relationship for a very long time.
>
> **Facilitator:** *The reason that you were able to get away with beating your wife for two years with no consequences was perhaps because you could get away with it. You have all of the power in the relationship.*
>
> **Group member:** *Yea, right, where is all this power you're talking about?*
>
> Many men do not necessarily feel as powerful as they are taught they should feel. Indeed, there appears to be a discrepancy between the collective power of men in our society and the perception of power in individual men. Kimmel (1994) eloquently stated the relationship between the reality and the perceptions of power: "Men's experience of powerlessness is *real*—the men actually feel it and certainly act on it—but it is not *true*, that is, it does not actually describe their condition" (p. 137). He later described men who claim powerlessness as having a "wind chill" psychology: "It doesn't really matter what the actual temperature is; what matters is what it feels like" (Kimmel, 2006, p. 218).
>
> In our society, we are faced with a collective male power that affords men advantage and privilege and with a collective of individual males who do not perceive that this power applies to them. This creates an interesting paradox: A way to help balance the power differential between men and women is conceivably to restore a sense of actual power in women and a sense of individual power in both women and men.
>
> Applying this sense of powerlessness to men who resort to fatal violence provides a stark reality. As Ewing (1987) noted, "The typical family killer is more likely to have been concerned about losing control over more than just his wife and family. His concern is more often with losing control with all aspects of his life, or at least those that he most values. He is a man who, in his own eyes, is or is about to become, a failure."

Men's adherence to hypermasculine attitudes is associated with proclivities to engage in acts of violence against women. In one study, males who scored high on a hypermasculinity scale reported

> **BOX 4.5**
> **Of Stereotypes and Substereotypes**
>
> The collection of data regarding stereotypes and substereotypes of various types of males and females by Deaux and her colleagues (Deaux, Winton, Crowley, & Lewis, 1985) allows for a comparison not only between masculine and feminine concepts, but of general and specific stereotypes. For each category, participants found the following characteristics to be most prototypical:
>
> **For women**
> - *Woman:* attractive, feminine, smart, sensitive, emotional
> - *Housewife:* cleans, cooks, cares for kids, stays busy
> - *Athletic woman:* muscular, fit, strong, aggressive, masculine
> - *Sexy woman:* good figure, long hair, good dresser, manicured nails, pretty face
> - *Business woman:* smart, well-dressed, unmarried, hard-working, organized
>
> **For men**
> - *Man:* strong, unemotional, macho, sexy, muscular
> - *Blue-collar working-man:* factory worker, hard-worker, middle-lower class citizen, uneducated laborer, union member
> - *Athletic man:* muscular, healthy, strong, fit
> - *Macho man:* muscular, hairy, attractive, self-centered
> - *Business man:* wears a suit, has an office with a view, has college education, is smart, has good appearance
>
> Stereotypes in general are likely to be inaccurate (to various degrees) when applied to specific individuals. Substereotypes are often created when faced with examples of individuals who are not consistent with already existing stereotypes (e.g., a male who adheres to feminist values). Hence, substereotypes allow the perception of having more accurate information of individuals and, ironically, allow the maintenance of stereotypes deemed inaccurate in the first place.

a greater acceptance of callous sex, both casual and coercive (J. P. Sullivan & Mosher, 1990). Men reporting greater hypermasculine attitudes also acknowledged a history of engaging in acts of sexual coercion against women and using force in dating situations (Mahoney, Shively, & Traw, 1986; Mosher & Anderson, 1986).

Recall in chapter 2 that Kilmartin's conditional model of violence includes pathology of the perpetrator. Although there are certainly some hypermasculine men who are not violent, both the theoretical and empirical relationships identified between hypermasculinity and men's violence against women support the conclusion that extreme forms of masculinity may be both toxic and pathological.

Hyperfemininity. Hyperfemininity is an exaggerated adherence to the stereotypical feminine gender role and includes the belief that women's success revolves around their sexuality and their ability to develop and maintain a relationship with a man. For those who adhere to hyperfemininity, sexuality has primary importance in both maintaining such a relationship and in affording the woman some power within it. Those who endorse this ideology also tend to believe that the rights and roles of women in society should be restrictive and traditional (Murnen & Byrne, 1991). For example, women who score high on the Hyperfeminine Inventory also tend to believe that marriage is more important than career and that their potential spouse should have an economically successful and prestigious job. Additionally, more feminine women have been found to react less harshly to depictions of sexual coercion (Murnen, 1998).

The concepts of hypermasculinity and hyperfemininity are mutually reinforcing and serve to perpetuate traditional gender roles and gender-based violence. Reiss (1986) found that in societies with a high incidence of rape, hypermasculinity is more likely to be endorsed as appropriate for males. In a meta-analysis that included 39 studies and 11 different attitudinal measures relevant to the perpetration of sexual assault, hypermasculinity was found to be the strongest predictor of sexual assault (Murnen, Wright, & Kaluzny, 2002). Murnen et al. (2002) go on to argue that, although hyperfemininity is not causally related to men's violence against women, it plays a supportive role. Hence, hyperfemininity may contribute to the attitudinal foundation that justifies, rationalizes, or minimizes instances of men's violence against women.

So far, we have discussed attitudes that help to provide the psychological foundations of patriarchy: attitudes toward men and masculinity, and toward women and femininity. These attitudes are more general constructs and do not directly assess the ensuing sexist attitudes that result from traditional views on gender.

Sexist attitudes. Sexist attitudes serve to provide foundations for gender-based violence on both a personal and social level. Peter Glick and Susan Fiske (2001a, 2001b) have extensively investigated two constructs that they have found to be related to the existence of gender inequality: ***hostile sexism*** and ***benevolent sexism***. Strong adherence to both may produce ambivalence toward women, a concept measured by the Ambivalent Sexism Inventory (ASI) (Glick & Fiske, 2001a).

Hostile sexism. Those who accept an attitude of hostile sexism are distrustful of women specifically, and gender relationships in general. They perceive women as seeking to control men either through sexuality or feminism (Glick & Fiske, 2001a). Hostile sexism is negative and strong, and fits Gordon Allport's (1954) classic definition of prejudice: "antipathy based upon a faulty and inflexible generalization" (p. 9). Moreover, hostile sexism has been found to be related to the concept of modern sexism described earlier in Box 4.2.

Benevolent sexism. Also known as the "women are wonderful" effect, this is the belief that women are to be cherished, adored, and protected (Glick & Fiske, 1996). (See Box 4.6 for a discussion of its chivalrous foundations.) Behavior that manifests from this attitude can be quite positive and helpful, as when a man carries a heavy box for a woman, or offers to help her work on her car.

On the surface, this attitude may appear positive, or at least benign in its impact on women. Such is not the case, however. Inherent in the idea that women are to be protected is the corresponding belief that women are weak and helpless. Furthermore, if women are to be protected, then men are placed in the dominant role of protectors. Here, the concept of "helping" disguises the dominance afforded to males and the imbalance of power between the sexes.

Although hostile sexism was found to be related to the concept of modern sexism conceptualized by Swim, Aiken, Hall, and Hunter (1995), benevolent sexism was not. Thus, the construct of benevolent sexism is tapping a unique form of sexism against women not previously identified (Glick & Fiske, 1996). After administering the ASI to over 15,000 men and women in 19 nations, Glick and Fiske (2001a) suggest that this form of sexism may be particularly insidious. There is a highly significant correlation between hostile and benevolent sexism, both of which predict gender inequality across cultures. The researchers argue that this juxtaposition of two forms of sexism allows some men (e.g., hypermasculine ones) and some women (e.g., hyperfeminine ones) to both love and hate women at the same time.

Benevolent sexism is also unique because women are more likely to endorse forms of benevolent than hostile sexism. Benevolent

BOX 4.6
Chivalry

The term ***chivalry*** comes from the French chevalier, a medieval knight or horseman. It refers to an attitude of protectionism over the weak, especially women. In the modern era, chivalry manifests itself in a series of gentlemanly behaviors that are thought to reflect a respectful attitude, such as opening doors for women, standing when they enter or leave the room, holding their chairs out so they can sit at a table, filling their drinks, and paying on dates.

Although chivalry is ostensibly intended to convey respect, we would argue that it is more of an effort to give the appearance of respect, although one can certainly be chivalrous and respectful at the same time. As such, stereotypical chivalry is a form of benevolent sexism that is used as a (usually nonconscious) strategy to get women to cooperate with unequal power between the sexes.

There is a great deal of difference between chivalry and respect. Respect involves listening to someone, valuing their opinions, and behaving on the basis of that valuing. Chivalry is a rigid set of rules based on the mistaken proposition that all women are alike. Chivalry might dictate giving flowers to someone who is allergic to them or opening the door for someone who does not wish for you do so. Respect would indicate the opposite behavior.

Etiquette columnist Miss Manners (Judith Martin) is reputed to have said, "A lady never fills her wine glass for herself. She looks wistfully into the bottom of her empty glass until the gentlemen in the room trip all over themselves to fill it for her." Although it sounds romantic, the bottom line is that if the woman wants another glass of wine, she has to depend on a man to get it for her. Chivalry is a set of behaviors that infantilizes women by allowing men to do all kinds of things for them that they are perfectly capable of doing for themselves, and it sets up a subtle, or not so subtle, power differential. She enjoys her power over men, but it's the kind of power that slaves have in relation to their masters—they can revolt, not do their jobs, and undermine their masters' authority, but their power is nothing compared to the masters' power.

As Glick and Fiske (2001a) have pointed out, benevolent sexist attitudes are reserved for women who cooperate with masculine power and privilege, while hostile sexist attitudes, or woman hating, are directed toward women who do not cooperate, such as lesbians, feminists, and women who refuse to conform their

> **BOX 4.6** *(continued)*
>
> behavior to masculine standards. Thus, at the systemic level, benevolent and hostile sexism are two sides of the same coin, as they both operate to deny women's humanity and power. Note that chivalry is a strong value in the U.S. Military, yet military men as a group commit high rates of violence against women (White, 2005). It is also noteworthy that many men have told us that they feel offended when women do not respond positively to their chivalric behaviors, which would seem to indicate that many of these men perform these behaviors in the service of their own self interests rather than as selfless acts for women. Glick (2005) also points out that most chivalric behaviors are "trivial niceties." If men want to help women, they should be willing to help with things that really matter, such as pay inequality, child care, and men's violence against women.
>
> We have found in the classroom that a critical discussion of benevolent sexism and chivalric behavior often results in confusion and frustration, especially for male students. If being nice to a woman (e.g., holding the door open for her) could actually be sexist, what behavioral options are left for respectful men? We suggest a simple solution for both men and women: Ask if you can be of help, and listen to the response.

sexism may have an appeal to some, particularly those who adhere to a hyperfeminine ideal. It is also likely that women who support benevolent sexism will be reinforced for endorsing it.

Attitudes toward rape. The attitudes specific to sexism pave the way for even more specific attitudes regarding men's violence against women. Most of the research in this area has involves investigation of attitudes regarding the crime of rape.

In her classic work on the subject, Susan Brownmiller (1975) noted that there are a plethora of myths and inaccurate stereotypes about rape, rapists, and rape survivors in our society. These ***rape myths*** generally take one of three forms:

1. *Women secretly wish to be raped,* and they find the idea of being physically forced to engage in unwanted sexual acts appealing. Note that this myth is impossible to refute (Burt, 1980).

2. *Most accusations of rape are faked,* and therefore one should be distrustful of women's allegations, believing that women routinely lie about rape to avoid the negative consequences of engaging in consensual sex. Recall from chapter 1 that the problem is actually quite the opposite: most women do not report the violence of men.
3. *Women cannot be raped against their will.* The argument is that any healthy woman could resist a rape attack if she really wanted to.

Utilizing feminist theory as her guide, Martha Burt (1980) developed attitudinal scales to assess rape myth acceptance (RMA) along with four attitudinal variables that she deemed theoretically relevant to attitudes toward rape. She argued that the acceptance of rape myths is part of a broader ideology of values and beliefs, as it is positively correlated with three broad attitudes: (a) adversarial sexual belief, or the belief that sexual relationships between men and women are fundamentally exploitative; (b) acceptance of interpersonal violence as a justifiable way to solve problems; and (c) the acceptance of traditional gender-role stereotypes. The strongest predictor of rape myth acceptance was an acceptance of interpersonal violence.

Lonsway and Fitzgerald (1994) have extended our understanding of rape myths by identifying the social and functional effects endorsing these beliefs. They point out that the acceptance of rape myths does more than just lead to cognitively based misconceptions about the crime of rape. It also serves to provide individuals and society the denial, minimization, and justification that ultimately support and perpetuate the existence of men's sexual violence.

In a review of previous research, Lonsway and Fitzgerald note that there have been surprisingly few consistent findings regarding rape myth acceptance, most likely due to theoretical discrepancies and psychometric issues. Those reliable findings that they identified include

- Men consistently report higher levels of rape myth acceptance than women.
- Those who report more negative attitudes toward women tend to have higher levels of rape myth acceptance.
- Those who adhere to traditional gender roles tend to have higher levels of rape myth acceptance.
- Higher levels of rape myth acceptance have been linked to men who report a greater likelihood of raping.

The researchers note:

> "We suggest that these four relationships are central to an understanding of rape myths; that is, the nomological net of RMA has at its core gender, traditional [gender] role attitudes, negative attitudes toward women, and likelihood of raping. Such a configuration conveys a powerful message about how RMA relates to other beliefs about women in our society" (Lonsway & Fitzgerald, 1994, p. 155).

We are in concurrence and find these conclusions generalizable to all forms of men's violence against women. It is the traditional conceptions of gender, that men are superior and women ultimately inferior, that function to offer men social roles with higher status and financial reward while offering women social roles of little social significance and less financial reward. Broad and sexist ideologies serve to support specific and inaccurate beliefs about gender-based violence, which also serve to perpetuate men's acts of violence against women.

Thus far we have discussed attitudes in a primarily general sense, referring to those endorsed within a society, or within groups or subgroups of individuals. In order to make sense of that which makes no sense, however, we must also take into account the individual attitudinal gymnastics in which both men and women may engage to make their cognitive worlds appear reasonable. The social psychological theory of ***cognitive dissonance*** can be helpful in explaining how individuals may alter attitudes so that they match feelings and behaviors, and perpetuate the existence of gender-based violence in the process.

COGNITIVE DISSONANCE THEORY

Consider the following examples:

- Sam professes to love his longtime partner Greta. When he wants to have sex and she does not, he holds her down and forces his penis into her vagina.
- John considers himself a decent man. John hits and kicks his girlfriend Hannah on a regular basis.
- Greg is so upset that his girlfriend Emily has broken up with him that he is willing to do anything to get her back. Greg follows Emily to school and work, and when she's out with her friends, even though Emily has repeatedly asked him to stop.
- Jacob considers himself a successful supervisor at his workplace. On occasion he has exchanged financial benefits to his female employ-

ees who submit to his coercive tactics to obtain what he would refer to as sex.

On the surface, each of these examples reveals glaring inconsistencies. Most general belief systems include the corresponding notions that men do not rape the women they love, decent men do not beat their girlfriends, stalking an ex-girlfriend is not likely to restore the relationship, and successful supervisors do not commit sexual harassment.

According to Festinger (1957), such inconsistencies may create cognitive dissonance, or tension that arises when one is simultaneously aware of two inconsistent cognitions (e.g., "I am a decent person," and "I am a batterer.") (Myers, 2005). This tension is psychologically uncomfortable and impels a person to reduce the dissonance. According to Festinger, "Just as hunger is motivating, cognitive dissonance is motivating. Cognitive dissonance will give rise to activity oriented toward reducing or eliminating the dissonance" (Festinger, 1957, p. 70). By reducing such dissonance, we are able to maintain a positive self-image, and once again feel good, smart, worthwhile, or safe (Aronson, 2004).

There are several possibilities for reducing the tension created by cognitive dissonance. One could, of course, change his or her behavior (e.g., John could quit hitting and kicking Hannah), effectively eliminating the source of tension. More commonly, self-justifying attitudinal changes take place in forms of rationalizations (attempting to make unreasonable behavior seem reasonable through excuses), denials (refusing to acknowledge reality), and minimizations (diminishing the seriousness of behavior or the outcome of the behavior). For men who commit violence, especially against those whom they presumably love, the possibilities are endless, and they are absurd if subject to any rational analysis. A rapist is likely to claim that the victim actually wanted him to force his penis into her vagina. A batterer may believe that it is his job as man of the house to teach his partner lessons, and thus violent behavior is sometimes necessary. A stalker may perceive his behavior as flattering to the victim, and a sexual harasser may discount the harm caused by his illegal behavior. All such self-justifications allow for the perpetuation of the violence.

However, it is not only those men who commit violence against women who experience cognitive dissonance in response to such violent episodes. On a nearly daily basis, all of us are exposed to alarming examples of men's abuse and violence against women, either personally or through local or national media. And many of us may be motivated to use dissonance-reducing strategies to create a sense of security within our own worlds. These strategies may include

- *Holding survivors of rape responsible for the rapist's attack.* Those who utilize this tactic may be threatened by the reality that anyone is vulnerable to attack.
- *Rationalizing that victims involved in abusive relationships could simply leave if they really wanted to.* Not only does this attitude prevent compassion for victims of men's ongoing violence, it eliminates the need to hold the perpetrator accountable and responsible for his violent behavior.
- *Diminishing the seriousness of stalking behavior, and the level of fear that is experienced by the stalker's target.* Stalking is a terrifying pattern of discrete behaviors that in isolation may not appear to be a "big deal."
- *Overlooking the sexual harassment of a supervisor because he is good for business.* The sexual harassment of company employees is not good for any business.

There are healthier means of reducing cognitive dissonance than finding a way to excuse the actions of the perpetrator (usually through finding fault with the survivor). Indeed, it seems quite reasonable to recognize that incidents of gender-based violence are illegal acts for which a perpetrator should be held accountable. Cognitive dissonance theory would suggest that if we recognize that incidents of gender-based violence are the responsibility of the perpetrators and work to hold them accountable, there would no longer be cognitive dissonance, and the motivation to find fault in the survivor could cease to exist.

SUMMARY

Social psychology is the study of the effect of situation, especially the presence of others, and conscious or unconscious judgments about others, on people's behavior. It offers a rich analysis of men's violence against women by helping to explain how inconsistent and often contradictory beliefs, behaviors, and feelings can exist simultaneously within a society and even within an individual. The attitudinal underpinnings of violence are more complicated than they might seem at first glance. For example, one could hold a belief in gender egalitarianism but at the same time continue to have sexist feelings and behaviors. A man may believe that he is respectful toward women when he is actually just being chivalrous by displaying a stereotypic set of gentlemanly behaviors based on the mistaken assumption that all women are alike. Gender-based violence is reinforced by the power differentials between men and women, which are in turn reinforced by social psychological processes that include ambivalent sexism, rape myth acceptance, and cognitive distortions.

KEY TERMS

Affective component
Antifemininity
Attitude
Automatic processing
Behavioral component
Benevolent sexism
Chivalry
Classically conditioned attitudes
Cognitive component
Cognitive dissonance
Femininity
Gender stereotypes
Hostile sexism
Hyperfemininity
Hypermasculinity
Implicit attitude
Masculinity
Modern sexism
Negative reinforcement
Operantly conditioned attitudes
Out-group homogeneity bias
Power
Prejudice
Privilege
Rape myths
Social psychology
Stereotype

CRITICAL THINKING QUESTIONS

1. Compare and contrast the following terms: attitudes, behavior, and cognitions.
2. Distinguish between **old-fashioned sexism** and **modern sexism**. What are the effects of modern sexism?
3. Describe some possible effects of the **out-group homogeneity bias**.
4. Comment on the statement "Stereotyping is a necessary cognitive process for all individuals."
5. What are possible consequences of stereotyping? Is it possible to not use stereotypes in one's perceptions of other individuals? Explain your answer.
6. How do culturally prevalent attitudes about males, females, masculinity, and femininity serve to support men's violence against women?
7. What are the advantages and disadvantages to conforming to one's gender stereotype?
8. Distinguish between **hostile sexism** and **benevolent sexism**. How are both of these forms of sexism harmful to both males and females?
9. Provide arguments for and against the suggestion that "**chivalry** should end in our society." Based on the arguments you provide, what is your conclusion about this suggestion?
10. Using the theory of cognitive dissonance, explain how it is possible for a person to abuse someone they presumably love.

Chapter 5

The Big Picture

Before moving to a discussion of prevention programs for men's violence against women, it seems appropriate to talk about the "big picture." As we have alluded to several times, the problem of men's violence against women is a problem for individual men but it is also embedded in larger social systems. The chapters that follow this one are mainly focused on prevention efforts in somewhat limited social contexts: individuals, small groups, and school and community organizations. Larger efforts such as The White Ribbon Campaign and Men Can Stop Rape are attempts to effect changes on a larger scale, mainly by raising awareness of the problem and promoting attitude change within national populations. As Rutherford and Chapman (1988) argued, "to produce a masculinity whose desire is no longer dependent on oppression, no longer policed by homophobia, and one that no longer resorts to violence and misogyny to maintain its sense of coherence....is a major political project" (p. 18).

However, attitude change is only one component of the remedy to a problem that has historical, economic, legal, legislative, cultural, and other social-structural attributes. A true "big picture" analysis takes these larger forces into account and proposes solutions that strike at the very foundations of the problem. With the assumption that the ultimate solution lies in a restructuring of the environment in which the problem occurs, this chapter provides a *macrosocietal perspective* on the causes, consequences, and solutions to men's violence against women.

THE HISTORICAL FOUNDATIONS OF GENDER INEQUALITY

The assumptions that underlie the macrosocietal hypothesis are, first, that gender roles are embedded within a society's division of labor, and, second, that in most modern cultures such gender arrangements support significantly greater power for men-as-a-group compared with women-as-a-group (Lerner, 1986). Although there is certainly great variation among individuals' levels of social power (e.g., a wealthy, white woman will be relatively powerful compared with a poor, minority man), in the aggregate, males "run the show." They control vastly more wealth and occupy a large majority of high government, business, and judicial positions. As we have noted throughout this book, in the United States, upper-income white men are by far the most dominant influencers of laws, labor arrangements, media and arts, and, in general, the cultural worldview of the populace. It is this power imbalance, an artifact of a historical gender-based division of labor, which supports men's violence against women. Therefore, although this violence can certainly be mitigated through education, law enforcement, and new legislation, it will never end completely until gender asymmetry is replaced with gender egalitarianism.

How did this power imbalance arrive on the scene? Based on the premise that gender is intertwined with work and family arrangements, an understanding of the history of work and the sexes is critical to an understanding of men's violence against women and its solutions. Following is a brief history of divisions of labor between the sexes.

A HISTORY OF GENDER AND LABOR

Human history can roughly be divided into four great eras based on the dominant forms of labor within societies: hunter/gatherer, agricultural, industrial, and post-industrial. Post-industrial society characterizes urban life in relatively affluent areas, but these other forms of societies still exist in many parts of the world.

Hunting and gathering was the only form of labor for more than 98% of human history. Based on anthropological and historical evidence, many scholars suggest that although there are variations in gender arrangements depending upon the circumstances of individual societies, hunter/gatherer groups are usually characterized by equality and cooperation between men and women. Many believe that gender was not an organizing principle in these cultures because there was no need for it to be so, as it made sense for the survival of the group for men and women to undertake similar foraging activities. Even in societies in which hunting was considered to be a masculine activity, women's labor accounted for a majority of the community food supply. Therefore, women were critical to the group's subsistence and held positions of social power. In these societies, which still exist in some parts of the world, violence against women occurs infrequently, and rape is nearly nonexistent—evidence that men's violence against women operates as a means for dominance over and subordination of not merely individual women, but women in general.

Agricultural societies began to appear around 3100 B.C.E. and ushered in a new set of economic demands. Prior to the development of modern machinery, much farm labor demanded upper-body strength and thus became men's work. It was an economic advantage to have many children, who could start to work at a young age and produce more food than they could consume. Therefore, women became most valuable as mothers, and over time, men began to control women's reproduction, and, by extension, their sexuality (Lerner, 1986). The most important work women could do in these societies was to give birth to as many children as possible during their childbearing years.

Hunter/gatherer societies were nomadic, but agricultural people were able to settle in one place for generations or even centuries. Private ownership, especially of land, came into existence and the intergenerational transmission of it was usually from father to son as a part of the institution of patriarchy, an arrangement by which males dominated in public life. Over time, men came to restrict women's movement and control other parts of their lives, and a stricter division of labor developed: "Man for the field; woman for the hearth." Men came to eschew "women's work"—childcare and other domestic duties—and masculinity came to be defined as antifemininity. Men who acted like women were shamed as unmanly. Boys were taught at an early age that femininity was far less worthy than masculinity, and gender equality was a threat to male dominance. Agricultural societies remain the bases for most of the world's industrial and post-industrial economies.

This change from hunter/gatherer egalitarianism to agricultural male dominance has been documented in the !Kung of Africa, a society that moved from a foraging to an agricultural economic base in the middle 20th century due to the influence of European occupation. Over the course of a generation, women began to contribute smaller proportions of the food supply and children began to segregate into single-sex play groups. Men increasingly limited women's mobility and refused to do what became regarded as "women's work." Aggression increased, including men's violence against women (Basow, 1992).

Because land became valuable in agricultural societies, it had to be defended, meaning that some members of the society had to be willing to risk their lives for the sake of the rest of the community. This task fell to men because of their upper-body strength, greater mobility (because men do not become pregnant nor nurse, and childcare can be seen as more optional for men), and the "expendability" of individual men's lives (stemming from the biological fact that relatively few men can father a great number of children). The designation of men to the important role of "defenders" placed them in the paradoxical roles of both protectors and warriors. The defensive posturing of this new warrior culture required the objectification of the enemies in order to engage in organized violence, which took the form of both killing the male enemy soldiers and humiliating them through the ritualistic rape of the women of conquered territories (Brownmiller, 1975).

To go from man to soldier requires colossal transformation. Men must be stripped of natural and vulnerable emotions if they are to perform the unnatural tasks of risking their lives on a regular basis, killing other men, and in some cases raping women. Hence, a masculinity that included objectivity, dispassion, and aggression became highly necessary and valued while natural and vulnerable feelings and empathy became associated with femininity—and women—and were disdained by men. (See Box 5.1 for a more current example of the derision of femininity.) Through this transformation, men and women came to inhabit very separate and unequal spheres of public and private life.

Cross-cultural researchers have demonstrated a significant connection between a society's level of sex segregation and level of men's violence against women (Coltrane, 1998; Sanday, 1981). Moreover, gender-based violence is also correlated with low levels

> **BOX 5.1**
> **Imagining the Self as a Person of the Other Sex**
>
> Researchers asked U.S. boys and girls from third to twelfth grade, "If you were to wake up tomorrow and discover that you were a member of the other sex, how would your life be different?" The results were revealing. Most of the students were sure that a change in sex would radically alter their lives.
>
> Girls reported that, if they were boys, they would be more assertive and self-reliant, express less emotion and more aggression, have more freedom, think less about their appearance, be freed from treatment as a sex object, perform different duties at home, and spend more quality time with their fathers.
>
> The boys imagined that, if they were girls, they would be quieter and more reserved, less active and more restricted, that they would worry more about their appearance, be treated as sex objects, worry about being the targets of perpetrators, and do fewer things with their fathers. Two boys put it succinctly:
>
> "If I woke up and I was a girl, I would go back to sleep and hope it was a bad dream."
>
> "If I were a girl, I'd kill myself."
>
> Clearly, boys and girls acknowledge the gender stereotypes that perpetuate the view that males are completely different, and better, than females (Baumgartner, 1983).

of men's participation in childcare (Coltrane, 1998). Thus, when men and boys learn to view the all-important work of raising children as being beneath them, they are predisposed toward devaluing, objectifying, and assaulting women. Since men-as-a-group dominate legal and political decisions, many assaultive men are not held accountable with negative social sanctions of any kind.

By the turn of the 19th century, agriculture had become so successful that a smaller proportion of the populace could produce enough food for all, and the Industrial Revolution moved a significant amount of labor from the farm to the factory. Because this work required physical strength and long periods of time away from the home, it became men's work unless there were male labor shortages, as in times of war. The gendered division of labor became even sharper, as did the ethic of antifemininity. Women's work was critical to family functioning, but much of it was unpaid, and men-as-a-group came to even higher levels of wealth-accumulation and control. Women (and children) were considered the legal property of their husbands. In fact, rape laws were originally property crimes against the husband and domestic violence laws were fashioned after animal cruelty laws, which came into existence first (Kimmel & Mosmiller, 1992).

In many parts of the world, warrior culture and economic conditions, and their resulting effect on social conceptions of masculinity, have set the stage for violence against women. However, significant cultural variations in beliefs about manliness provide evidence that, rather than being a hardwired reality, masculinity is socially constructed around the basic needs of the society. From this perspective, there is a "family resemblance" to masculinity because of commonalities in the histories of various cultures and men's violence against women can decrease if social and economic influence forces changes in the social ideations around what it means to be a man.

Anthropologist David Gilmore's (1990) *Manhood in the Making* is a comparative study of masculinity within several cultures. In most, masculinity was defined by strength, risk-taking, avoidance of femininity, aggression, and sexual initiative. Moreover, men were thought to achieve manhood through some sort of rite of passage, usually involving physical discomfort or pain, rather than merely growing into it, hence the title of the book. But there were two striking exceptions that lend support to the social-structural hypothesis: Tahiti (Polynesia) and Semai (central Malaysia). In both, men are gentle, non-competitive, and nonviolent. There is little ideology of women as property and little sexual jealousy. In fact, gender is not much of an organizing principle in the society; women and men are thought to be similar. Gilmore remarked that foreigners visiting Tahiti were amazed at the

> bizarre [by Western standards] lack of sexual differentiation on the island ...Tahitian women had a remarkably high status and were permitted to do almost everything that the men did...Men are no more aggressive than women; women do not seem 'softer' or 'more maternal' than the men...there is no stress on proving manhood, no pressure on men to appear in any significant way different from women or children. Men have no fear of acting in ways Westerners would consider effeminate. During dances, for instance, adult men will dance together in close bodily contact, rubbing against each other without any anxiety... (p. 202–203)

What social forces have caused these two cultures to be so different from the rest of the world? Because of unusual circumstances, there has never been any use for masculinity to be defined by dominance, aggression, or antifemininity. In both of these cultures, there is plenty of land and food, thus no competition for scarce resources. Importantly, there has been no warfare or any other labor (such as dangerous hunting or fishing) that puts its citizens at risk. Therefore, there has been no need to socialize anyone to be willing to die on behalf of the society, no warrior culture, and no need to differentiate men from women in social ideologies. Gilmore describes the unusual circumstance and histories of these two cultures:

> There is no want of natural resources and thus no economic incentive to strive or to compete, no agonistic ethos, no open market for skills. Because the economy is cooperative, ambition is devalued. There are no serious hazards in the external world that the men are expected to defend against ... Neither society feels threatened by invaders; neither engages in warfare. There is little pressure for worldly success. There is no concept of a secluded private sphere of women and children that men must protect. Men have no interest in defining themselves as different from or superior to women, or as their defenders. In short, there is little basis for an ideology of manhood that motivates men to perform under pressure or to defend boundaries (pp. 217–218)

As post-industrial society continues to develop, gender roles are becoming less and less relevant to aspects of life besides reproduction, as the gendered division of both work and family labor is evaporating. Labor-saving devices mean that men's upper-body strength is no longer an economic asset; there is virtually no work that men can do and women cannot. When available, reproductive technologies allow people to control the timing of reproduction and the size of families. Children are no longer an economic asset; hence, families are tending to become smaller. Because a single income is less often sufficient for most families than in the past, and because many women want to claim their right to be full economic partners in society, paid labor settings are becoming increasingly heterogeneous. Moreover, we are seeing a sharp increase in men's participation in childcare and other family work, albeit still far short of equal responsibility for domestic labor.

As women slowly attain a more equal share of wealth and institutional power, we should come full circle to the gender-egalitarian character of foraging societies. Of course, this is a very slow process, and we do not anticipate its completion within our lifetimes. However, if one accepts the argument that gender is embedded in economic arrangements and the division of labor, then gender power asymmetry and gender-based violence should change in response to the evolution of systems in which the sex of the person occupying the work or family role is irrelevant in most social settings. As psychologist Sandra Bem told her children, "What sex you are doesn't matter unless you're trying to make a baby."

We are not suggesting that institutional, governmental, educational, or individual efforts to end men's violence are unnecessary, or that gender development will work this problem out by itself. Nor are we suggesting that the march forward to equality is a linear one, as we have certainly seen times when the wheels seem to be turning backwards, most notably in early 21st century United States, which has been marked by an upsurge in the power of socially conservative politicians and a renewed culture of belligerence. As evidence of the latter, witness the popularity of "reality television" in which viewers revel in the bullying of powerless contestants, or the continued popularity of so-called "professional wrestling" (which is neither professional, nor is it wrestling) which continues to ratchet up its level of violence and humiliation, increasingly directed at female characters. At this writing, the United States is the only industrialized nation that has not yet ratified the United Nations Convention on the Elimination of all Forms of Discrimination Against Women (CEDAW) treaty (un.org/womenwatch/daw/cedaw/states.htm, 2006).

But at the same time, a "big picture" analysis reveals that larger societal forces are taking us in the right direction. Non-agricultural societies are more gender-egalitarian than agricultural ones, and urban areas, which are more likely to have a wide economic base, are more gender-egalitarian than rural ones. In the last several U.S. presidential elections, the more liberal, gender-progressive candidate carried every major city.

CULTURE AND VIOLENCE

Intimate partner violence takes place in a cultural context that supports it. Historically, mainstream U.S. society has endorsed men's domination of women, even to the point of violence (Landes, Squyres, & Quiram, 1997). In 1996, a Maryland man fatally shot his wife when he found her in bed with another man. He was found guilty, and the male judge in the case apologized to the defendant when he sentenced him to prison, saying that mandatory sentencing guidelines gave him no choice and suggesting that any man in the same set of circumstances would have done the same thing (Childress, 1996).

In the early 1990s, football star O. J. Simpson pleaded "no contest" to a domestic-violence charge and was required to attend counseling sessions (which he completed by telephone), pay a small fine, and perform some community service. A few years later, he was charged with murdering his wife and her companion. Although he was found not guilty, he was judged to be responsible for these two deaths in civil court. Simpson's status as a former star athlete was doubtless a factor in the leniency of the original sentence and the failure of the legal system to hold him accountable for his crime. Had he committed this violence in a gender-egalitarian social context, the outcome would likely have been different.

Thus viewed, men's violence against women is a consequence of economic and political systems that render women relatively powerless compared with men (Lepowsky, 1999). Most individual men do not condone nor directly participate in this violence, but the cultural atmosphere that endorses men's dominance of women dictates that, as long as men's power, aggression, and dominance are central features of the social meanings attached to masculinity, a disproportionate number of those who participate in violence will be male.

Gang rape is an extreme manifestation of negative cultures of masculinity and the abuse of power. Although most fraternity members or individual athletes do not commit such criminal acts, members of these organizations are disproportionately involved in these crimes (O'Sullivan, 1991). Perhaps because of their homosocial nature, some fraternities and athletic teams may have a tendency to endorse violent ideologies and a level of organization that allows for an aggregation of power, dominance, and group allegiance. Moreover, under circumstances of high emotional arousal, such as in heavy drinking and/or viewing of sexually oriented material, some group members may lose their sense of individuality and thus their moral compass, a phenomenon known as deindividuation, which also takes place during riots and other instances of collective violence (Deiner, 1980).

At this writing, several members of the Duke University lacrosse team stand accused of the sexual assault of a sex worker (known in lay culture as an "exotic dancer" or "stripper") whom they hired to perform at a party. According to news reports, the sex worker was an African-American woman who attended nearby North Carolina Central University, a poor, historically Black college. She was under the impression that only five men would be in attendance and was surprised to find more than 40 men, all team members, at the house when she arrived. Allegedly, some of the men yelled racial slurs at her while she danced and threatened to assault her with a broomstick. She reported that, later in the evening, three men shoved her into a bathroom and assaulted her for about 30 minutes (Holley & Sweezey, 2006).

It is important to note that, at this writing, these are all allegations and nobody has been convicted of any crime. But this situation is a quintessential illustration of the way in which social forces enable men to be violent against women. Many Duke students come from wealthier families, and lacrosse is a popular sport in affluent parts of Long Island, New York, and elitist Baltimore prep schools. Some of the players could afford to hire the sex worker, who was a student at a relatively poorer institution and in all likelihood did not benefit from the level of privilege of most students attending Duke. The team constitutes the kind of homosocial male organization that often is characterized by the display of antifeminine and homophobic attitudes. One of the players had suggested in an e-mail that he was going to kill the sex worker, whom he referred to as a "bitch." Coaches often use antifeminine and homophobic slurs to shame their players into masculine conformity and risk-taking, thus contributing to the maintenance of these toxic attitudes. Moreover, 98% of the men on the team were white and some allegedly made overtly racist comments to the sex worker. Thus, the power imbalances of race, class, and gender all came together that evening, perhaps with disastrous results.

In *Our Guys: The Glen Ridge Rape Case and the Secret Life of the Perfect Suburb*, Bernard Lefkowitz (1997) paints another chilling account of the influence of community attitudes on gender-based violence. In 1989, a group of teenaged boys, all popular athletes, gang-raped a developmentally disabled girl in the basement of one of the boys' homes in the affluent suburb of Glen Ridge, New Jersey. Although many of these boys had created havoc within their school and communities, including vandalism (in one case, causing thousands of dollars of damage at a house party), bullying, and indecent exposure in a classroom, they were never held accountable for their misbehavior because of their popularity and the status of their families. At the trial, a defense attorney referred to the victim as a "Lolita" who had seduced the boys, implying that male sexuality is under the control of females—in this case, a girl with an I.Q. well below normal. Three of the defendants were finally jailed eight years after the crime. Lefkowitz clearly indicts the entire community in the crime and attributes it to "jock culture," male dominance, and a "boys will be boys" attitude.

Boswell and Spade (1996) asked a group of women at a university to list the fraternities where they felt the most and least safe, based on their knowledge of sexual assault incidents. The researchers identified four relatively safe (low-risk) fraternities and four relatively dangerous (high-risk) fraternities. Participant observers attended parties at the fraternity houses and wrote detailed descriptions of the social atmospheres of the various organizations.

The observers characterized parties at low-risk fraternities as friendly and noted that there were a lot of conversations between men and women. There was not much crude behavior such as sexual displays, cursing, or derogatory comments about women, and women's bathrooms were clean and well-supplied. At the high-risk houses, observers noted a marked separation of the sexes and heavier drinking. The music was often so loud that having a conversation was virtually impossible, and so interactions between men and women were mainly limited to dancing and drinking. There was more hostility toward women, sexually crude displays, and the bathrooms provided for women were filthy, sometimes to the extent of being unusable. In the morning after the parties, men from these houses often shouted derogatory comments to women as they walked home after spending the night there. Men from low-risk fraternities often had steady girlfriends and long-term relationships with women, but the men from high-risk fraternities lost status within their groups if they engaged in these kinds of relationships; thus there was a pervasive attitude that women are only for sex and that predatory sexual behavior was acceptable.

There are many other stories of similarly horrific behavior by groups of men or boys, supporting the conclusions of anthropological studies by Sanday (1981; 1996) and Lepowsky (1999) in which the researchers demonstrate a strong connection between violence against women and two variables: social separation of the sexes and cultural attitudes that communicate women's subordination to men. The power distinction between the sexes in these incidents is striking, with clear messages that men's bonds are threatened if the men behave respectfully toward women.

Thus, men's violence against women is strongly related to gender asymmetry in power and its consequent patriarchal culture. When there are social demands for men to display a superiority and disconnection to the feminine ideals and to women themselves, there will always be men who attack women in an attempt to assert a defense against feelings of powerlessness, a pattern that Whiting (1965) labeled "Masculine Protest." Thus viewed, gender-based violence is motivated by the need for men to feel superior to women.

Anthropologist Peggy Sanday (1981) has noted that rape is virtually nonexistent in 44 non-patriarchal societies, and that only 18% of cultures, including that of the United States, are "rape prone." The striking cross-cultural variation in these hate crimes is a strong piece of evidence in support of the hypothesis that social-structural conditions have a powerful effect on gender relations and power assertion.

TOWARD SOLUTIONS

If these long-standing cultural characteristics are a central determinant of the epidemiology of men's violence against women, then it will never be completely eradicated unless and until the basic power asymmetry between men and women is eliminated. Although we take this position, we do not want to imply that people should simply sit back and wait for these changes to take place. A quote attributed to Bertha Calloway well illustrates our stance: "We cannot direct the wind, but we can adjust the sails." In this context, changes in social structural conditions are the "wind." The "sails" are the variety of ways in which we can influence cultural, legal, educational, and political forces to minimize the impact of this striking difference in power between men-as-a-group and women-as-a-group.

Beginning in the 1970s, we have begun to see some of these changes in the United States. In the legal arena, "rape shield laws" have been helpful in limiting defense attorney's tactics of playing on jurors' prejudices against women. Before the enactment of these laws, it was acceptable for a lawyer to introduce as evidence a victim's prior sexual history and imply that the act in question was consensual because the victim liked to have sex. Slowly, people began to realize that a history of consensual sex is completely irrelevant to a rape. The marital exemption to rape laws has also become legally excluded. Hence, the reality of rape in marriage is both acknowledged and criminalized. And the corroboration requirement that physical evidence must be presented in order for a conviction to occur has also been eliminated (Allison & Wrightsman, 1993).

For cases of partner violence, legislatures have mandated arrests for perpetrators of domestic violence if there is probable cause that a crime has been committed. This practice precludes discretionary judgment of police officers often motivated to keep the family unit intact. Most recently, stalking laws and protection-from-stalking orders have been legislated and implemented.

Innovators within the criminal justice system are also learning better ways of holding perpetrators legally accountable for their crimes. It is common for perpetrators of intimate partner violence to intimidate and threaten their partners during the prosecution phase, causing the victim to become fearful and likely reluctant to testify in court against the perpetrator. Without the testimony of the victim, the likelihood of conviction without a plea bargain decreases tremendously. Appropriately, both investigators and prosecutors have begun advancing the strategic collection and presentation of evidence that allows for successful trial prosecution without the testimony of the victim. Investigators can accomplish this goal by undertaking a thorough collection of evidence immediately after the crime, such as photographs, eyewitness accounts, 911 tapes, and recordings of interviews with the victim. The creation of psychological profiles of defendants that match perpetrator characteristics can also be helpful for prosecuting attorneys as they weave motive and evidence into a comprehensible story (Wrightsman, 2006).

In the political arena, the Violence Against Women Act has been enormously helpful in investing significant amounts of federal money into research, education, and legal efforts to fight the scourge of gender-based violence. The U.S. Congress renewed this legislation in 2005, and advocacy groups exert considerable pressure on lawmakers to maintain and increase the resources allocated to prevention and intervention.

We can also "adjust the sails" with a variety of educational and grassroots advocacy efforts, described in the next two chapters. The "wind" is blowing in the right direction—not fast enough for activists or survivors, but the "sails" are getting better and better.

SUMMARY

Men's violence against women is embedded in the historical inequality between the sexes, a phenomenon strongly related to a division of labor that confers disproportionate social and economic power to men-as-a-group relative to women-as-a-group (albeit with great variation among individuals within these groups). Gendered violence will only become a thing of the past when this inequality is eliminated.

The forces that forged the power imbalance between the sexes are changing in an egalitarian direction because of labor-saving devices, reproductive technologies, and the rise of the dual-income family. But gender inequality has been dominant in the world for thousands of years and will not disappear in short order. In the meantime, political, educational, and legal reforms will help to minimize the negative impact of larger societal forces that have rendered women relatively powerless compared to men.

KEY TERMS

Macrosocietal perspective

CRITICAL THINKING QUESTIONS

1. How does the division of labor between the sexes relate to gender-based violence?
2. Societies of hunters and gatherers dominated the vast majority of human history. Why is there little evidence of the existence of men's violence against women in these societies?
3. Describe some of the psychological modifications that might be needed to become a soldier. What are the consequences of these changes?
4. Comment on the question: "If you were to wake up tomorrow and discover that you were a member of the other sex, how would your life be different?"
5. Describe the distinctions between "low risk" and "high risk" fraternity houses. How might the distinctions between these houses be related to gender-based violence?

PART III

Intervention and Prevention

Chapter 6

Responding to Gender-Based Violence: Intervention

When a man perpetrates violence against a woman and the incident is reported, intervention may begin either for the survivor, the perpetrator, or ideally, both (secondary victims—friends or family of the survivor—may also benefit from professional services). As mentioned in chapter 3, the survivor is likely experiencing far-reaching emotional consequences. Receiving intervention in the form of support or counseling can be vital to recovery. Intervention for the perpetrator is also critical to decrease the likelihood of recidivism. In this chapter, we discuss intervention strategies that have been developed as we struggle to deal with the consequences of men's violence against women.

Our short history of working to stop men's violence against women has taught us an important lesson: intervention, which consists of responses to violence after the fact, is important, but is only part of the answer. Efforts to intervene, by definition, always refer to reactive rather than proactive measures.

We first discuss intervention models and techniques that are being used to help survivors go through the process of healing. In the second part of this chapter, we review programs that attempt to hold offenders of these crimes accountable for their actions, and provide them with tools aimed at preventing them from committing further acts of abuse and violent crimes.

INTERVENTION FOR SURVIVORS

Intervention for survivors may occur on both personal and public levels. Given the prevalence rates discussed in chapter 1 and the very real consequences of victimization discussed in chapter 3, it is imperative that both immediate and long-term support is available to survivors. Failure to intervene can have lasting negative effects. For example, Koss, Heise, and Russo (1994) found that as much as five years after the assault, female rape survivors (even if they did not label their experience as rape) visit their physicians nearly twice as often than those with no reported assault histories.

PERSONAL INTERVENTION

Although not seeking available services does not mean that one will never recover, professional intervention the form of psychological, emotional, medical, and/or legal support can speed this process (Ledray, 1999).

Psychological and Emotional Intervention. The most accessible and visible source of psychological and emotional help is likely to be a local women's crisis center (Koss et al., 2003) where the staff is specially trained to provide advocacy and support to survivors. These specialists can (a) accompany the survivor to the hospital, the police station, and/or the criminal trial of the offender, (b) provide resources (e.g., clothing and toiletries, access to technology), (c) make referrals to professional mental health services, (d) provide group and individual psychotherapy or support counseling, and (e) offer information and education (cf. R. Campbell & Martin, 2001; J. P. Sullivan & Gillum, 2001). Researchers have demonstrated that survivors who access local crisis centers or obtain counseling from clergy found these services beneficial to their healing (Campbell, Wasco, Ahrens, Sefl, & Barnes, 2001). Advocates from local crisis centers can also serve as liaisons between survivors and other intervention sources such as the medical and legal systems.

Psychotherapy. Qualified staff in women's crisis resource centers, as well as other licensed professionals (e.g., social workers, counselors, psychologists) can benefit survivors tremendously through the provision of psychotherapeutic services which can provide both short-term and long-term benefits for survivors of trauma.

Effective psychotherapy must begin with an appropriate diagnosis. As stated in chapter 3, survivors of abuse and trauma frequently experience posttraumatic stress disorder (PTSD). Others may not meet the criteria for an actual diagnosis, but will likely experience symptoms that are consistent with those of PTSD (e.g., intrusive thoughts, avoidance behavior) or depression. Once the professional makes an accurate diagnosis, he or she can formulate a treatment plan (Sanford, 2003).

There are a variety of different treatment options for those experiencing symptoms of PTSD, including behavior therapy, cognitive-behavioral therapy (CBT), eye-movement desensitization and reprocessing (EMDR), and group treatment (Whealin, 2004).

Behavior therapy. The major assumption of behavior therapy is that emotions, cognitions, and behaviors are learned, and can therefore be unlearned. The therapist's task is to identify maladaptive emotions, cognitions, and behaviors and help the client to modify them in a healthier direction.

One type of behavioral therapy that has been found to be effective for survivors of sexual assault is **stress inoculation training (SIT)** (Falsetti & Bernat, 2000). This therapy was originally developed by Meichenbaum (1977), but was tailored by Kilpatrick, Veronen, & Resick (1982) to treat the specific fears and anxieties that rape survivors experience. There are three phases to SIT: (a) education, (b) skill-building, and (c) application.

Educational phase. In the educational phase, survivors learn the general dynamics of classical conditioning and how they contribute to the learned response of fear. Survivors also examine cues in the environment that can trigger such fears. For example, if a man with a mustache was the attacker, any mustache can become associated with fear. Survivors also learn relaxation techniques that are incompatible with anxiety responses.

Skill-building phase. In the skill-building phase, survivors learn techniques that can help them to reduce their fears through two distinct types of exercises. One revolves around reducing the physiological sensations related to anxiety and fear (e.g., rapid breathing, tenseness). Here, survivors learn forms of deep breathing (e.g., diaphragmatic breathing) or specific relaxation techniques such as progressive muscle relaxation (Falsetti, 1997). A second skill is inhibiting fearful thoughts. Psychotherapists may teach techniques such as thought stopping, mental rehearsal, or guided self-talk to discourage thoughts that may produce fear.

Application phase. In the final phase of SIT, survivors seek to apply the skills that they have learned to control their fears, self-criticisms, and general avoidance behaviors in their everyday lives.

SIT generally takes 10–14 sessions and has been found to be an effective technique for reducing rape-related fear and anxiety in both uncontrolled studies (Kilpatrick et al., 1982; Veronen & Kilpatrick, 1982) and controlled studies (Resick, Jordan, Girelli, Hutter, & Marhoefer-Dvorak, 1988).

Cognitive-behavioral therapy. The focus of cognitive-behavioral therapy (CBT) is on working with cognitions to change the way that the survivor thinks and feels about the self and environment, as well as unwanted behaviors that have resulted from the trauma. Specific cognitive-behavioral therapies that have been found to be effective for survivors of violence include prolonged exposure and cognitive processing therapy (Falsetti & Bernat, 2000).

Prolonged exposure. The concept of prolonged exposure (PE, also known as *flooding*) is based upon theories of learning and information processing. PE rests on the assumption that repeated exposure to fearful images and memories will serve to reduce those fears. For example, viewing a frightening movie will usually result in a fear response, but chances are that the fear response would not be as great if the movie were viewed a second time. If one were to see this movie over and over again, it would lose its power to invoke a fear response. Through PE, repeated exposure allows for the abuse and/or assault to lose its power over one's emotions.

During PE, the survivor is asked to recount his or her story in as much detail as possible. The narrative is then repeated several times during each therapy session in order to reduce the fear associated with the memory. Survivors may also be asked to cognitively confront situations that are not dangerous, but are associated with the traumatic event, and therefore have become associated with fear and danger (e.g., dating, dark places).

PE has been found to be an effective treatment technique for rape survivors with PTSD, and superior to no treatment, traditional counseling, and SIT in reducing symptoms of PTSD (Foa, Rothbaum, Riggs, & Murdock, 1991). A brief version of PE has also been found to decrease PTSD symptoms in rape survivors shortly following the attack (Foa, Hearst-Ikeda, & Perry, 1995). PE has also been found to be more effective than SIT (without exposure), as has a combination PE-SIT for both sexual and physical assault survivors who met the criteria for PTSD.

Cognitive processing therapy (CPT). Developed by Resick & Schnicke (1993) to treat survivors of rape and sexual assault, CPT is based an information processing model and combines components of both exposure therapy and cognitive restructuring. The primary objective of CPT is to integrate the rape experience by dealing with the emotional consequences of the rape, as well as any cognitive distortions (e.g., "My world is not safe.") or maladaptive and inaccurate beliefs (e.g., "It was my fault.") concerning the rape.

Survivors begin the integration process through a form of exposure. They are asked to write narratives of the assault in detail, and to also write about the meaning of rape to them, as well as issues relevant to their recovery, including safety, trust, power, self-esteem, and intimacy (Falsetti & Bernat, 2000). Additionally, survivors are educated about feelings, the relationship between cognitions and emotions, and are encouraged to identify "stuck-points" in their narratives that preclude full emotional processing regarding the assault.

In an uncontrolled study, CPT has been found to decrease symptoms of PTSD for survivors of rape, reducing the reported levels of PTSD from 90% pretreatment to 0% post-treatment, and reducing levels of depression from 62% to 42% (Resick & Schnicke, 1993).

Eye Movement Desensitization and Reprocessing (EMDR). Developed by F. Shapiro (1989), this recent approach rests upon an Adaptive Information Processing (AIP) model, and was designed to specifically treat those who are experiencing symptoms of PTSD. The technique was theoretically driven by the assumption that human memory is stored in related networks organized around the earliest relevant event, which contain related thoughts, images, emotions, and sensations. The AIP model further assumes that if a traumatic experience for which a network is created is not fully processed, that memory will remain intact and traumatic, and will become the basis for psychological dysfunction.

Through AIP, EMDR seeks to reduce the negative impact of the traumatic memory network by reconnecting it with a positive and adaptive network of information. EMDR can begin after the therapist has ensured through evaluation and education that the survivor has basic coping skills for handling emotional distress. The client is first asked to focus upon an element of the traumatic network while engaging in a dual attention activity (e.g., visually following the therapist's finger as it moves across the visual field), until the client is able to focus upon this element without experiencing distress. Once this goal is achieved, the client is asked to focus upon a more positive, preferred belief while similarly engaging in the dual attention activity.

EMDR has been found to be effective for crime victims, police officers (Baker & McBride, 1991; Kleinknecht & Morgan, 1992; Page & Crino, 1993; F. Shapiro & Solomon, 1995), and sexual assault victims (Hyer, 1995; F. Shapiro, 1989; B. Shapiro 1991). The theoretical rationale underlying EMDR, however, has been called into question. A review of the research does not find that the inclusion of eye movements within treatment sessions adds therapeutic effectiveness beyond the value of cognitive and emotional reprocessing. In a review of practice guidelines for those experiencing Acute Stress Disorder or PTSD, the American Psychiatric Association noted, "It would therefore appear that it is the common sharing of trauma exposure techniques and emotional reprocessing that is principally responsible for treatment gains" (2004, p. 36). Hence, while many researchers on the effectiveness of EMDR judge the technique to be useful, it may not be more effective that other cognitive behavior or exposure therapies.

Group Treatment. According to the National Center for Post-Traumatic Stress Disorder, group work is often helpful to survivors of trauma, as it offers a safe place for individuals to talk about their experiences. By sharing one's story and listening to the stories of others, the survivor may develop a stronger sense of trust and self-confidence. Group work may also serve to reduce feelings of isolation.

A common theme can be extracted from each of these treatment options: confronting the reality of the traumatic event(s) in a safe environment is helpful to the recovery process. Research reveals that these treatment techniques also counter powerful and inhibiting myths regarding recovery: that recounting the assault is psychologically harmful, and that gender-based violence is something that one must simply "get over." Although repeated exposure to painful memories is certainly not a pleasant experience, the outcome of this process suggests that it is worthwhile and offers hope for healing to survivors.

Medical Intervention. There are distinct advantages to seeking medical services. If an attacker has physically injured the survivor and/or has put her or him at risk for pregnancy and/or sexually transmitted diseases, it is important that the survivor obtain medical attention as soon as possible after the attack and continue receiving these services for as long as is professionally recommended.

For sexual assault or rape survivors, a Sexual Assault Nurse Examiner (***SANE/SART nurse***) may be available at the hospital to conduct a ***rape kit*** examination to collect legal evidence (Ledray, 1999). In many jurisdictions, before the examination can be conducted, law enforcement must be contacted and will be present during the collection of any evidence (although not necessarily within the physical presence of the victim). It can be empowering for a survivor to choose to have this examination conducted, especially if he or she is interested (or may later become interested) in pursuing prosecution of the attacker. The survivor's body is the most important source of evidence in a rape case (Lonsway, 2000).

However, undergoing a rape kit examination may entail a risk of re-victimization. When a survivor agrees to undergo it, it is usually in the immediate aftermath of the assault (up to 72 hours) (Lonsway, 2000). The procedure calls for the survivor to completely disrobe and surrender his or her clothing to police and submit to the swabbing of every body orifice. Hair samples, if available, will be pulled from the head and the pubic region. Pictures are likely to be taken, including those using a ***culpascope***, a camera that is inserted directly into an orifice. This procedure would be an unnerving experience for anyone, and it is obviously even more difficult for someone whom a rapist has recently victimized.

For victims of intimate partner violence (IPV), evidence collection often includes videotaped interviews with the victim and nearly always includes photographs of her injuries. It is important to follow up with additional photographs two or three days later, because it takes time for the full impact of bruises to appear.

Legal Intervention. Contacting law enforcement offers the possibility of offender accountability, justice, and an increased sense of security for the survivor (at least eventually). Reporting an assault to police is the only recourse available for survivors wishing to pursue legal accountability for the offender. (We discuss offender accountability in more depth later in this chapter.)

There are a variety of reasons that a survivor may not report the assault. In one study, the most common reason cited was fear of the perpetrator and, interestingly, the survivor's minimization of the assault as a "minor, one-time incident." For both male and female victims of IPV, the most frequently cited reason for non-reporting was the concern that the police could not do anything about the perpetrator's violence and abuse. The second and third most prominent reasons cited, respectively, were a fear that the police would not believe them (females were significantly more concerned about this possibility than males) and that the violence would be trivialized by police (male victims were significantly more likely to expect this occurrence than females; Erwin & Vidales, 2001). Erwin and Vidales (2001) cited National Violence Against Women (NVAW) estimates of reporting rates for stalking that indicate similar findings: Of the 48.1% of females and 63.8% of males who did not report, fully 100% of them believed that police could not do anything about the crime. Over 90% of non-reporters also feared that police would not believe them. As we will see, these concerns may not be unfounded.

Seeking medical and/or legal services may entail additional risks for victims and survivors. Although there have been nationwide efforts at educating both medical and legal professionals about the dynamics of gender-based violence, these professionals have traditionally not been comprehensively trained in this area (Lonsway, 2000). J.C. Campbell & Soeken (1999) found that rape victims who sought services reported, on average, two experiences with medical and/or legal services staffs that served to re-traumatize them, illustrating the need for ongoing public intervention education for relevant professionals.

PUBLIC INTERVENTION

Public intervention generally takes on one of two forms: (a) advocacy or (b) education, although these two enterprises can sometimes be difficult to distinguish from each other. Public advocacy refers to working to effect change (e.g., in laws or public policy) that supports the reduction of men's violence against women. Through the advocacy work of grassroots organizations that began in the 1970s, we have seen the criminalization of marital rape, intimate partner violence, and stalking (cf. Fagan, 1996). Sexual harassment is now defined as a civil rights violation, and sexual assault and rape laws in most states have been strengthened and made gender-neutral (Allison & Wrightsman, 1993; Largen, 1988). Within many police departments, we have seen "mandatory arrest" requirements (e.g., a police officer must make an arrest in an IPV investigation if he or she finds probable cause that someone has committed a crime), and some district attorney's offices have implemented "no drop" policies for charges (Fagan, 1996). That is, once an arrest is made, prosecution must go forward.

Public education involves providing information to individuals or specific populations (e.g., law enforcement personnel, state representatives, families of survivors) with the ultimate objectives of improving support services for survivors and holding perpetrators accountable for their crimes. See Box 6.1 for an example of one form of public education.

Intervention work depends critically on having an infrastructure of service organizations. Currently, there are more than 2,000 shelter and service programs in the United States. In 1978, over 100 battered women's advocates from all across the nation gathered in Washington, DC to attend the U.S. Commission on Civil Rights hearing on battered women. They collectively organized the National Coalition Against Domestic Violence (NCADV). Today, along with other related local and national organizations, the NCADV continues to operate at the personal, social, and national levels by offering personal intervention to survivors through advocacy and support, and also by educating the public and influencing public policy. Domestic Violence Awareness Month (October) and Sexual Assault Awareness Month (April) are now local and national events that serve to continue educate the public about these important issues. Since 1993, the United Nations has identified men's violence against women as an international human rights issue.

INTERVENTION WITH PERPETRATORS

There are two primary possibilities for dealing with the perpetrator: (a) legal processes and (b) psychological intervention. Like intervention work with survivors, however, there are no clear boundaries between these interventions. For example, it is not uncommon for a perpetrator to enter the legal system and be mandated into a psychological intervention program as part of his sentence. Ideally, effective psychological intervention could preclude the necessity for further legal intervention; however, when psychological intervention is not effective, (e.g., the perpetrator re-offends), it is important that further legal intervention be immediate and swift.

BOX 6.1
Reducing the Risk of Rape and Sexual Assault

For decades, advice-often confusing and inconsistent-has been offered primarily to girls and women on how to protect themselves from attackers, especially sexual predators (Morgan, 1986). Currently, this counsel takes one of two forms: (a) avoiding dangerous situations (risk reduction) and (b) learning how to effectively respond to an attack (resistance awareness).

Risk reduction: Limiting one's activities (e.g., not walking alone at night, avoiding being with a man without any others present, staying with friends) may help one to avoid an attack. Learning and following basic safety guidelines can affect the level of exposure to danger or risk. Asking women to curtail their activities, however, is founded upon (and serves to support) the unrealistic expectation that women can control the actions of potential perpetrators. To attempt to limit when a woman goes out, with whom she associates, where she goes, or even what she wears only serves to implicitly hold women responsible for men's violence against them. Moreover, public avoidance behavior is only useful in reducing the risk of stranger attacks, which, as we have seen, are a small percentage of total assaults. Limiting women's freedom is a form of social control that reinforces gender inequality between men and women, which is at the heart of gender-based violence (Corcoran, 1992).

Resistance awareness: Potential victims can also learn how to resist being raped after a perpetrator attacks. Bart and O'Brien (1985), compared women who were targets of attackers who failed to carry out the rape with cases in which the attacker completed the rape. The researchers found that multiple and active response strategies (e.g., more than one of the following: screaming, running, hitting, kicking, or biting) by the targeted victim were associated with non-completed rape. It appears that these behaviors, which are antithetical to the feminine stereotype, are related to impeding the efforts of a rapist.

This is not to say that a perpetrator's ability to complete his assault hinges on the response of the victim. All victims respond to the best of their abilities when attacked, regardless of the situation. To question the adequacy of a victim/survivor's response to an attack is unwarranted, and as with risk reduction, implicitly assigns part of the responsibility for the rape to the survivor.

> **BOX 6.1** *(continued)*
>
> Although it is helpful to know basic safety guidelines as well as defensive strategies for potential attacks, it is also important to acknowledge two implicit assumptions underlying these measures. First, this approach assumes that those who are attacked will be able to respond to the attack rationally and reasonably. Second, as mentioned previously, it implies that victims are responsible for the outcome of a perpetrator's criminal behavior. Both of these assumptions carry with them a level of absurdity. It is noteworthy that in spite of all of the advice, men's violence against women remains prevalent. Ultimately, if a predator is intent on committing abuse and violence, a victim's response may only be a factor to the extent that it will affect the abusive and violent tactics that the perpetrator finds necessary to complete his assault.

It is very rare for a perpetrator of violence to voluntarily seek intervention, except insincerely in order to give the appearance that he is concerned about his behavior in anticipation of legal proceedings. In most cases, therefore, a necessary prerequisite for offender accountability is law enforcement notification. Although a police report guarantees an investigation, it does not ensure that the offender will be arrested. Many stages of protocol must be followed for accountability from the criminal justice system to occur, each governed by due process rules. At every stage, perpetrators of violence may escape accountability. (See Box 6.2 for a summary of each of these stages.)

CRIMINAL JUSTICE INTERVENTION

The intervention focus on survivors may help to explain why the rate of men's violence against women remains alarmingly high. Reduction of violence can only occur by addressing perpetration, and survivor services can only come after an assailant has committed the crime. Historically, the business of dealing with attackers has been left solely to the criminal justice system. In the following sections of this chapter, we review further how the system has traditionally responded to reported incidents of gender-based crime.

In 1999, the National Center for Policy Analysis (NCPA) published *Crime and Punishment in America*. This report stated that, in general, crime rates were decreasing, in part because accountability

> **BOX 6.2**
> **The Criminal Justice System**
>
> The criminal justice system of the United States is founded upon the values of due process and protection of citizens' rights at every stage of involvement within the system. Following is a summary of all steps that must be taken in order for a perpetrator of a crime to be held legally accountable for his or her actions.
>
> When a police report is filed, or police are notified of a crime (Step 1), they are obligated to investigate and determine if there is a reasonable likelihood (*probable cause*) that a crime has occurred. If so, an arrest is warranted (Step 2). If there is no evidence (e.g., bruises or cuts on a victim, property destroyed, etc.) that a crime has been committed, an information report will be written by the police officer, and the investigation will cease. If there is probable cause, a search for a suspect begins (Step 3). Law enforcement agents make an arrest if they can identify and apprehend the suspect (Step 4), and then forward a report of their investigation to the local district attorney, who decides whether he or she will prosecute the person who has been charged (Step 5). If prosecution occurs, there may be a plea agreement (where the defendant pleads guilty, usually to a lesser charge), or the case will go to trial, where a judge or jury renders a verdict of either guilty or not guilty (Step 6). It is only at this juncture, which can take weeks, months, or even years to reach, that sentencing can occur (Step 7) for a defendant who is found guilty. A judge may then order the defendant into treatment, impose a jail or prison sentence, or both.
>
> One exception to this process is *diversion*, in which a district attorney may, for example, essentially put a prosecution on hold while a defendant enters some form of treatment. If the offender takes responsibility for his criminal actions and successfully completes an intervention program, the original charges may be dropped.
>
> Diversion is an important option, and it can serve to expedite the accountability process; however, it is not appropriate in many circumstances. If, for example, the criminal justice system is dealing with a serial rapist (and, as we discussed in chapter 2, most are) or a batterer who has antisocial personality disorder, diversion is never appropriate. It is important for a judge to always consider the safety of the survivor and that of possible future victims when making decisions regarding offender adjudication.

was increasing; convicted offenders were being incarcerated for longer periods of time. The average expected punishment for both serious assault and burglary doubled between 1980 and 1997. The average expected punishment for murderers and rapists tripled. Currently, convicted murderers receive an average of 41 months (approximately 1,230 days) in prison. The average sentence for a convicted rapist is now 128 days.

It is encouraging that a rapist convicted in 1997 could expect to spend three times longer in prison than a one convicted in 1980, but the fact that this translates into a sentence of 128 days is very discouraging. It suggests that common myths and misperceptions regarding the crime of rape remain strong. See Box 6.3 for current examples of myths regarding the crime of rape.

REPORTING GENDER-BASED VIOLENCE

Gender-based violence is highly underreported. It is difficult to assess exactly what proportion of victims and survivors report these crimes (see Box 6.4 for a look at these data). Reluctance to do so is nearly universal and stands in stark contrast to victims' reactions to other major crimes. As previously discussed, there may be many reasons for this hesitancy, but a major concern revolves around survivors' fears of how they may be treated by the criminal justice system. This apprehension is quite realistic, as involvement in the criminal justice system can lead to re-victimization (Greenfield & Rand, 1998; Koss, 2000; Orth, 1993).

FROM ARREST TO CONVICTION

As stated earlier, the legal process can be interrupted at any point following investigation, arrest, charge, or prosecution. A look at the cessations of legal procedures reveals a highly selective process for eliminating cases from the system of men being charged with violent crimes against women.

Perpetrators of gender-based violence do not always leave evidence. Sex offenders may experience erectile dysfunction or not ejaculate during their assaults (Groth, 1979). They may not cause physical tears or bruises on the victim. Nonphysical forms of abuse, such as economic or emotional abuse, are not violations of the law. Also, as mentioned earlier, stalking can exist without any physical contact, or even without the victim's awareness of the stalking behavior. When the violence does not include these factors, the offenders of these crimes are unlikely to face legal consequences.

> **BOX 6.3**
> **Denying the Reality of Gender-Based Crime**
>
> In September 2004, two 18-year-old men, Brian K. Ussery and William N. Haney, who had been convicted of rape in Douglas County, Kansas, were in court awaiting sentencing. They had admitted to (along with two other men) supplying alcohol to a 13-year-old girl. When she became intoxicated, they each took turns penetrating her vagina with their penises. The girl testified four different times about the assaults before the judge accepted the plea agreement.
>
> The sentencing guidelines for these crimes directed a penalty of 13 years in prison. The actual sentence for each of these men was 60 days in jail, plus probation. Given that they had already been incarcerated for more than 60 days prior to the plea bargain, the offenders walked out of the courthouse immediately following the pronouncement of their sentences. Judge Paula Martin explained that there was "substantial and compelling reason" to give the felons lighter sentences. She looked directly at the young girl in her court and said, "You were an active participant in your own rape." Clearly, the judge subscribed to the myth that men and boys cannot control their aggression and sexuality, and therefore it is up to women and girls to do so, even in the case of a young teenager in the company of adult men. The judge further justified the sentence by inferring that this victim was not harmed as much as some other rape victims. The following week, the young girl mutilated her arms and attempted suicide (Westlander, 2004).
>
> Prosecutors appealed this sentence and, based on orders from the State Court of Appeals, Judge Martin resentenced the two men. Consistent with recommendations of the Court of Appeals, she ordered Haney to serve 82 months in prison and Ussery to serve 65 months (Wilson, 2005, personal communication).

In 1997, the Bureau of Justice Statistics (BJS) reported that about half of all reported rapes are cleared by arrest. Size of jurisdiction did not have an effect on these rates. Based on these same data, BJS reported that 80% of those who were arrested were also prosecuted. Forty-eight percent of those arrested for rape were convicted. In about 92% of the cases not resulting in conviction (32% of all cases in which there was prosecution), the cases were dismissed.

BOX 6.4
Reporting Rates for Gender-Based Violent Crime

Researchers have attempted to estimate the ratio of committed to reported crimes. Estimates vary widely.

Rape and sexual assault. Koss, Gidycz, and Wisniewski (1987) found that 1 in 20 (5%) of those who said that someone had sexually assaulted them reported the crime to the police. Statistics collected in the 2002 National Crime Victimization Survey (NCVS) by the U.S. Department of Justice, however, reveal a reporting rate of 53.7% (Rennison & Rand, 2003). According to the NCVS, reports of rape to the police increased 23% in a three-year period, from 30% in 1999. Interestingly, similar good news had been brought in 1991, when the U.S. Department of Justice issued a report saying that 53% of victims report rapes to the police (Associated Press, 1991). The reality of reporting rape and sexual assault may lie somewhere in between these discrepant statistics, but both indicate a high non-reporting rate. Interestingly, the NCVS found that the form of violent crime that was most likely to be reported to law enforcement was robbery (71%).

Reporting rates for rape are even lower for male than for female victims (Pino & Meier, 1999), perhaps because shame and guilt are even greater for men than for women, given the reality of homophobia and demands for male dominance (Kilmartin, 2007). Pino & Meier (1999) found that the only significant predictor of male victims' reporting was the presence of physical injury: men were eight times more likely to report the crime when they needed medical attention for injuries than when they did not. For women, several variables were found to be predictive of reporting: (a) the presence of physical injuries, (b) when the offender was a stranger, (c) when a weapon was present, and (d) when the offender also stole property from the victim. Note that each of these factors is associated with the stereotype of "real" rape (Estrich, 1987). Interestingly, the most significant predictor of reporting rape in this study was when the attacker also committed theft. Under this circumstance, survivors were more than four times more likely to report the crimes. Because of the stereotype of rape and the perceptions of nebulous boundaries between sex and violence that exist in our society, perhaps theft is more clearly identifiable as a crime than rape.

> **BOX 6.4** *(continued)*
>
> ***Intimate partner violence.*** The reporting rate for IPV is also low. In early research, Walker (1979) reported that only 10% of the over 400 women who shared stories of their husbands perpetrating repeated incidents of abuse and violence against them said that they had ever reported the crime, due primarily to their belief that the police could not deal with the crime effectively. (It is important to remember that this study did not include a random sample of participants.) Recently, the NCVS reported that about half (53% of females and 46% of males) of those whom a partner assaulted reported the incident to law enforcement (Rennison, 2000). These statistics are quite similar to the 1993 NCVS statistics of reporting rates of 48% for females and 47% for males.
>
> ***Stalking.*** In the National Violence Against Women (NVAW) survey, researchers found that 55% of females and 48% of males who were aware that a stalker was pursuing them reported the problem to law enforcement (Tjaden & Thoennes, 1998). The National College Women Sexual Victimization (NCWSV) Study conducted in 1997 showed much lower reporting rates. Although 93.4% of female targets of stalkers reported that they had confided in someone about the crime, only 16.9% reported it to law enforcement. It is possible for a perpetrator to stalk someone without his or her awareness, which would, of course, make it impossible to report. Thus, the likelihood of underreporting in this crime is even higher than for other forms of gender-based violence.
>
> There is always a margin of error in scientific surveys. Although the actual rates of reporting are very difficult to assess, these studies all point towards the unmistakable conclusion that gender-based violence is highly underreported. At worst, up to 95% of survivors do not report their experience to the police. At best, only about half bring awareness of the crime to law enforcement. Thus, the majority of those who commit gender-based violence are never confronted by anyone within the criminal justice system.

Extrapolating from the most encouraging data reported here, out of 100 rapes, about 50 (at most) will be reported, about 25 will be prosecuted, and about 12.5 will result in conviction; however, experts in the field argue that this conclusion based on BJS statistics is extremely optimistic. Lisak and Miller (2002), who conducted a study of undetected sex offenders, estimated that only about 1 out of 100 rapists is likely to be convicted. In earlier research, Bienen (1983) estimated the conviction rate to be between 2% and 5%.

Arrest rates for other types of crime vary with the nature of the crime and specific characteristics associated with events surrounding it. Fernandez-Lanier, Chard-Wierschem, & Hall (2002) analyzed IPV arrest rates in the state of New York by county. They reported that, on average, police officers arrest one of every three suspects present at the crime scene. This percentage nearly doubles when the perpetrator has caused a physical injury. They also reported wide variability by county in arrest rates, ranging from 30% to 87%. According to Fagan (1996), the prosecution of perpetrators who commit violence against their partners remains low in many communities, at 10% or less of those arrested.

According to the NVAW study on stalking, about half of all victims of stalking report the crime. About 25% of reports resulted in an arrest. Of those arrested, prosecutions took place for 13.1% of those who stalked women and 9% of those who stalked men. Of those prosecuted, the conviction rates were 52.8% and 60% for those who stalked female and male victims, respectively. Extrapolating from these data, out of 100 stalkers, about 50 are reported, about 12.5 are arrested, about two are prosecuted, and only one is convicted.

It is clear that legal accountability for gender-based violence offenders is difficult to accomplish. Intervention efforts must continue in attempt to strengthen the legal consequences for gender-based violent offenders (see Box 6.5 for an innovative model of community intervention for intimate partner violence).

It is clear that most perpetrators of gender-based violence are not held accountable by the criminal justice system. Of those who are, most will not go to prison. In 1997, the U.S. Department of Justice Bureau of Justice Statistics issued a report stating that approximately 265,000 adult sex offenders were under the care, custody, or control of correctional agencies in the United States. Of these, almost 60 percent were living in communities, either while on probation or parole. In 2003, of the 4,073,987 persons on probation, 10% were perpetrators of gender-based violence (3% sex offenders, 7% IPV offenders).

There are emerging trends regarding the supervision and management of these offenders. In 2004, the Lane Council of Governments (funded by the United States Department of Justice) submitted a national report on the management of sex offenders in the

> **BOX 6.5**
> **Police Response Advocacy Intervention Programming**
>
> In 2004, the U.S. Department of Justice funded a $300,000 grant for a county in Southeast Kansas to implement the "Police Response Advocacy" project. This project, aimed at increasing offender accountability, involved inter-agency collaboration between the local crisis resource center, law enforcement, the district attorney's office, the offender treatment center, and a regional university. The grant funds several important positions, all specialized to intervene with perpetrators of gender-based violence, including
>
> - A detective who only investigates reported cases of gender-based violence.
> - A special prosecutor who solely prosecutes those arrested for gender-based violent crimes.
> - A police response advocacy coordinator, available to victims of gender-based violence at the scene of the crime after it has been secured by law enforcement agents.
> - A records analyst, who is deputized by the county sheriff's office and is therefore privy to otherwise confidential data collected by law enforcement. The records analyst writes "offender histories" that are made available online to law enforcement agents responding to a call, or to the special prosecutor. The records analyst also collects data on the adjudication of every call related to a gender-based violent crime and provides summary reports to a committee representing all relevant agencies.
>
> The assignment of a records analyst is a unique and important position. It is not uncommon for police to receive a call that, even when it is clearly IPV related, is labeled as another kind of incident. For example, a citizen calls to complain that neighbors are being loud. The officers arrive at the scene and find a husband shouting at his wife. Shouting at one's spouse is not a crime, but doing it persistently in public meets the criteria for a charge of disorderly conduct (disturbing the peace). The records analyst would be able to see the report, identify it as clearly IPV related, and include it in the offender history. This information can help to provide a context to police officers who may receive future calls regarding the same perpetrator, or to the district attorney who is assessing the possibilities for prosecution.

> **BOX 6.5** *(continued)*
>
> The collection of data by the records analyst and the distribution of the results of the data analyses serve the important function of holding agencies accountable. The records analyst regularly provides statistics on arrest, prosecution, and conviction rates to the committee. These data also reveal the types of interventions imposed on offenders who are convicted and sentenced, as well as follow-up data on the success of these intervention programs.

community. They cite four best practices that are critical for effective management of these offenders: (a) collaboration, (b) victim-centered approach (which we will hereafter refer to as survivor-centered), (c) clear and consistent policies, and (d) sex-offender specific treatment. These recommended practices may go beyond the supervision of sex offenders and serve as guidelines for effective community supervision of perpetrators who commit other forms of gender-based violence.

Collaboration. Collaboration among all agencies and individuals charged with specific responsibilities in the management of offenders is critical. This practice includes (a) the survivor, (b) the supervising agency, (c) the advocacy community, (d) the treatment agency, (e) law enforcement, (f) defense attorneys, (g) judges, (h) prosecutors, (i) school and social service officials, (j) the offenders' family, and others. Effective interagency collaboration allows for shared information about offenders and coordinated intervention.

Survivor-centered approach. The most comprehensive and responsible approaches to treatment keep the needs and safety of survivors as its primary goal. In this regard, concern for survivors guides community policy development.

Clear and consistent policies. It is important for communities of all levels (state, local, and agency) to have memoranda of understanding (MOU) that clearly outline how cases will be investigated, prosecuted, and adjudicated. It is also important to have comprehensive policies on community supervision and specific roles for each agency relevant to this supervision.

Sex-offender specific treatment. Mandated specialized treatment is an integral component of effective treatment for sex offenders.

According to this report, the three most important factors for effective sex offender programs include programs that (a) hold offenders at the highest level of accountability, (b) are survivor-centered, and (c) are limited in the level of confidentiality that they offer to the offender. (We discuss these features more thoroughly later in this chapter.)

Historically, treatment for sex offenders has been a controversial issue. Law professor John Q. Lafond put it simply: "In the 1980's, American states made the decision that sex offenders were not sick; they were bad." (Kersting, 2003, p. 52). The imposition of longer prison sentences, and sex offender registration laws that require all convicted sex offenders to register in their community (see Box 6.6) are consistent with this attitude. Although some states offered treatment, the general consensus was that these treatment programs were ineffective (Kersting, 2003).

TREATMENT FOR PERPETRATORS

Given that most perpetrators of gender-based crimes are living in our communities, it is critical to provide effective treatment. Although some have questioned the efficacy of such treatment programs in the past, recent research hints at an emerging optimism (Kersting, 2003). In 2002, Karl Hanson and his colleagues published a meta-analysis on the effectiveness of treatment for sex offenders (Hanson et al., 2002). For the first time, this analysis indicated a significant difference between recidivism rates for sex offenders who were treated and those who were not. (See Box 6.7 for a discussion on recidivism rates in general.).

The approaches of intervention programs vary widely. Programs for those who commit IPV, for example, are more specialized than other types of treatment programs, as they incorporate monitoring (e.g., regular conversations with the survivor) and accountability (e.g., a requirement that the offender takes responsibility for his actions, limited assurances of confidentiality).

Group work is considered the most common form of treatment for both sex offenders and IPV offenders. Specially designed treatment programs for sexual harassers and stalkers are not in place (Wakefield & Underwager, 1991; Stucky Halley, 2004). The rationale

BOX 6.6
Sex Offender Community Notification

In 1994, the U.S. Congress passed the Jacob Wetterling Crimes Against Children and Sexually Violent Offender Registration Act. This law required all states to develop programs that include the identification and registration of lifelong sexual predators. In 1996, Megan's Law provided an amendment to this Act and required that all states provide public access to information about sex offenders in their community. Megan's Law was founded upon the assumption that public information would allow parents to inform their children about who was dangerous and thus make it more difficult for perpetrators to re-offend (Lane Council of Governments, 2003). Since the enactment of these federal mandates, scholars and advocates have debated their utility. In 2003, the Lane Council of Governments identified several potential benefits to this legislation:

- Aiding in the development of stronger bonds between law enforcement and members of the general community.
- Increasing the ability for the public to protect itself.
- Improving public education on the nature of sex offenses.
- A tool for managing sex offenders in the community.

Schram & Milloy (1995) empirically examined the effectiveness of registration notification, comparing 90 sex offenders who were subject to notification with 90 who were not. They found no differences in further arrest between these groups after 54 months. There was, however, a significant difference in the time of rearrest. Offenders subject to notification were more likely to be rearrested more quickly than those not subject to notification.

There are potential negative consequences of registration and notification mandates. The Lane Council of Governments (2003) summarizes their strong concerns about these consequences, including

- It may provide a false sense of security to the public.
- It distinguishes sex offenders from other criminals who commit crimes that are equally horrific (e.g., child abuse).
- It has been found to be related to a decrease in the reporting of domestic child sexual abuse (Freeman-Longo, 1996).

> **BOX 6.6** *(continued)*
>
> - It does not focus on primary prevention (techniques that address the entire population), or secondary prevention (techniques that address the at-risk population before any offense). (See chapter 7 for a discussion of different types of prevention.)
> - It is costly and time consuming.
> - It places responsibility for public safety on the community rather than the offender.
> - It could undermine treatment by disconnecting the offender from community support and reducing offender accountability.
> - It could limit the offender's ability to function in the community.
>
> In 2006, a young man murdered two registered sex offenders in Maine. He was able to target the victims easily because their addresses and pictures were available from sex offender Web sites (CBS News, 2006). Thus, sex offender registries may expose offenders to victimization at the hands of vigilantes.
>
> Juxtaposing the potential benefits of registration and notification mandates with the potential negative consequences, one point becomes clear: There is vast frustration over both the existence of sexual violence in our society and current attempts to resolve this issue.

for using group approaches is that these perpetrators are generally highly manipulative; however, their tactics can be quite subtle and are more likely to be identified and confronted by others who have behaved in similar ways than they are in individual therapy. Although this argument may make intuitive sense, there is little empirical data to support this conclusion (Wakefield & Underwager, 1991).

Treating sex offenders. Treatment approaches for perpetrators of sexual assault vary from organization to organization, all with the goal of relapse prevention. There are three primary approaches to sex offender treatment: (a) cognitive-behavioral, (b) psychoeducational, and (c) pharmacological (Lane Council of Governments, 2003).

The cognitive-behavioral approach. Most sex offender treatment programs rely upon a cognitive-behavioral approach. This comprehensive treatment model is founded upon psychological

> **BOX 6.7**
> **Recidivism Rates Among Sex Offenders**
>
> R. Karl Hanson and Monique T. Bussiere (1998, 2002) undertook studies on recidivism and found surprisingly low rates. In 1998, they found a 13.4% recidivism rate in a meta-analysis that included 23,393 sex offenders from 61 studies. In 2002, the recidivism rate obtained was consistently low (10% and 17.3% for the experimental and control participants, respectively). These findings are encouraging and offer hope in the face of mounting public skepticism. Hanson noted, "Even when we're talking with law enforcement officials, they'll guess demonstrated rates to be in the 70s or 80s, so real rates of 10 to 20 percent surprise everybody" (Kersting, 2003, p. 52).
>
> This finding, however, stands in stark contrast to the findings of those studying undetected rapists that the majority of sexual assault perpetrators are serial offenders (e.g., Lisak and Miller, 2002; see also chapter 2.). It is possible that the detection factor is critical in explaining this discrepancy. The majority of perpetrators in research on recidivism involve those who have been arrested, convicted, and sentenced for their crimes. In essence, they have been held legally accountable for their behavior. None of the sex offenders studied by Lisak and Miller (2002) had been arrested. This finding supports the contention that legal accountability is critical for effective intervention, and that without it, the criminal behavior is likely to recur.
>
> It is also likely that there is a level of undetected recidivism. Hanson and Bussiere (1998) acknowledged that the detected rates of recidivism are likely to be underestimates. They report that the most common measures of recidivism in research were reconviction (84%), arrests (54%), self-reports (which could lead to rearrest) (25%), and parole violations (16%). These measures are certainly important, but they are not exhaustive.

theories of learning and information processing. Cognitive-behavioral therapy targets deviant arousal, distorted cognitions, deficits in social skills, and behavior patterns that lead to offending through several distinct therapeutic components (Hall, 1996). The approach typically includes various forms of aversion therapy (where deviant fantasies are associated with negative consequences), sex education, social skills training, and techniques used to confront cognitive distortions.

The psychoeducational approach. The pscheducational approach stresses increasing the offender's concern for the survivor and recognition of responsibility for his offenses. Raising empathy for the survivor is a critical component of sex offender treatment. It includes not only acknowledging the criminal behavior, but becoming emotionally aware of its effects.

The pharmacological approach. The pharmacological approach utilizes chemotherapy to help reduce sexual arousal. Anti-androgens such as Depo Provera (medroxyprogesterone acetate) reportedly lower the sex drive in males by reducing the level of serum testosterone. Critics of this approach point out that although drugs may inhibit sexual appetite, they may not control the aggressive tendencies that are at the heart of sexual violence (Thompson, 1984).

In practice, these approaches are not mutually exclusive. Programs are increasingly utilizing tools from several models. Research supports this practice, and narrows the most effective components of sex offender treatment to three: (a) offender accountability, (b) survivor-centering, and (c) limited confidentiality (Center for Sex Offender Management, 2000; Lane Council of Governments, 2003).

Offender accountability. For many programs, a fundamental prerequisite to successful completion of treatment for perpetrators is that they acknowledge their criminal behavior and accept responsibility for their actions. With this approach, there is no room for blaming the victim. Cognitive distortions such as denial (e.g., "I didn't do it."), rationalization (e.g., "She really wanted it."), or minimization (e.g., "She enjoyed herself.") are identified and confronted (cf. Perkins, Hammond, Coles, & Bishopp, 1998).

Physiological tools for facilitating offender accountability include the penile plethysmograph and the polygraph. The plethysmograph measures erectile response to various stimuli. Although this technique is invasive, it can be used to not only help design treatment programming for individual offenders, but to assess the veracity of offender self-reports through an independent measure of sexual arousal to deviant stimuli. The Association for the Treatment of Sexual Abusers (ATSA) has developed guidelines for the use of the plethysmograph with sex offenders.

The polygraph is a device designed to detect deception. Although its validity has been questioned by many experts (cf. Wrightsman, Greene, Neitzel, & Fortune, 2002), it is helpful for the purposes of accountability in this context. It can be used to not only obtain an accurate sexual and criminal history of the offender, but also to address specific behaviors or allegations that an offender is denying and to monitor ongoing compliance with treatment requirements (Lane Council of Governments, 2003). Especially when the offender believes that the device will detect lies, he will be motivated to give accurate information to the polygraph examiner.

Survivor-centered approach. Another important component of effectiveness is that attention be focused upon the survivor and the impact that the perpetrator's sexual offense had on him or her. As mentioned earlier, many programs incorporate efforts to increase empathy for survivors into their program.

Limited confidentiality. For the purposes of survivor and community safety, sex offenders in treatment are not guaranteed full confidentiality. If a perpetrator admits committing additional crimes during treatment and the criminal justice system is not aware of these criminal acts, therapists are required to report these acts to the authorities. This practice can be especially difficult for perpetrators at the beginning of therapy, as it requires them to take full responsibility for all of their criminal behavior, not just the crimes for which they have been arrested or convicted (Kersting, 2003).

TREATING OFFENDERS OF INTIMATE PARTNER VIOLENCE

Although programs designed to treat perpetrators of IPV use a variety of methods, some core components are common across programs (Saunders & Hamill, 2003). Saunders (1996) identified numerous interventions that could be classified along several dimensions based on their underlying assumptions. These include (a) skills training, (b) cognitive approaches, (c) gender role resocialization, (d) methods aimed at acknowledging power and control tactics, (e) family systems approaches, and (f) trauma-based approaches.

Skills training is guided by social learning theory and focuses upon the behavioral deficits and excesses of offenders. The approach utilizes both role playing and positive role modeling of group leaders to help perpetrators learn alternative behavioral responses to their specific negative emotions and their potentially negative behavioral consequences.

The cognitive approach. The cognitive approach includes the assumption that faulty thinking serves as a foundation for negative emotions and subsequent abusive behavior. This approach attempts to help the perpetrator analyze specific episodes of abuse or violence in an attempt to get to the thoughts and beliefs that accompanied it. See Box 6.8 for an example.

EFFECTIVENESS OF INTIMATE PARTNER VIOLENCE PROGRAMS

Over thirty studies have been published on the effectiveness of IPV programs. Very few, however, rely on experimental design (Saunders & Hamill, 2003; see also Aldarondo, 2002; Gondolf, 2002). An exception is the research of Jackson et al. (2003), who compared participants of 8-week- and 26-week-long programs with offenders who did not undergo any intervention. They found significant behavioral improvements for those who attended the 26-week program, but no differences between attenders and nonattenders of the shorter program. Hence, a longer program appears to be more effective in effecting behavioral change in perpetrators.

Pandya & Gingerich (2002) investigated factors that predicted progress in IPV perpetrators. They found that those who were able to (a) acknowledge responsibility for their behavior, (b) conclude that the costs of their violence outweighed the benefits, and (c) identify a specific problem within themselves that they could address were more likely to make progress than those who were unable to achieve these ends. Interestingly, the "problem" was different for each of the offenders in this study. Additional factors found to be important for change include the development of survivor empathy, the reduction of dependency upon one's partner, and improved communication skills (Scott & Wolfe, 2000).

Recent meta-analyses, however, suggest that although participation in IPV programs is more effective than doing nothing, overall these effects are small, particularly when information from partners regarding any change in the perpetrator are used as outcome measures (Babcock, Green, & Robie, 2004). Given the inherent problems of experimental design when evaluating such programs, this outcome is not particularly surprising (Saunders & Hamill, 2003) In one quasi-experimental, multi-site study, more moderate and positive effect sizes have been found (Gondolf & Jones, 2001)

Yet the rate of recidivism is still high. When police records only are used, it ranges from about 10 to 20 percent. Across the research,

> **BOX 6.8**
> **The Duluth Model Control Log**
>
> The control log used as part of the pyscheducational program of the Duluth Model (Paymar & Pence, 1993) encourages IPV perpetrators to conduct a power analysis of their behavior by breaking down specific episodes of violence or abuse into seven component parts.
>
> ***Actions.*** The perpetrator describes-as specifically as possible-the situation and the actions used to control. These behaviors may include statements, facial expressions, gestures, tone of voice, or physical contact. When possible, information obtained from the survivor may be used to corroborate the statements of the perpetrator.
>
> ***Intents and beliefs.*** The perpetrator identifies the source of the behavior-What did he want to happen in this situation? It is possible that the actual intent of behavior is beyond his awareness?-especially at the beginning of doing a control log.
>
> ***Feelings.*** Identifying the emotions that the perpetrator was experiencing at the time of the event can be a difficult task. The Duluth Model utilizes the concept of the funnel effect to provide an analogy of the way that men are taught to handle negative emotions. People experience a variety of negative emotions, including fear, insecurity, shame, disappointment, and sadness. These feelings, however, are often experienced as unacceptable, especially for hypermasculine men. According to this model, the unacceptable negative emotions may quickly turn to anger, a more "comfortable" negative emotion for many men. Becoming aware of the vulnerable emotions that give rise to anger is an important part of the process.
>
> ***Minimization, denial, and blame.*** Here, perpetrators identify ways in which they ultimately blamed their partner for their abuse and violence. What excuses did they make? How did they explain their behavior after the fact? Did they acknowledge the effects that their behavior had on their partners? For instance, a perpetrator might say, "I hit her because she made me mad," assigning the source of the action to the victim. It is essential that the perpetrator come to the understanding that violence is the sole responsibility of the person who commits the crime.

BOX 6.8 (continued)

Effects. The perpetrator identifies specific effects that the violent behavior had on them, their partners, and others. He learns to recognize not only the negative outcomes for his partner and others, but also the short-term advantages that may have resulted for him (e.g., he gets to leave; the children go to their rooms.).

Past violence. The offender identifies how current actions may have been associated with past violence and identifies the effects of this past violence. For example, perpetrators may have a facial expression that they regularly use to intimidate and threaten their victims. Even when they do not use violence, these tactics serve to control their victims, who live in fear of the next attack.

Non-controlling behaviors. Finally, the perpetrator identifies alternative behaviors, given the same feelings and situation. What could he have done differently? This component is critical in helping the offender learn to replace destructive behavior with more appropriate and healthy behaviors.

Control logs are done in groups so that others can contribute to the discussion and help to hold the offender accountable.

Gender role resocialization. This approach attempts to help perpetrators identify stereotypic masculine pressures and the effects of these forces, including the paradoxical effects of male dominance and male insecurity (cf. Saunders, 1984). Those who utilize this approach encourage perpetrators to step out of the "box" of masculinity that serves to facilitate their violence.

Awareness of control tactics. As discussed in chapter 1, IPV is founded upon an entire system of power and control tactics (cf. Pence & Paymar, 1993). In some programs, emphasis upon these tactics is offered, along with attempt to increase survivor empathy in perpetrators through developing an awareness of the effects of these tactics on the survivors.

The family systems approach. The family systems approach assumes that couples unknowingly engage in repeated cycles of interaction that may culminate in abuse (cf. Neidig & Friedman, 1984). The goal is to analyze and change these patterns. This is the most controversial approach, as critics argue that considering IPV a relationship issue implicitly holds victims responsible for the criminal actions of the perpetrator in the relationship (Saunders & Hamill, 2003).

> **BOX 6.8** *(continued)*
>
> **Trauma-based approaches.** Trauma-based approaches are founded on the assumptions that IPV offenders have likely experienced childhood trauma (e.g., witnessing parental violence as a child, being abused as a child), and that survivor empathy may develop through resolution of this trauma.

approximately one third of partners report that abuse recurred within one year following treatment (Saunders & Hamill, 2003). When studies extend beyond one year posttreatment, recidivism rates rise to as high as 41% (Aldarondo, 2002; Bennett & Willliams, 2001). It is important to acknowledge that these data nonetheless suggest that those who are reported to have re-offended are in the minority.

SUMMARY

It is clear that the development and implementation of intervention strategies for both survivors and perpetrators of gender-based violence is a difficult endeavor. Nonetheless, given the vast numbers of both victims and perpetrators, it is critical that we emphasize the importance of undertaking these efforts. Professionals working in this area must continue to work to identify practices that provide the most effective support to survivors and the best mechanisms for holding perpetrators accountable, as well as providing them with professional psychological interventions.

KEY TERMS

Culpascope
Diversion
Funnel effect
Intervention
Probable cause
Rape kit
Resistance awareness

Risk reduction

Sexual Assault Nurse Examiner (SANE/SART nurse)

CRITICAL THINKING QUESTIONS

1. Intervention is an important part of supporting victims and survivors of gender-based violence. What are the most important components of such intervention? Why?
2. Why might a victim or survivor of gender-based crime be reluctant to seek help or to report her experience to law enforcement?
3. What is the distinction between *risk reduction* and *resistance awareness*?
4. What are the most effective techniques for holding a perpetrator accountable for his actions?
5. Sex offender community notification is a federal mandate requiring all states to provide public access to information about sex offenders in their community. In your opinion, do the benefits gained from this mandate outweigh the costs? Provide support for your opinion.
6. What are the critical components of effective psychological interventions for perpetrators of gender-based crimes?
7. Why might it be easier for some males to become angry than to experience other unpleasant emotions? What are the consequences of converting other feelings into anger?

Chapter 7

Gender-based Violence: Toward Prevention

We have established the clinical and social psychological foundations that can help us understand the prevalence and dynamics of gender-based violence. We have consistently argued that sex-based inequities in power, supported by consequential stereotypical attitudinal and behavioral expectations of men and women, combine to create vulnerabilities in both men and women for victimizing and victimization, respectively.

We have also repeatedly argued that the majority of men do not rape, abuse, stalk, or sexually harass women. Although this fact can—and should—serve to de-normalize gender-based violence (e.g., rape is something that most men do not do), it does not—and should not—serve to absolve men or women who do not commit such crimes from responsibility for the existence of its high prevalence rates, and ultimately for reducing these rates (see Box 7.1 for a discussion of blame and responsibility in the context of gender-based violence).

> **BOX 7.1**
> **On Blame and Responsibility**
>
> It is not uncommon for men to feel defensive about the issue of gender-based violence, and thus reluctant to join in the work of men's violence-prevention programs. The epidemic prevalence of the problem, juxtaposed with the fact that men commit the majority of these crimes, can lead to feelings of shame and blame. Although gaining a sense of awareness concerning the issues of men's violence against women may naturally lead to negative emotional reactions, such feelings are not inevitable and often not helpful.
>
> There is an important distinction between the concepts of blame and responsibility in this context. According to Shaver and Drown (1986), blame is present when an offensive act occurs and the actor's justifications or excuses for the act are judged to be invalid or unacceptable. Two important elements must be satisfied for blame to be assigned. First, the event must be negative in nature. As Shaver (1985, p. 3) points out, "people are never blamed for doing good." Second, it must be intentional. Using this definition, we find that the perpetrator of an act of violence is unquestionably and exclusively to blame in spite of his unacceptable minimizations, rationalizations, and denials.
>
> The placement of blame is both theoretically and practically significant because it precludes the possibility of blaming others—most of all, victims. But what about responsibility? Theoretical conceptualizations of responsibility are more complex and multidimensional than those for blame. After reviewing the foundational work of both Heider (1958) and Hart (1968) regarding the concept of responsibility, Phillip Shaver (1985) concludes that attributions of responsibility are dependent upon
>
> - *Perceptions of the stimulus person's causal contribution to the outcome.* Did the perpetrator commit direct acts of sexual assault, rape, partner violence, stalking, or sexual harassment?
> - *Awareness of the consequences.* Did the perpetrator know that he might induce fear or pain upon his victim?
> - *Intentions for the event to occur.* Did the perpetrator resolve to physically or psychologically damage his victim?
> - *Degree of volition.* Did the perpetrator engage in his or her actions freely?

BOX 7.1 *(continued)*

- *Appreciation of the moral wrongfulness of the action taken.* Did the perpetrator understand that what he or she was doing was illegal, immoral, or wrong?

Shaver argues that as each of these components increase, so will attributions of responsibility. Upon analysis, these criteria support the conclusion that, once again, perpetrators are exclusively responsible for their acts of gender-based violence. Even if an offender does not label his intended actions as criminal or violent, (e.g., violence rationalized as attempts to "teach her a lesson" or "get her back"), or anticipate all of the effects of his intended actions (e.g., visible bruising), he is still solely responsible for his criminal and violent acts. He should have known better, even if he did not.

This is not to say that there is a disconnection between the issue of gender-based violence and men (or women) who do not offend. Indeed, although the majority of men who do not commit such crimes are not responsible for the behavior of those who do, they are detrimentally affected by it. The impact is so insidious that it has actually been described as a "benefit" for men: men who rape, stalk, or harass women saturate the masculine stereotype to the point that men who do not commit these acts are, by definition, the "good guys." Hence, a "good guy" is defined in terms of the negative behaviors that they do not commit, as opposed to any positive behaviors in which they engage. This ideology results in a very low standard of behavior for males in a patriarchal society.

It is time to raise the bar, and time for men to take responsibility. When it comes to preventing violence, there is nothing more powerful than a group of men coming together and taking a stand. Through education and awareness, men can learn to appropriately confront their peers when they express sexist and inappropriate attitudes, or engage in behaviors that show disrespect to women. And once men take on the responsibility of educating themselves and others on these issues, they commit themselves to being change-makers as opposed to passive bystanders.

MOVING TOWARDS VIOLENCE PREVENTION

Jackson Katz (2003), a leading anti-sexist male activist, articulates the need for work in gender-violence prevention: "It is time we tried something new. Men's violence against women, children, and other men has persisted at pandemic rates for far too long. This violence, in particular domestic and sexual violence, has destroyed too many families, torn away at the fabric of our communities, and absorbed a tremendous amount of precious resources."

Efforts at prevention can be described as occurring on any of three levels (Wolfe & Jaffe, 2003). **Tertiary prevention**, or *relapse prevention*, involves attempts to prevent a problem behavior from recurring once it has already taken place. Within this context, tertiary prevention efforts might include batterer education programs or legal disincentives. The goal of **secondary prevention** is to identify at-risk individuals and work to reduce the risk factors that create vulnerability to problems. Educational programming for men in fraternities or on athletic teams (in which masculine or hypermasculine standards of behavior are often encouraged, and which show much higher levels of gendered violence than other male populations) on violence prevention would be considered secondary prevention. Finally, **primary prevention** involves working to reduce the incidence of a problem within the entire population. In terms of gender-based violence prevention, this effort would involve the introduction of concepts such as new values, ways of thinking, and the development of new relationship skills (Wolfe & Jaffe, 2003) (see Box 7.2 for a discussion on resistance awareness versus prevention).

Although all forms of prevention are important and necessary, primary prevention is most critical to the eradication of gender-based violence because these efforts challenge the foundational structure that allows this violence to exist and effects profound social, cultural, and economic changes that balance the power between the sexes (Lang, 2002).

THE INVOLVEMENT OF MEN

The elimination of men's violence against women rests critically on men's involvement in primary prevention efforts (Katz, 2003; Kilmartin & Berkowitz, 2005; Lang, 2002). According to James Lang (2002), this participation is necessary because men are central to violent acts and because violence is central to identity as a man in

> **BOX 7.2**
> **Resistance Awareness vs. Prevention**
>
> Traditionally, efforts to reduce the incidence of gender-based violence have been aimed at controlling or modifying the behavior of potential victims, usually females (Koss & Harvey, 1991; Corcoran, 1992). Golda Meir, former prime minister of Israel, tells the story of a time when incidents of rape and sexual assault were increasing. Government officials' "solution" was to establish a curfew—for women (Allison & Wrightsman, 1993). Similarly, when news stories surfaced about the alarming prevalence of sexual assault at the Air Force Academy, the then Commandant suggested that the problem was caused by male and female cadets occupying the same dormitories and announced plans for segregating the population by sex. In other words, the problem is that men are raping women, and the solution is getting rid of the women. For decades, programs to educate women and girls have taken the form of ***resistance awareness.*** Educators advised them to either restrict their behavior (e.g., don't walk alone, don't wear short dresses or skirts) so that they might avoid being attacked, or to learn how to "effectively" respond when attacked (e.g., fight back, scream) (Morgan, 1986).
>
> Being educated on resistance-awareness techniques can be empowering for girls and women who are taught to fear gender-based violence-particularly rape-from an early age (Gordon & Rigor, 1989). However, resistance awareness does not guarantee that one will be able to successfully avoid victimization. Moreover, education and knowledge of resistance awareness for females has not reduced the prevalence rates of gender-based violence-an effort that requires a cognitive and social shift towards the concept of prevention, which is about change at both the individual and social level. "Prevention provides an escape from a negative life course, and helps to develop competency and knowledge that leads to a more desired life course in general" (Veinot, 1999, p. 1).

those cultures that give greater value to masculinity than to femininity. Additionally, men are more likely to be in positions of power in nearly every organizational sphere, and hence they are in better positions to effect positive change for both women and men. Hence, while men are the center of the problem, they are also an important part of the solution. As bell hooks (1992) noted, "...men have a tremendous contribution to make....in the area of exposing, confronting, opposing, and transforming the sexism of their male peers" (pp. 570–571). Since gender-based violence has been historically defined as a "women's issue" (Katz, 2003), and because masculinity is culturally defined as the "not feminine," men who engage in these social change efforts must be especially courageous, independent, and risk-taking (Kilmartin & Berkowitz, 2005). Men's organized efforts began in the late 1980s and early 1990s, with scattered and isolated programs (see Box 7.3 for an interview with a Don McPherson, a man committed to ending violence against women). Chapter 8 provides descriptions of several current programs.

Historically, a majority of men have served as silent observers to other men's gender-based violence and sexism (Berkowitz, 1994; Kilmartin, 2007). For example, when boys or men make sexist jokes or remarks, other males may either say nothing or laugh along with the others in an effort to win the approval of their peers. Because of the pressures to conform to the antifeminine standards of masculinity, these boys and men are likely to remain silent even when they feel uncomfortable.

Research on social norms suggests that, indeed, *most* males report feeling uncomfortable when they are exposed to behavior that is sexist or degrades females. Most boys and men, however, believe that their emotional discomfort to sexist behaviors is isolated from the emotional responses of other men (Berkowitz, 1994; Kilmartin, Green, Heinzen, Kuchler, & Smith, 2004; Kilmartin, Conway, Freidberg, McQuoid, & Tschan, 1997). (See chapter 8 for more on this topic.)

The logical converse to this reality that most men and boys are not comfortable with sexism is that most males are comfortable with concepts of peace and equality even though the masculine stereotype does not encourage them to speak out publicly in favor of them. It does not require a huge leap to go from the understanding that men value peace and equality to the proposition that men, in fact, might want to participate in ending violence, especially if they understood that being part of the solution to the problem of violence is a noble—and positively masculine—endeavor. Indeed, in our work, we find that men are often relieved to find that there are other men interested in taking responsibility for the safety and well-being of their community and in doing violence-prevention work.

BOX 7.3
An Interview with Don McPherson

Don McPherson is the founder and executive director of the Sports Leadership Institute at Adelphi University and is one of the nation's leading educators and advocates for the prevention of men's violence against women. In fall 2005, he volunteered his time to talk to us about his work.

When did you get involved in violence-prevention work? What brought you into this work? *Specifically in late 1994, when I was hired at Northeastern University to run a program called Athletes in Service to America, one of the components of the program was Jackson Katz' MVP program. (He had not met Jackson previously.) It was a National program and I was expanding the programs of the center to four different communities across the country. One of those programs was Jackson's program. During that time, I discovered that this problem is more evident than it's ever been and this culture and the work is not done and I think it is needed now more than ever. The other thing that attracted me to it, and has kept me alive in it, is...if we're going to prevent this and change this, there is a whole other piece about masculinity that expands the definition of masculinity. This works simultaneously with violence against women. Unfortunately, I think that toxic masculinity is a more pervasive problem than domestic violence. For example, my father...he was a great dad, not violent, not abusive, but so much of himself he did not share with his children. He was a police officer and very traditionally masculine...the stoic man, but gentle, kind, and loving. He was impacted negatively by this. I think that he is now a man who doesn't necessarily regret his past because it was all he knew, but he understands the negative implications of his past masculinity. I realize, too, that he was one of the lucky ones. He was able to be that person and still be a successful dad. I know many, many, many more dads of friends and people close to me whose dads were hypermasculine and who never came around, or who died before they could tell them that they loved him and hear that back. We must educate men about this.*

Can you tell us about your current program in Adelphia, New York? *I am the Director of the Sports Leadership Institute at Adelphi University. Currently, it's a little separate from the violence-prevention*

BOX 7.3 *(continued)*

work that I do. We run leadership workshops in high schools, work with parents in the community. The work is primarily centered on school issues, such as bullying, alcohol, drug use, and those types of issues.

Within our leadership program, I have developed some of the fundamental elements of violence-prevention work. For example, language issues, and getting kids to understand gender-based language is a fundamental element.

We work with the leaders of the schools. We want to teach kids about the invisible kids at school, or who are virtually invisible to our culture. Basically, we want the kids who have social status to recognize those who don't, by pointing it out, quite deliberately. We want to sensitize them to those students; especially those in the earlier grades…they don't just disappear.

Don, I would guess you were one of the "popular" kids in school. So how did you get to this understanding?
I think that if you're an honest person, you see inequities. Sometimes you benefit from this at times, as in the case of being popular. Sometimes you experience the disadvantages of this; in my case as a Black man. I remember on news reels, Black people having hoses turned on them, or dogs turned on them. I grew up with a reality that I was special, and I was more special than other Black people because I was being recognized, appreciated, and even exalted by White culture.

How did that feel?
(Pause) Confusing. You asked earlier about the impact of my father's stoic nature on me. I believe his stoic nature protected me at that time, and taught me how to keep things very close to the vest. No matter how much injustice there was, there was still right and wrong. During this period, it was taking an honest look at things. My childhood was full of contradictions and different worlds. We never moved, but unlike everyone else in my family, I went to three different schools. Public…Catholic…public, predominantly Black middle school, and public, predominantly White high school. I was Black, I was talented, and sport was seen as the way out, although I avoided the idea that sports was my only way out.

When one person is oppressed we are all oppressed. I truly believe that. When I sit with a group of men, without women, I feel

BOX 7.3 *(continued)*

the oppression against women. It just occurred a couple of weeks ago. I'm sitting with a group of men who are married men, nice guys, and they were looking at the women half their age and talking about them in ways that were objectifying them. I said something, and I left. It's offensive to me. If I stay silent, I'm part of the problem. And yet, because I am a man, and I am honest about it, I feel it. It is on the acute level of our daily interactions.

Your success in the world of football is quite impressive. How important do you think that this success in sports has had on your ability to do violence-prevention work? Can you talk about the role that sports has on both violence and violence-prevention work?

I spent most of my life in the 70s and 80s, when I was changing schools and changing high schools, I spent a lot of time by myself and thinking about it at the time. At Syracuse, I had all this talent to play football and I enjoyed it and I loved it, but I didn't understand it. I used to write letters to God...why did you give me all this talent? I know now why, because it gives me the platform to do this work.

I did a lot of things in my career in hindsight to sabotage my own career; I didn't want to be a star. I changed high schools, for example. I was asking colleges about being a Black quarterback. (They would quit recruiting me.) I wrote letters to all 28 NFL teams and said don't recruit me if you are considering me for another position. I was very good at quarterback, and I didn't want racism to preclude my ability to be a quarterback. What I did, I did with integrity, and didn't allow the endeavor to dictate my identity, which is what I continue to do today. And I want to encourage others to do so as well. And I am aware that all people see when I walk in the door is someone who used to play football. I find it a little offensive that I am known as an athlete. I've been doing violence prevention work for 18 years, professionally for 11 years, and yet people still refer to me as an athlete. I haven't touched my toes in 10 years.

With regard to coaches of sports teams, what do you see as their role to both gender-based violence and violence-prevention work? What are effective techniques of involving coaches in this work?

Until the world of sports is more honest about how it perpetuates narrow masculinity, and how coaches contribute to this, the

BOX 7.3 *(continued)*

constructed of toxic masculinity is not likely to change. I think it's difficult, though. I think we expect too much from our coaches, and we expect things that are impossible, quite frankly, with regard to this issue. If you want for coaches to get involved in this work, then that would go a long way, but to expect the institution of coaching to involve violence-prevention work is not reasonable at this time. Coaches interested in this would have a difficult time with other coaches. I see coaches as part of the solution. But their job is to teach, to nurture, and to teach kids how to compete. With coaches, you want boys to be tough and to compete. You also want girls to do this. We expect that coaches are going to be addressing the issues of violence, when what we need to do is have coaches address the issue of gender identity.

With regard to techniques of violence prevention for coaches, it's a matter of talking with them about the narrowness of masculinity, and comparing this with the narrowness of the given sports. The more you know in sports, the better decisions you'll make about sports. The more you know about gender, the better decisions you'll make about gender-related decisions, and the more broadly masculinity (or femininity) will be defined. Generally speaking, the more limited one is the poorer decisions they will be. This is about broadening the emotional toolbox of a person.

What we can do is help coaches to understand the benefits of broadening the concept of gender and gender identification. The challenge is how to we teach our boys to be better without degrading girls? These messages must come from our culture and be assimilated into our sports institution. So much of the language that we use in our culture comes from the sports world, or from military speak, and we live in a capitalistic society with a zero sum game: I win, you lose. (You're either in the box, or you're not.) We have got to get to a point where we think beyond a "win/lose" paradigm, which does not come from sports vernacular.

There seems to be momentum gaining in the violence-prevention work, particularly with regard to bringing men into the movement. What factors have been most critical to building this momentum? What can be done to positively impact this work?

I think that there has been an exceptional job of organizations around the country with regard to highlighting the statistics, and

BOX 7.3 (continued)

have been absolutely amazing at discussing issues that people don't want to discuss and raising awareness of the problem. Unfortunately, a lot of this has been done in reaction to high-profile cases, very horrific cases. Without this attention, more and more of this would be happening. The violence prevention work has really shown light to the problem. There have been extraordinary and courageous women as well who were willing to show their face as victims and survivors of violence.

All of this has raised the awareness for men, as well as their consciousness. Then I think you have the next level of men who have been very courageous in this other discussion about masculinity. Enough men have been intrigued about masculinity and how it has contributed to the problem. And some of these men are brave enough to confront their contribution to the problem if they don't get involved.

What do you see as "best practices" in men's violence-prevention work? What do you see as critical elements of such programs?

I think the critical elements are engaging men in the discussion as part of the solution. The tone of blaming all men for the problem is counterproductive, and I think that tone has been heard in the past very clearly. Today, there is a lot less of that. Women have embraced men in doing this work, women who have been entrenched in the issue, and who appreciate men, including myself, who stand up and speak out. It's easier for men to get involved when they're not going to be blamed. This is sad, but important. I hate that word blame-blame and fault. Does someone always have to be vilified?

What do you see as the future of violence-prevention work?

I think the future is in addressing masculinity, and acknowledging that we are part of the problem if [we] remain silent to the structures of an oppressive system. Once we do that, we have the unavoidable recognition that with power comes responsibility. We also have to look at how the global oppressive system and global violence. How can we speak about violence-prevention when we go to war?

I think we will continue to incarcerate, and rehabilitate, but the dialogue about violence-prevention work will become more global, and it's going to be a respect movement.

> **BOX 7.3** *(continued)*
>
> **Why don't you want to call it a peace movement?**
> *I tend to shy away from language that is commonly used. And, I think that peace sometimes for people expresses a Pollyannic world of hope that people cannot connect to. For example, I don't think that if you ask for evidence of violence in our society, people would think first of the war in Iraq. Lack of war, however, does not mean peace, even though peace is seen as the opposite of war.*
>
> *The irony of America is that our culture is trained not to think about these things, not to confront them, not to deal with the difficult questions. We are also trained to be very self-centered and self-absorbed, and it's hard to be empathetic when you're so self-absorbed. When we come upon people in need, (or are invisible,) or people in general, what questions do we ask? Martin Luther King Jr. once told a story that I believe is relevant: Three men came across a beggar. They were all leaders, men of power. The first man didn't help because he was afraid that he might be attacked, and his congregation would suffer. He was thinking of the people that he served. The second person worried that if he helped he might get hurt, he could be killed. The third asked the question, if I do not help this man, what's going to happen to him?*
>
> *The message from this is that we will be selfish. But we shouldn't live this way. We should live our lives by asking ourselves, what's going to happen to them? We have got to consider the impact of our behavior. I think about this every day...and this is another byproduct of my status and notoriety. I found out the impact I can make. You don't just meet someone and then disappear. You realize that your behavior matters and it makes a difference. Just smiling at someone, being nice to them can make a profound difference. We must help those who are suffering.*

The bystander approach to prevention utilizes the principle of social norms and encourages the silent and vast majority of men who are against gender-based violence to express their disapproval of sexist behavior in other men through appropriate confrontation. For several reasons, men can affect men in different ways than women can affect men. First, because patriarchy affords more power to men than to women, men may have a greater ability to influence other men. Second, there may be a (mis)perception that men who confront sexism and violence against women are working against their self-interest (Aronson, 2004). Therefore, their credibility is increased and their ability to persuade others increases. Finally, much of men's sexist behavior occurs in gender-exclusive contexts, precluding the opportunity for women to respond to it.

Kilmartin and Berkowitz (2005) suggest a developmental progression for men's violence-prevention programs in various communities. A community may begin with a one-time awareness program like a nationally known speaker's presentation or a theatrical piece that sheds light on the issues. Such an event could plant the seeds for an evolution into important formal and/or informal discussions among men, among women, and between men and women about issues related to gender-based violence. Local schools and universities might provide a forum for a panel discussion on the issues.

A next step would be the development or adoption of an identified curriculum aimed at a specific audience. Universities and colleges might offer a course on gender-based violence, or incorporate the topic into already existing courses (e.g., Men and Masculinities, Gender Studies, or Women's Studies). Middle and high schools could incorporate violence-prevention curricula into various classes (e.g., health class) or other activities (See Box 7.4 for an example of a high-school violence-prevention curriculum). Any of these efforts may lead to strategies that promote environmental social change, including the formation of men's programs aimed at violence prevention.

A third step in program development is the movement toward peer-administered programs and environmental educational strategies. Especially within school settings, well trained peer educators can be very effective, since people are more likely to be influenced by those whom they perceive to be similar to them. Environmental approaches include public awareness campaigns, social norms interventions, and public service advertisements. All of these efforts are sustained movements toward cultural change.

The final stage of program development is a full integration of violence prevention into the institutional aspects of the community. In schools, this outcome would include highly effective policies; information about the problem and its solutions that enters into the mainstream of student life in the classroom and elsewhere; and social-structural gender egalitarianism, with women and men holding similar levels of institutional power. In communities, it would also involve effective laws, well trained intervention and prevention

> **BOX 7.4**
> **Safe Dates: A Dating-Violence Prevention Curriculum**
>
> Safe Dates is a school-based program designed by Vangie Foshee and Stacey Langwick to prevent incidents of psychological, physical, and sexual abuse in the dating relationships of middle- and high-school students. Program goals include
>
> - Changing adolescent dating-violence norms.
> - Changing adolescent gender-role norms.
> - Improving conflict resolution skills in dating relationships.
> - Promoting awareness of community resources for dating violence.
> - Promoting help-seeking by victims and perpetrators.
> - Improving peer help-giving skills.
>
> The program consists of five components: a poster contest, parent materials, a teacher-training outline, a play script entitled "There's No Excuse for Dating Abuse," and a nine-session curriculum. The topics addressed in the nine-session curriculum include
>
> - Defining Caring Relationships.
> - Defining Dating Abuse.
> - Why Do People Abuse?
> - How to Help Friends.
> - Overcoming Gender Stereotypes.
> - Equal Power through Communication.
> - How We Feel, How We Deal.
> - Preventing Sexual Assault.
>
> Safe Dates is one of several violence-prevention curricula that innovators have created in an attempt to change knowledge, attitudes, and behavior on the issues of gender-based violence. It is somewhat unique, however, in that researchers have empirically investigated its effectiveness. The results are promising. In a four-year follow-up, researchers found a 56% to 92% reduction in reports of physical, serious physical, and sexual dating violence (modelprograms.samhsaa.gov) in addition to both primary and secondary prevention effects on all six of the goals for males and females of all races.

personnel, an overall commitment to primary prevention, and swift remedy following negative incidents.

In 2002, the Centers for Disease Control and Prevention (CDC) initiated a large contract, "Evaluation Assistance for Projects Designed to Prevent First-Time Male Perpetration of Sexual Violence," in which it sought to identify the programmatic efforts being implemented throughout the United States and assist in the improvement of some of these programs (Clinton-Sherrod, Gibbs, Vincus, Squire, Cignetti, Pettibone, et al., 2003). Investigators identified 37 existing programs that either involved both sexes or were primarily for men. Although this research was primarily geared toward the prevention of sexual violence, many of the identified programs crossed boundaries into other domains of gender-based violence.

TYPES OF GENDER-BASED VIOLENCE-PREVENTION PROGRAMS

The CDC acknowledged wide variations among the programs with regard to several criteria, including populations served, media used to convey the message, goals and objectives, theories or scientific bases for the approach, levels of program evaluation, and staff capacity. CDC was able to identify four types of gender-based violence prevention programs, each with its own advantages:

One-time awareness/educational workshop and theatrical performances. Fourteen programs were "one shot" efforts at violence prevention, such as bringing a nationally recognized speaker to a college campus for consulting with administrators and presenting to an audience of students. The positive effects of these programs are most likely short-term (Clinton-Sherrod et al., 2003). However, these efforts can serve to inspire audiences to work towards the development of more fully integrated prevention programs.

Ongoing, open-forum discussion groups. Five of the identified programs used available media or other nationally accessible educational tools to promote regular and honest discussion of the issues. Especially with single-sex groups, open-forum discussions can be critical to the development of both individuals and programs. These efforts must also include honest discussions of sensitive topics such as fear or hostility toward the other sex, homophobia, specific feelings (especially fear), sexuality, pressures that women and men feel to act in gender-consistent ways, and relationships (Kilmartin & Berkowitz, 2005). Especially in the beginning, it is critical that group members feel safe to explore their emotions without feeling uncomfortable or fearing that their comments might be perceived as offensive; a single-sex atmosphere tends to support this feeling of safety (Earle, 1992; Kilmartin & Berkowitz, 2005).

Multiple-session, curriculum-based prevention interventions. Sixteen of the programs identified by the CDC were of this type. The durations of the programs varied from a few weeks to a few months. Many utilized a mentoring model in which the curriculum is delivered by peer (or slightly older) presenters. Those programs that have a planned, ongoing curriculum that is presented over time have been found to be the most successful in terms of effecting attitudinal change (Clinton-Sherrod et al. 2003).

Environmental change strategies. Generally, these types of programs are aimed at promoting cultural change. Specifically, they are geared toward changing attitudes and behaviors that support the existence of gendered violence and include efforts at promoting awareness of the issue, protesting violence against women, and encouraging others (primarily men) to be actively and personally involved in reducing gendered violence. The CDC recognized the White Ribbon Campaign and the work of Men Can Stop Rape as two such efforts (see chapter 8).

MEN AND WOMEN DOING PREVENTION WORK

Based upon both theory and research, it is clear that single-sex, peer-facilitated, interactive men's programs are most effective at preventing men's gender-based violence (Berkowitz, 1994; Clinton-Sherrod et al., 2003). This conclusion creates the possibility for an awkward paradox: women, who are most likely to be targets of men's gender-based violence, are faced with the reality that it is men who must solve this problem. A direct possible implication of this paradox is that in order to solve gender-based violence, women need men. Hence, we are once again faced with the possibility of perpetuating a power differential of men having more influence (e.g., men being more important) than women. It is premature, however, to stop at this conclusion and its implications, which rest upon the false assumption that gender-based violence is a woman's issue. At a deeper level of analysis, both men and women will benefit from the eradication of violence and thus both are critical to prevention work.

WOMEN AS ACTIVE PARTICIPANTS IN THE MOVEMENT

It is important to acknowledge that women are and always have been at the forefront of the movement as agents of social change. Women can learn to appropriately confront inappropriate and sexist behavior when they experience or are exposed to it, raise awareness of the issue, and support both men and women who go beyond stereotypes and step into their individuality—including women who are strong and independent and men who are strong and sensitive. Indeed, strength, independence, and sensitivity are all qualities that can help support a social movement.

The involvement of women in men's violence-prevention programs is critical for two primary reasons. First, for men to develop a grasp of the issue of gendered violence, it is important that they pause to truly listen to the stories of women regarding the experiences and observations of being female in a patriarchal society. Hence, it is important for women to be able to share their experiences and insights effectively.

It is also critical that women observe (either directly or indirectly) the process of men's violence-prevention efforts, offering feedback, constructive criticism, and support to those who are engaged in this work. It is critical that men are accountable to women as they embark upon this work. Ultimately, men and women must work both separately and together to prevent gender-based violence. As anthropologist Margaret Mead noted, "Never doubt that a small group of thoughtful, committed citizens can change the world."

GOALS OF VIOLENCE-PREVENTION PROGRAMMING FOR MEN

To accomplish the ultimate goal of eliminating gendered violence, we must reach a number of intermediate goals. Indeed, it is the personal and interpersonal growth and learning of individuals that will ultimately lead to the modification of social norms in a society. As South African civil rights martyr Steve Biko noted, "Change the way people think, and things will never be the same."

Such personal growth and learning can be facilitated by membership in a group aimed at a higher purpose, such as a men's gender-based violence-prevention program. Kilmartin and Berkowitz (2005) identify the following goals as important to men's programs:

To educate men about the effect of gender on their lives. For individuals who belong to privileged groups, these social advantages are often invisible (See Box 7.5 for some examples of men's privilege). That is, they tend not to reflect on or understand the privileges granted to them. Much like older siblings who often hold privileges, this advantage is not revealed until it is perceived and identified by the younger siblings.

Similarly, the risks associated with these privileges are also often unrecognized. Hence, both the emotional and psychological risks of subscribing to the masculine standards (e.g., the inability to express emotional pain, the pressure to "fight" for your honor, or the increased likelihood of abusing your partner) are often ignored.

To invite men to explore gendered issues. Gendered issues that are most relevant to the prevention of gender-based may include:

- Gender stereotypes. Until gender was "discovered" in the 1970s (Smiler, 2004), the concepts of masculinity and femininity were unquestioned prescriptions for behavior for both men and women. In violence-prevention programs, it is critical to examine the role of gender on both the lives of individual males and females, and on the lives of women and men as gendered groups. It is important to honor the positive elements of both masculinity and femininity and also to identify the negative social pressures that individuals feel to think and act in stereotype-consistent ways, as well as the consequences of these pressures (see Box 7.5 for a discussion of "The Box.") Ultimately, men can work together to deconstruct the concept of masculinity, and then to recreate it.
- Fear of women (*femiphobia*) and hostility toward women (*misogyny*). The following statements reveal the femiphobia and the misogyny that can exist in a patriarchal society:

  "My triplet daughters' names—Kimmy, Kirsty, and Kathy—all start with K because I struck out three times."—Gary Adams, former UCLA basketball coach, on why he used K, the symbol for a strikeout in baseball, for his daughter's names.

  "Microphones are like mistresses. They can't answer back. You control them."—Larry King, talk-show host.

> **BOX 7.5**
> **"The Box" of Masculinity**
>
> In his film, "Tough Guise," Jackson Katz uses a box as an analogy to demonstrate the pressures that men exert on one another to stay within the boundaries of culturally defined masculinity. Within the "box" are stereotypical masculine characteristics such as aggression, heterosexuality, and low emotionality. Boys and men often go to great lengths to stay within these boundaries out of fear of appearing feminine or unmanly. Doing so, however, takes great energy. It is natural to cry, to want to spend time with female friends and partners, to be loving, to express feelings other than anger, or to have a close relationship with another man.
>
> When boys and men step outside of the box, they are often punished by others(usually males) to validate the practice of masculinity within a patriarchal system. Hence, it is very threatening to males when they observe another male stepping outside of the box. This punishment usually takes the form of antifemine (e.g., "You play like a girl!") or homophobic (e.g., "That's gay.") ridicule. Through this process of punishment, boys learn early in life to conform to the masculine gender behaviors that are required of them by "stepping back into the box." Thus, male peer groups often use shame and the threat of relegating the boy to a social underclass to police the boundaries of acceptable masculinity.
>
> Men who participate in gender-aware violence-prevention programs can reduce their perceived pressure to stay within the box. By creating a social climate that honors and reinforces individuality, men encourage one another to be themselves rather than merely "going along with the program."

"I'm scared to death of women and money. Those two things have caused more creatures' downfall than any other."—Jimmy Swaggart, televangelist.

"Most are fairly stupid. I don't like many of them."—Timothy Dalton, actor, about women.

- Because boys and men are strongly and soundly punished for expressing feminine attitudes or behaviors, femininity becomes associated with danger, fear, and disgust. Fear is a natural emotion, but it is viewed as unacceptable for the masculine boy or man to experience or express it. However, the one negative emotion that is socially acceptable for men is anger. Therefore, many men learn to funnel their femiphobia into anger, hostility, and violence towards females.

Men can learn to successfully confront any discomfort they may have about femininity or females that they may have been conditioned to experience so they can unlearn any violent tendencies.

- Fear of gay men (a form of homophobia). The perceived association between gay men and femininity is longstanding in Western societies and has encouraged the endorsement of many myths and stereotypes regarding gay men. For a man to love another man is the epitome of antimasculinity. Homophobia serves to perpetuate hypermasculine myths and stereotypes and trap men into rigid masculinity (Kilmartin, 2007). Through honest discussion, heterosexual men can learn that not only is it all right to accept and respect gay men, but it is possible—and healthy—to have nonsexual, close relationships with other men. Men's psychological intimacy with other men may reduce unrealistic expectations that they might place on their female partners to solely and successfully nurture all of their emotional needs, or to suffer the consequences when they act out their inner conflicts.
- Anger and other feelings. It is important to recognize that emotions are human experiences. Although the expressions of emotions are variable, and are influenced by both gender and culture, the experience of basic emotions, like disgust, anger, fear, happiness, sadness, and surprise, is universal (Myers, 2005). Men can learn the benefits of expressing their feelings (e.g., greater psychological and physical health) and can also identify the costs of both experiencing and expressing strong and consistent levels of anger (e.g., less intimate relationships, risk of physical health, vulnerability to committing violence).
- Sexuality. In his qualitative research, Pollack (1998) tells the stories of boys who feel pressured to engage in sexual intercourse because of the association of male sexuality with conquest, power, and status. The perceived connection between power and sexuality serves to create a gateway to the possibilities of committing rape and sexual assault.
- Feelings about fathers and other men. Researchers are increasingly identifying the costs of poor parenting by fathers (Kilmartin, 2007). David Lisak (1991) reports that, among the undetected rapists that he interviewed, the most striking finding was that the rapists consistently reported feelings of bitterness and disappointment towards their fathers. The positive involvement of fathers is related to high self-esteem, egalitarian gender beliefs, belief in the importance of the father's role, and a mature understanding of children and of the parent-child relationship (Erickson & Gecas, 1991). For young men entering adulthood and preparing to start families, it is critical to

consider the impact that their relationships with their fathers have had on them as adults.
- Relationships. The stereotype of masculinity is that men are independent and self-sufficient, have sexual relationships only with women, and have "working" relationships with other men. Intimate relationships with other men are forbidden in the world of masculinity. This prohibition may help to explain why both women and men indicate that their friendships with women are more intimate, enjoyable, and nurturing than their friendships with men (Rubin, 1985; Sapadin, 1988). Through these programs, men can learn the value of strong and respectful interpersonal bonds with women and other men. Having respect within a relationship greatly inhibits the likelihood that power-and-control dynamics will exist, and hence increases the likelihood that the relationship will be free of abuse and violence.

To facilitate empathy for women, other men, and the self. *Empathy* is the sympathetic awareness of another person's distress. To be empathic with others, it is critical to have an awareness of one's own distress. Men who have experienced childhood sexual abuse and have been able to acknowledge the emotional pain of that abuse showed a tendency to have more peaceful relationships than those men who denied their emotional pain (Lisak, 1993). Hence, ***empathy for the self*** is a critical component for the development of both personal health and positive relationships. However, through the process of socialization, men and boys are taught to deny most of their feelings of distress. This acculturation may help to explain why women express more empathy for others than men, even when they are enduring similar experiences (Batson, Sympson, Hindman, Decruz, Todd, Jennings, & Burris, 1996). The experience of empathy among men involved in men's violence-prevention work is critical to programmatic success. To experience empathy for oneself, other men, and ultimately, for women helps men to rediscover their humanity, which precludes the possibility for violence. It is also important for men involved in this work to understand that although it is beneficial for them to be empathic towards women, it is not helpful to pity or patronize them, which reinforces a power differential that provides the foundation for gender-based violence in the first place.

To associate masculinity with dignity and individual choice. As noted earlier, there are many honorable components to masculinity. Strength, courage, independence, risk taking, and other positive masculine attributes can be brought to bear in violence-prevention efforts. Because of their tendency to inhibit the expression of their non-masculine, or especially feminine qualities, these components of men's individualities are frequently hidden and unnoticed. To redefine the concept of masculinity as one that involves dignity and individual choice allows men the freedom and flexibility to be authentic. Ultimately, this newly defined concept of masculinity encourages the development of men of integrity.

To define and denormalize gender-based violence and the underlying negative attitudes toward women. Statistically, rape and sexual assault, IPV, stalking, and sexual harassment are not normal events, nor are the attitudes of those who commit these crimes. The beliefs that a woman might enjoy rape or needs to be told what to do, that regularly giving unwanted letters and flowers will eventually win someone's love, or that it is reasonable to exchange sex for employment benefits, must be met with strong disapproval by other men.

Although violence is not normal, the attitudes that support it are *normative*. In spite of the statistical and psychological abnormalities of criminals, the underlying negative attitudes towards women that serve to support the perpetration of violence are pervasive. It is not unusual to hear men who have never committed a violent act nonetheless tell derogatory jokes about women or refer to women by animal names or the names of their genitals. Such negative attitudes must ultimately be challenged and de-normalized in order to effect change towards nonviolence. When the foundations that support gendered violence are eradicated, so will the violence itself.

To identify the characteristics of healthy relationships and learn the skills needed to develop these kinds of relationships. It is not enough to ask men to not engage in abusive or violent behaviors. Men have both the potential and the responsibility to be full participants of egalitarian relationships with their friends, partners, and children. For both women and men, relationships that are perceived as fair and equitable are significantly more satisfying than those perceived as inequitable (Fletcher, Fincham, Cramer, & Heron, 1987; Hatfield, Traupmann, Sprecher, Utne, & Hay, 1985; Van Yperen & Buunk, 1990). (See Box 7.6 for a discussion of healthy relationships and Box 7.7 for a discussion on privilege.)

> **BOX 7.6**
> **Having Healthy Relationships**
>
> One of the ways in which we can prevent gender-based violence is to promote healthy attitudes founded on concepts of mutual respect and egalitarianism. Developing a relationship takes time and occurs through a process of reciprocal self-disclosure (Derlega, Metts, Petronio, & Margulis, 1993). As relationships grow, partners will reveal more and more of themselves to each other. This process creates a foundation of knowledge about partners—their strengths and limitations, successes and failures—and this awareness means that we have the ability to both benefit or hurt our partners and the relationship in significant ways.
>
> Both the process and the outcome of self-disclosure are feminine-defined phenomena, as are many of the skills that are related to healthy relationships—for example, the abilities to demonstrate care and concern and to be emotionally expressive are related to longevity in relationships (Blumstein & Schwartz, 1983). Good communication (both listening and talking) is critical for healthy relationships (Garner, 1991), but typically masculine expressions (e.g., inattentiveness, or lack of affection) are related to dissatisfaction (McAdams, Lester, Brand, McNamara, & Lensky, 1988). Therefore, for men to have successful relationships, they must be willing to step into the world of culturally defined femininity.

To learn how to positively affect other men and women. When men come together as a group and address the topics of gender and gendered violence, they have the opportunity to learn and grow personally. The next step is to go beyond a sense of awareness about the issue to developing a sense of responsibility for its prevention. Men must serve as nonviolent role models for other men and boys behaving in ways that challenge traditional masculine stereotypes, developing close and respectful relationships with other men and women, and having discussions about the issues of gender and power and how they relate to violence. Overall, the ultimate goal of such awareness and commitment:

To contribute to the overall intellectual, moral, and psychological development of men and women, boys and girls. Learning about gender, violence, and the connections between the two has developmental implications that go beyond the content of the subject matter. An awareness of the dominant culture's pressure

> **BOX 7.7**
> **On Privilege**
>
> In "Teaching About Being an Oppressor," Steven Schacht (2004) identifies various "advantages" that he experiences on a daily basis by virtue of his being male, including
>
> - *When I go to lease/buy a car or home (or to have work done on them), I can expect to not only be treated in a far more professional manner than women (who are often patronized in these business transactions), but in most cases, to ultimately pay less for the product or service.*
> - *If I am sexually active, even promiscuous, I can largely count on not being seen as a slut, a whore, or a prostitute.*
> - *If I am married or even cohabitating, I can count on my "wife" doing most of the housework and being responsible for most of the childcare should we have children, regardless of whether she works or not.*
> - *Should I decide to rape a woman in my quest to feel superior, I can rest assured that it is highly unlikely that she will report my misogynist criminal activity to the police. If, however, I should incur the unfortunate charge of rape, unlike any other crime, I can count on my accuser's life and status to simultaneously be on trial to determine if she is worthy of being named my "victim."*
> - *When venturing out in public I can reasonably rest assured that I will not be sexually harassed or sexually assaulted.*
>
> Such privilege is often invisible (Kimmel, 2004). That is, those who are privileged are not likely to notice that they have advantages that others may not have. Michael Kimmel (2004) describes a revealing moment while participating in a discussion group on feminism:
>
>> *In one meeting, a white woman and a black woman were discussing whether all women were, by definition, "sisters" because they all had essentially the same experiences and because all women faced a common oppression by men. The white woman asserted that the fact that they were both women bonded them, in spite of racial differences. The black woman disagreed.*
>>
>> *"When you wake up in the morning and look in the mirror, what do you see?" she asked.*
>>
>> *"I see a woman," replied the white woman.*
>>
>> *"That's precisely the problem," responded the **black** woman. "I see a black woman. To me, race is visible every day, because I am not*

> **BOX 7.7** *(continued)*
>
> *privileged in our culture. Race is invisible to you, because it's how you are privileged. It's why there will always be differences in our experience."*
>
> *As I witnessed this exchange, I was startled, and groaned—more audibly, perhaps, than I had intended. Someone asked what my response had meant.*
>
> *"Well," I said, "when I look in the mirror, I see a human being. I'm universally generalizable. As a middle-class white man, I have no class, no race, and no gender. I'm the generic person!"*
>
> When we think of inequality, we most always think of how some individuals or groups are minimized or hurt by it—and awareness of one's own privilege allows one to make this estimation.

on people to conform to gender expectations puts people into a position to resist this pressure when it conflicts with one's life goals. It can also generalize into greater ability to think critically about other cultural pressures to conform to areas unrelated or tangentially related to gender, such as politics, literature, and media. Since violence is a moral issue, education about this problem can serve to give a person a heightened sense of other moral issues. Gender and violence education can help people become more conscious of their worlds and thus put them into better positions to manage their lives.

In the film *Men's Work: Fraternity Brothers Stopping Violence against Women*, (described in more detail in chapter 8), a group of men learn about sexual assault and its prevention and then they give presentations on the topic to their fraternity brothers. In the process, they become better leaders and more sensitive men. They develop better relationship skills, and they become better engaged in, and more aware of, the personal and political worlds. Thus, apprehending the subject of men's violence against women can result in many benefits beyond those directly associated with the topic, just as learning music or a foreign language can result in a general enhancement of one's skills and sense of self.

SUMMARY

We will never solve the problem of men's violence against women until we are able to bring effective prevention to those who have already offended, those at high risk, and the general population of men and boys. Historically, males have been underrepresented among those who facilitate prevention efforts because gender-based violence has been defined as a women's issue. However, it is critical that men take the lead in educating other men about the connections among violence, cultural masculinity, and privilege. Men who do so find that engaging in this process enhances their lives.

KEY TERMS

Empathy
Empathy for the self
Femiphobia
Misogyny
Primary prevention
Resistance awareness
Secondary prevention
Tertiary prevention

CRITICAL THINKING QUESTIONS

1. How does men's violence against women hurt women who have not been directly affected by such violence? How does men's violence against women hurt the majority of men who do not commit such acts?
2. In his interview, Don McPherson speaks about the "invisible kids." What does he mean by this? What makes a person invisible? What are the consequences of feeling invisible?
3. How it is possible for one's privilege to remain invisible in spite of experiencing greater social and/or public visibility than those in less-privileged social positions?
4. Women have been engaged in working on the issues of gender-based violence for decades. Only recently have men begun to get involved. How can men and women work best together to ultimately eliminate gender-based violence?

5. As discussed in this chapter, Jackson Katz uses "the box" as an analogy for understanding the social pressures that are exerted upon individual males. There are similar pressures placed upon females to behave in ways that are consistent with their gender stereotype. Think about your own unique qualities. Which of these would fall into the box of masculinity? The box of femininity? Which of these are irrelevant to the concept of gender?
6. Acknowledging the positive qualities of masculinity is important to engaging men in the work of gender-violence prevention. Identify some of these positive qualities. Can you identify men you know who demonstrate these characteristics?
7. What can you, as an individual, do to help both yourself and those around you feel the freedom to behave "as they really are"?

Chapter 8

Model Prevention Programs

Although the effort to prevent men's violence against women is still a relatively recent phenomenon, committed individuals and organizations have developed a variety of innovative approaches. In this chapter, we describe some of the best programs currently in practice. Some introductory considerations are warranted. First, primary prevention strategies focus on men and boys. Since males perpetrate the vast majority of gender-based violence, reducing its incidence requires their participation. Second, most of the programs we describe focus on sexual assault. Since a large number of prevention programs originated in colleges and universities, and since sexual assault is epidemic in these settings, the tendency of programming experts is to focus on this problem more than on other forms of gendered violence, although there is increasing attention to stalking and dating violence. Awareness of these latter forms of violence is more recent than for sexual assault, hence programming that addresses them is less well-developed. Third, the amount of empirical evidence for the effectiveness of these efforts differs among programs, but is scant in most cases. There is a strong need for extensive research into the effects of prevention efforts on behavior change. Finally, most programming takes place in higher education settings. Of the 37 existing prevention programs that researchers for the Centers for Disease Control and Prevention (discussed in chapter 7) identified, 19 were located on college campuses, and many of the remaining programs had affiliations with higher education (Clinton-Sherrod et al., 2003).

The leadership of institutions of higher learning in prevention efforts is probably due to several factors. First, colleges and universities are typically populated by 18–22 year olds, a high risk group that is also somewhat of a "captive audience." There are opportunities for contact in classrooms, orientation sessions, school organizations, and the relatively confined environment of the campus. Second, a full awareness of gender-based violence seems not to have penetrated the mainstream culture; hence, a lack of interest in its prevention. Indeed, many people outside of academe believe that violence is solely a product of the perpetrator's personality and that therefore it is not preventable, thus there is more of an emphasis on reactive efforts such as prosecution and incarceration. For violence prevention efforts to go mainstream into our communities, it is critical that we understand that this violence is preventable. And finally, colleges and universities tend to be places that foster an awareness of social problems and a commitment to contribute to their solutions. But we are also seeing an increase in progressive community organizations, such as women's resource centers, that are organizing prevention activities.

Following are descriptions of several model prevention programs (presented in no particular order).

THE SOCIAL NORMS APPROACH

In the late 1980s, researchers such as Michael Haines, H. Wesley Perkins, and Alan Berkowitz began to develop environmental interventions to reduce binge drinking on college campuses. Their approach was based on research indicating that college students overestimate the amount that the average student drinks, and that they therefore experience social pressure to binge drink in order to conform their behavior to perceived norms. The researchers hypothesized that if students would come to understand that their peers actually drink less than they previously believed, they would feel less social pressure to over-imbibe and would reduce their use of alcohol. The researchers surveyed large groups of students and launched several public information campaigns to publicize the discrepancy between what students think about peers' average consumption and how much students actually drink. This approach continues to generate controversy, but there is some empirical support for its effectiveness (Haines, 1997).

Alan Berkowitz (see Box 8.1) has been a leader in applying the social norms approach to other kinds of campus behavioral problems, especially sexual assault. The basic approach is based on several assumptions:

1. Sexual assault is a product of cultural sexism.
2. Male peer support is an important factor in either encouraging or inhibiting sexual assault.
3. Most men overestimate the degree of their male peers' sexism and rape-supportive attitudes.
4. Well-designed methods to communicate the discrepancy between actual attitudes and perceived attitudes will result in a change in men's perceptions of their peers.
5. A positive change in perceptions of peers' attitudes will encourage men to make efforts to undermine peer support for sexual assault and ultimately result in a reduction of this violence.

The second and third assumptions have received some empirical support. Kilmartin, Conway, Friedberg, McQuoid, Tschan, & Norbet (1999) have demonstrated large discrepancies between college men's actual and perceived attitudes toward women—men believed that other men were more sexist and rape supportive than they actually were. In this same study, the researchers also demonstrated that a public information campaign could reduce the distorted perception of the average male on campus, at least in the short run. Kilmartin, Green, Heinzen, Kuchler, & Smith (2004) replicated this finding and also demonstrated that a brief (30-minute) presentation by a male peer (see description below) was effective in reducing the distorted perception of other men's sexism and rape-supportive attitudes in a three week follow up. It remains to be seen, however, how durable this change in perception is.

The procedure for doing social norms programming begins with a preliminary investigation of the attitudes of interest (see chapter 5.). In the above studies, researchers used scales such as the Ambivalent Sexism Inventory (Glick & Fiske, 2001b) to measure general levels of sexism, the Rape Myth Acceptance Scale (Burt, 1980), and an informal measure of men's discomfort with sexism displayed by their male peers. Researchers interested in other forms of gender-based violence could find measures that tap into the attitudes thought to underlie the specific behavior of interest (e.g.,

> **BOX 8.1**
> **An Interview with Alan Berkowitz**
> *Centre for Leadership for Women*
> *(www.leadershipforwomen.com.au)*
>
> Diane Rogers Healy (DRH), Center for Leadership for Women (CLW), Australia: *Welcome to the CLW interview series. Thank you for agreeing to this interview.*
>
> Alan Berkowitz (AB): *I am honored that you asked me to be interviewed by the Centre, and I am happy to contribute whatever I can to your important work. One of the best ways that men can demonstrate leadership is by supporting the leadership of women, so thank you for giving me a chance to do this.*
>
> DRH: *Can we start by hearing a bit about how you got involved in this work and why you choose to work in the area of preventing violence against women?*
>
> AB: *Social justice work has always been one of my passions. I grew up in a community where I was able to witness injustice and the unconscious racism of my neighbors and this made me want to do something to make a difference. I was also inspired by the Civil Rights movement and the political changes taking place in the United States in the 1960's. In the 1980's in my first job working in higher education I noticed that as a result of the feminist and women's movements there was a lot of attention being paid to the emotional needs and political consciousness of women, but almost no attention to the needs of men. Young men were confused, feeling on the defensive, and without an understanding of themselves as men and how they needed to change. As a result a colleague and I founded a program at Hobart College called "Men and Masculinity" that offered workshops and trainings for men about gender issues. One of the offshoots of this program was my work with men to prevent violence against women. This has been a critical element of my professional identity ever since.*
>
> DRH: *I understand that one of your favourite sayings is: "You can't be part of the solution until you understand how you are part of the problem."*
>
> AB: *Yes, it is. I have always felt that we have a responsibility to be active in creating the type of world we want to live in. This saying is actually a variation of one that was popular in the United States in the 1960's: "you're either part of the solution or part of the problem." I love the revised version of this quote for two reasons.*

BOX 8.1 *(continued)*

First, it makes it clear that we have to change ourselves in order to create change in the world and that there will always be something in us that is "part of the problem." For example, as a man committed to ending sexism and violence against women I have had to learn about my unconscious sexism and male privilege, a process that is ongoing. Second, the revised version of the quote substitutes "both/and" thinking for "either/or" thinking. Either/or thinking is responsible for many of our current problems and polarized discussions. The solutions that we need for many of the world's problems are "both/and" solutions. Unfortunately the leadership of my own country is currently one of the worst offenders in fostering "either/ or" thinking.

DRH: *In your consulting work, in which ways do you find that people are part of the problem?*

AB: *Well, this can take many forms. As I said, as men we need to begin to see our own sexism, with the help of women who are willing to be our allies, and use our privilege against itself. This is true for other oppressions as well—for instance, racism, heterosexism, classism, etc. Actually, most of what I will say here about men's role in ending violence against women will be true for other issues as well-whites ending racism, Christians ending anti-Semitism, etc. Often people are naive in how they approach a problem and think that they know the answer without having done their homework and without being accountable to the groups they are trying to help.*

In my work on social norms theory we have found that many leaders hold misperceptions that contribute to the problem. For example, young people may think that their peers drink alcohol and have more sex than they really do, which causes pressure to engage in these behaviors. Yet the leaders who are trying to solve these problems are often guilty of believing and spreading the same misinformation about young people that contributes to the problem to begin with.

DRH: *To what do you attribute a shift in the field of sexual assault prevention to address the role of men in ending violence against women? When did this shift occur?*

AB: *This shift has been taking place gradually over a period of years and is now gaining momentum and critical mass. Ending violence against women has always been seen as the province of*

> **BOX 8.1** (continued)
>
> women, first because all the original leaders on these issues were women; second, because women were skeptical about men's involvement; and third, because men did not step up to the plate to be part of the work. But seeing violence prevention as only the responsibility of women is an example of thinking that perpetuates the problem. Many women advocates and leaders have come to the understanding that it is important to have male partners in the work who can speak with and understand men. At the same time, men have become more aware of violence against women because of the many courageous survivors who have chosen to not be silent. So there is a growing awareness that men have a role to play in this issue, but that it must be alongside of and as accountable to women.
>
> DRH: *In many of your writings you have argued that men underestimate the extent to which other men are uncomfortable with sexist behavior towards women? What problem does this pose for men and why do you advocate strategies to reduce this discomfort amongst men?*
>
> AB: In my own personal experience there have been many times when I was uncomfortable with oppressive behavior and was silent because I thought that it did not bother others. One of the beautiful things that can happen in an all-male workshop with honest dialogue is that men will come "out of the closet" and express their discomfort with some men's behavior. This experience led me to design survey questions that ask men how uncomfortable they are with certain situations, and how uncomfortable they think that their male peers are with the same situations. We almost always find that men are uncomfortable but think that their peers are not. Many others have replicated this research and it has been extended to other issues such as racism and homophobia.
>
> DRH: *What is the Social Norms Theory and why do you believe that social norms interventions focusing on peer influences, have a greater impact on individual behavior than biological, personality, familial, religious, cultural and other influences?*
>
> AB: The example I just gave of men thinking that other men are not uncomfortable is an example of social norms theory. Social norms theory says that we often misperceive what others think and do. For example, people tend to overestimate unhealthy behaviors and underestimate healthy behaviors in groups that they belong to.

BOX 8.1 *(continued)*

These misperceptions then have an effect on what people do. In one study that I conducted with colleagues we found that men underestimated other men's willingness to intervene to prevent sexual assault and that the single biggest predictor of men's willingness to intervene was whether they thought other men would intervene. This finding reveals the reason why men's programming is effective-because the biggest influence on men is other men. This is due to sexism and men's not taking women seriously. The idea is to use this reality against itself in order to change it.

One of the reasons why correcting misperceptions is effective is because they are easier to change than the other influences you mention-personality, family, etc.

DRH: How do you use the Social Norms Approach to assist men develop into women's social justice allies in ending violence? What has been the level of success of this approach?

AB: In the United States the social norms approach has been very effective in addressing alcohol use, cigarette use, driving while intoxicated, and driving without seatbelts. It has been used in Canada and the Great Britain. For those who are interested there is a summary of the social norms literature on my website, www.alanberkowitz.com. This approach is also being used to address violence against women and there are indications that it can be effective. Most of this research is still in the formative stage but I feel that it is promising.

The idea behind the social norms approach is that misperceptions influence how we act. For example, if I would like to act differently as a man my willingness to do so may be influenced by how I think other men will react. Information that other men actually feel the way that I do will give me permission to try new behaviors. The social norms approach offers a methodology for providing information about true norms-in this case, what men actually feel-in the form of group discussions or social marketing media.

By the way, there is an interesting way of looking at male socialization from a social norms perspective. It turns out that most men are uncomfortable with many of the ways that we have been taught to be men, but we think that we are alone in our discomfort. For example, a man might think that it is ok for a man to express sadness, but he will refrain from doing so if he incorrectly thinks that other men don't agree. So telling men the truth about what men

> **BOX 8.1** *(continued)*
>
> *feel gives us permission to act differently than we have been taught to act as men.*
>
> DRH: *What types of programs do you offer that focus on men's role in preventing violence against women and what is their structure? Do you run programs for men who perpetrate domestic violence?*
>
> AB: *Most of my work is as a consultant helping others develop effective programs on health and social justice issues. This can take the form of designing effective rape prevention workshops for men, or helping in the design and implementation of media campaigns that provide men with accurate information about what other men do. Because most of my work is in the area of prevention I don't usually work with perpetrators.*
>
> DRH: *Do men voluntarily join your programs when promoted or are they recommended to join by a third party working with them?*
>
> AB: *One of the dilemmas in working with men is that most of us don't begin by seeing ourselves doing this work. So we need to be invited in. This can take place by being nominated by a man we respect, by learning about violence against women from women we care about, or by attending a required workshop that opens our eyes to the problem. Many men want to do the right thing and will be receptive to helping if they are recruited as allies and approached with respect rather than guilt and/or blame.*
>
> DRH: *In terms of the program focus, which focus have you found most beneficial for participants: building empathy towards victims, the development of personal skills, learning to intervene in other men's behavior, re-socialization of male culture and behavior?*
>
> AB: *Well, you just gave a great list of the different approaches to working with men! They are all effective in different ways, but some ask men to change more than others. For example, it is important that men have empathy for victims and understand the trauma of victimization, but this approach can leave men in the role of wanting to help women without changing ourselves. Similarly, we all need to have the personal skills to ensure that sexual intimacy with a man or woman is consenting, so this is essential, but having these skills only prevents someone from being a perpetrator, it doesn't help them to change others. So teaching men to intervene against*

BOX 8.1 *(continued)*

the problematic behavior of other men is critical to social change and it is essential because men care so much about what other men think. Finally, since part of the problem is with how men are socialized to be men, any program examining gender socialization is valuable.

These approaches can be ranked according to how deeply they take men into the process of understanding ourselves "as part of the problem" and how they help us make the necessary changes.

DRH: How have you worked with the media to change the larger environment?

AB: The social norms approach was originally developed using media as a way of announcing the true norm. In many countries including Australia there are creative uses of media to educate men about their role in preventing violence against women: for example, the "Violence Against Women -It's Against All the Rules" and the "Violence Against Women-Australia Says No" campaigns. When this media includes statistics about what men actually feel and/or do then it is considered "social norms marketing" media. These statistics let men know that other men like them care about these issues and will support them in taking action.

DRH: In the all-male rape prevention programs that you have conducted, do you find that such programs are more effective when conducted in separate gender groups than in co-educational formats? Why?

AB: Most of the research addressing this subject has been conducted in the United States with college students. The findings are clear-both men and women benefit more in separate gender groups. This is because men and women start out with different levels of awareness of the issue, have different learning goals, and are more comfortable discussing the issue with their same-gender peers. This has also been my experience conducting many all-male workshops. There is also value in co-educational workshops and these can help foster dialogue and present each gender with the other's perspective. But my personal experience and the accumulated research suggest that it is better when possible to start this work in separate gender groups. This is parallel to the experience of the women's movement, which began with all-female consciousness raising groups.

BOX 8.1 *(continued)*

DRH: *How do you get University students to understand and observe the Guidelines you advocate for consent in intimate relationships and in particular that they are free to choose not only at the initial point for sexual intimacy but also at ensuing points of interaction?*

AB: *I have found that the best way to get young people to understand how to ensure consent is to present them with ambiguous scenarios in which it is not clear if consent is present. We then discuss these scenarios and the men present have vigorous discussions presenting their points of view about the presence or absence of consent. When men see that there are a variety of opinions among other men it gets them thinking and re-examining their own assumptions. For those who are interested, there is an article on my website that outlines these consent guidelines.*

DRH: *With researchers who study the male gender role finding that masculinity is often defined in opposition to femininity -which is devalued or seen as less desirable- are you satisfied with the approaches of the American education system to socialize boys to value the female sex and their own feminine qualities?*

AB: *This is one of those "both/and" discussions. I believe that as part of our human inheritance we have both "female" and "male" qualities within each of us. Our full emotional and spiritual development as human beings requires that we develop both of these and find a balance between them that works, which will be different for each person. Because men have been taught to de-value and neglect our feminine side, it is important that we learn to accept it and express it. As we value the feminine inside of ourselves we will also learn to respect the feminine outside of us, and vice-versa. Even as I say this I can feel a certain discomfort within myself in talking about my feminine side. This is because men's socialization to devalue the feminine is so deep that it feels awkward to me as a man to talk about my femininity. This is another good example of a situation where either/or thinking (male or female) needs to be replaced with both/and thinking (male and female).*

DRH: *What are some of the frustrations and highlights of working in this field?*

AB: *The highlight is that I am a better human being as a result of this work. We often tell men that they need to care about violence against women because it hurts the women we care about. This is*

BOX 8.1 *(continued)*

true but what we often forget to say is that it hurts us as well. When a women walks across the street because she is afraid of me she is making a good decision but I feel bad being seen as dangerous. Violence against women therefore hurts me directly and not only indirectly. All of us want to be effective and make a difference. One of my great blessings is that I have been given the opportunity to make a difference by helping men take responsibility for ending violence against women. Another highlight is the tremendous progress we have made in figuring out how to involve and engage men. We have very far to go but we can still appreciate where we have come from. The frustration, of course, is that there is so much to do and the problem is immense. It is a great spiritual challenge to maintain optimism and faith in the face of so much injustice. My spiritual mentors have taught me that it is possible to remain positive, effective, and joyful in the face of overwhelming challenges. It feels right to end this interview by acknowledging their great influence in my life.

Alan Berkowitz is an independent consultant who helps colleges, universities, public health agencies, and communities design programs that address health and social justice issues. His expert opinion is frequently sought after by the U.S. government and professional organizations, and he is well known for scholarship and innovative programs addressing issues of substance abuse, sexual assault, gender, social norms, and diversity. Alan has developed model rape prevention programs for men and programs on men's issues, is a co-founder of the social norms approach, and is the editor and founder of *The Report on Social Norms*. He received a Ph.D. in Psychology from Cornell University in 1981 and has received five national awards for his professional contributions and activities. More information about Alan and his work can be found at www.alanberkowitz.com.

Diann Rodgers-Healey, who conducted this interview, is the founder of the Australian Centre for Leadership for Women. Diann has conducted extensive interviews with well-known leaders-mostly women-that are posted on the Centre's website, and she has written extensively and produced programs on women as leaders. Diann also works as a strategic planning consultant for schools and organizations to help them develop vision, mission, and core principles, and also provides leadership, guidance, and coaching to individuals. More information about Diann can be found at www.leadershipforwomen.com.au.

hostility toward women). Each participant fills out the surveys anonymously and the researchers collect the forms. Then participants receive the same surveys, but with different instructions. In the 1999 study, the researchers asked men to complete the survey based on the perceived attitudes of "a male student on this campus whom you know well," and then gave a third set of surveys with the direction to describe "the average male student on this campus." In the 2004 study, participants reported their own attitudes, and then they completed the same surveys describing "the average man in this room."

In both studies, the researchers compiled mean scores for all scales for self-ratings (the "actual averages") and scores for ratings of others (the "perceived averages"). The discrepancies between the actual averages as reported by the men and the perceived averages as estimated by them were quite large, indicating that men believe that other men are much more sexist and rape-supportive than they actually are.

The next step is to undertake an information campaign to correct the cognitive distortion. In the 1999 study, this effort took the form of displaying posters with the results of the research in prominent campus locations, and also placing large advertisements in the campus newspaper. Follow-up research indicated a significant reduction in perceived negative attitudes of the average male student, but surprisingly, the ratings of "a male student whom you know well" did not change.

In retrospect, one possible reason for this finding is that the advertisements targeted average male attitudes with the assumption that men would view their peers as average; however, the "average male" is an abstraction and "a man whom you know well" is a real person. The researchers therefore undertook the 2004 study with the goal of giving concrete feedback about the attitudes of the actual men in the room, based on the social norms intervention model that Far & Miller (2003) used successfully in challenging students' perceptions of other students' drinking.

In this latter study, Kilmartin and his research team utilized a two-group design. Participants in the control group completed the surveys and were dismissed. Experimental group participants completed the surveys, and then a male member of the research team gave a 30-minute presentation in which he explained how cognitive distortions develop and why it is important in the prevention of sexual assault to correct these distortions. Then he gave the participants feedback on the considerable extent of their groups' misperceptions. At three-week follow-up, experimental participants had reduced their distortions for most measures relative to control group participants. It remains to be seen whether this effect endures for longer time periods.

The advantage of the social norms approach is that the entire population of men can participate and learn how they can contribute to the solutions for gender-based violence. If done well, the message is an empowering and positive message that promotes respectful behavior and integrity. The difficulties of undertaking these campaigns is that it can be time consuming and expensive to do the research, and the construction of credible social norms messages depends critically on (a) an in-depth understanding of the audience, (b) the culture of the targeted environment, and (c) the method used to communicate the message. For instance, one should not use a school newspaper as a medium on a campus where few students read it. Berkowitz (2005) recommends paying very close attention to the social context in which the intervention takes place.

MENTORS IN VIOLENCE PREVENTION

The Mentors in Violence Prevention (MVP) program was founded in 1993 at the Center for the Study of Sport in Society at Northeastern University in Massachusetts as an effort to encourage student-athletes to take a leadership role in preventing gender-based violence. Two of its most visible proponents are social activist Jackson Katz and former All-American and professional football player Donald McPherson. Because it targets an at-risk group, male athletes, MVP could be considered a secondary prevention effort; however, this program also seeks to involve female athletes, and so it also has a risk reduction component.

The MVP program utilizes a mixed-sex, ***bystander approach***. Generally, a male and a female co-facilitator present scenarios in which there is a risk for violence. Audience members are asked to imagine themselves as bystanders and discuss how they would react. For example, in one scenario, a woman has had too much to drink at a college student party and a man is trying to get her to kiss him. Participants are first asked if this is a realistic scenario, and the vast majority of college students agree, many having witnessed similar occurrences. Then the facilitators ask: What would you think and do if you were present when this was happening?

> **BOX 8.2**
> **10 Things Men Can Do to Prevent Gender Violence**
> *by Jackson Katz*
>
> 1. Approach gender violence as a men's issue involving men of all ages and socioeconomic, racial, and ethnic backgrounds. View men not only as perpetrators or possible offenders, but as empowered bystanders who can confront abusive peers.
> 2. If a brother, friend, classmate, or teammate is abusing his female partner-or is disrespectful or abusive to girls and women in general-don't look the other way. If you feel comfortable doing so, try to talk to him about it. Urge him to seek help. Or if you don't know what to do, consult a friend, a parent, a professor, or a counselor. Don't remain silent!
> 3. Have the courage to look inward. Question your own attitudes. Don't be defensive when something you do or say ends up hurting someone else. Try hard to understand how your own attitudes and actions might inadvertently perpetuate sexism and violence, and work toward changing them.
> 4. If you suspect that a woman close to you is being abused or has been sexually assaulted, gently ask if you can help.
> 5. If you are emotionally, psychologically, physically, or sexually abusive to women, or have been in the past, seek professional help now.
> 6. Be an ally to women who are working to end all forms of gender violence. Support the work of campus-based women's centers. Attend "Take Back the Night" rallies and other public events. Raise money for community-based rape crisis centers and battered women's shelters. If you belong to a team or fraternity, or another student group, organize a fundraiser.
> 7. Recognize and speak out against homophobia and gay-bashing. Discrimination and violence against lesbians and gays are wrong in and of themselves. This abuse also has direct links to sexism (e.g., the sexual orientation of men who speak out against sexism is often questioned, a conscious or unconscious strategy intended to silence them. This is a key reason few men do so).
> 8. Attend programs, take courses, watch films, and read articles and books about multicultural masculinities, gender inequality, and the root causes of gender violence. Educate yourself and others about how larger social forces affect the conflicts between individual men and women.
> 9. Don't fund sexism. Refuse to purchase any magazine, rent any video, subscribe to any Web site, or buy any music that portrays girls or women in a sexually degrading or abusive manner. Protest sexism in the media.

> **BOX 8.2** *(continued)*
> 10. Mentor and teach young boys about how to be men in ways that don't involve degrading or abusing girls and women. Volunteer to work with gender violence prevention programs, including anti-sexist men's programs. Lead by example.

The scenarios are presented in a "playbook," which, in sports, is a plan for performance during a game. The analogy is that a playbook is a set of strategies for practicing an athlete's role so he or she can react and help the team in the game situation. The parallel to the party situation is that one usually needs to think about and practice an effective reaction to respond effectively in a situation. These scenario presentations then evolve into broader discussions of (a) sexism, (b) popular culture, (c) media representations of women and men, and (d) the damaging effects of men's conversations when they derogate women.

The MVP program communicates that the bystander role is not neutral; it can either condone or help to prevent violence. Programs range from 90-minute single presentations to a 22-hour training over three days. An independent evaluation attests to the effectiveness of these efforts (www.sportinsociety.org). MVP also publishes a curriculum and offers free publications ("10 Things Men Can Do to Prevent Violence against Women" and a similar handout on what women can do; see Box 8.1) and trains people within organizations to continue using the curriculum as part of their ongoing violence prevention efforts.

MEN CAN STOP RAPE

Founded as an incorporated nonprofit organization in 1997, Men Can Stop Rape (MCSR) developed from D.C. Men Against Rape, a volunteer organization founded in Washington, DC in 1987. The basic premise of this group's work is that rape and other forms of gender-based violence are learned behaviors that can be unlearned. Originally titled the Men's Rape Prevention Project (MRPP), MCSR is a profeminist organization that offers a variety of programs, including the Men of Strength Clubs (MOST Clubs), the Strength Campaign, and the Frederick Douglass Awards.

The Men of Strength Clubs are a unique offering in which organizations of young men learn to take leadership in ending men's violence against women. These clubs are mostly organized in schools and community organizations. They provide a space in which male youths can (a) support one another, (b) learn about the connections between toxic masculinity and violence, (c) explore healthy visions of what it means to be a man, and (d) undertake social justice work. In an extensive outcomes research project over a two-year period, Stephanie Hawkins (2006) demonstrated that these clubs effected durable and positive changes in members' (a) awareness of inappropriate behaviors, (b) self-reported likelihood to confront these behaviors in other boys, and (c) feelings of being understood and respected by their peers.

The Strength Campaign is a public awareness effort to educate about the problem of sexual assault and promote healthy visions of male sexuality. It uses images of young men and women with slogans such as, "My strength is not for hurting, so when I wasn't sure how she felt, I asked," and, "My strength is not for hurting, so when guys disrespect women, we say that's not right." The original Campaign used posters of these images as well as larger advertisements on public buses and bus shelters. MCSR sells these posters, which have now appeared in all 50 states and more than 20 countries.

The Frederick Douglass Awards are an annual event to honor men and boys who are at the forefront of the effort to end sexual assault. MCSR also offers a variety of presentations and workshops, both to direct service recipients and to professionals. They provide consultation and technical assistance to organizations who want to create or improve local programming in sexual assault prevention and provide links to various resources on their Web site (www.mencanstoprape.org).

THE WHITE RIBBON CAMPAIGN

In December, 1990, Marc Lepine, armed with weaponry, entered a classroom at a Montreal, Canada's E'cole Polytechnique. He ordered all of the women to line up against the wall and, after declaring his hatred of feminists, shot 14 of the women dead as the men were forced to watch. He then committed suicide. On the first anniversary of this "Montreal Massacre," tens of thousands of Canadian men participated in The White Ribbon Campaign, a grassroots activism effort. The white ribbon is a statement that one will not commit, condone, or remain silent about men's violence against women. The White Ribbon Campaign has grown into the largest effort in the world of men working to end gender-based violence.

Many men have imported the White Ribbon Campaign into their countries and communities. Typical activities include distributing ribbons; raising money for rape crisis centers, domestic violence shelters, batterer treatment programs, and other organizations that deal directly with the consequences of men's violence against women; and undertaking public information campaigns. Most campaigns also encourage men to sign a pledge to never commit, condone, or remain silent about violence against women. Research on one U.S. college campus indicated that students' awareness of the problem of men's violence against women and their attitude toward the problem both improved as a direct result of the campaign (Kilmartin, Chirico, & Leemann, 1997).

The White Ribbon Campaign is significant in that it was the first social movement undertaken in which violence against women was identified as a men's social issue and emphasized men's responsibility in violence prevention. The White Ribbon Campaign Web site (www.whiteribbon.ca) contains a wealth of information and resources for those who want to institute the Campaign at their local level.

ONE IN FOUR

John Foubert founded not-for-profit National Men's Outreach for Rape Education (NO MORE) in 1998. Later, the organization changed its name to "One in Four." It provides consultation and training on sexual assault prevention for males and is the umbrella organization for male sexual assault peer education groups which also use the title "One in Four," named after the famous statistic that one in four college women is a victim of sexual assault or attempted sexual assault (Koss, Gidycz, & Wisniewski, 1987; see chapter 1). One in Four chapters are active on several college and university campuses.

The major activity of these groups is "The Men's Program: How to Help a Sexual Assault Survivor: What Men Can Do." This program is grounded in research that indicates that the most effective sexual assault prevention is undertaken by peer educators with all-male groups in an interactive format (Berkowitz, 1994). The goals of the presentation are to give the male audience information about how to help women recover from rape and how to understand sexual coercion from the point of view of the victim through an empathy induction technique, which also results in an increased aversion to rape.

The program begins with the peer educators stating the goals of the program and making it clear that they do not wish to blame men for sexual assault. Rather, they want to enlist men as allies in the effort to end this violence. Then, they define sexual assault and provide statistics on its prevalence.

The presentation then proceeds to the *Police Rape Training Video*. This is a brief lecture given by a police officer in which he describes in rather graphic detail two men raping a (generic) male police officer. The lecturer uses the second person in his description (e.g., "You get out of the car to move the trash can in the alley") to facilitate participants' identification with the protagonist in the story. Peer educators then cite similarities and differences between the perpetrator's rape of the police officer and the common experiences of a female victim when an acquaintance rapist attacks her. The program proceeds with general information on how men can help to end rape and specific information about how to help a survivor and concludes with a general discussion.

The Men's Program is perhaps the best current empirically-supported prevention effort. Foubert (2005) reports that participants in the program showed decreased rape myth acceptance and lower self-reported likelihood of raping extending to at least seven months following the presentation. Theoretically, this attitude change is the result of material being presented in a way that is relevant to the audience and motivates listeners to attend. According to the Elaboration Likelihood Model, this method results in central rather than peripheral information processing and tends to effect longer term change than other approaches. Information on One in Four and the Men's Program is available at nomorerape.org.

THE FRATERNITY VIOLENCE EDUCATION PROJECT

Deborah Mahlstedt founded the Fraternity Violence Education Project (FVEP) at West Chester University (PA) in 1989. FVEP is a secondary prevention program—one that is aimed at an at-risk population: fraternity members. The FVEP is a multiple-session, curriculum-based program that involves fraternity members as peer educators.

Men who participate in the project make a full-year commitment to it. During the first academic semester, they take part in a seminar on gender-based violence and receive academic credit for their participation. This seminar is run by FVEP members who were trained during the previous year, with occasional presentations by faculty members. Like The Men's Program, the approach of the seminar is to provide a single-sex, peer-led, interactive space in which men can learn about sexual assault and relate it to their own lives.

After they have completed the seminar training, participants undertake presentations to their own fraternities in teams of two. Thus, they deliver information to men with whom they have ongoing relationships, taking advantage of the effect of enhanced persuasion that occurs when audience members perceive themselves as similar to those who present the information. Moreover, these presenters, who have raised their consciousness about gender-based violence, are also often present at fraternity parties, which frequently constitute a high-risk environment for sexual assault. FVEP participants have been trained to intervene in potentially violent situations.

Men's Work: Fraternity Brothers Stopping Violence Against Women (available from insightmedia.org) is a videotape that follows the experience of several FVEP members as they undertake their training seminar and make their presentations. It shows these men discussing many issues related to dating violence, especially power dimensions and sexual objectification. The videotape is not really a "how to" presentation that explains fully how one can initiate the program. Rather it is a story of the process of personal and interpersonal change within the peer educators, who are interviewed throughout. *Men's Work* provides an illustration of an oftentimes overlooked aspect of peer education: that it has a positive effect on not only the audience, but also the development of maturity and interpersonal competencies in the educators. In fact, Mahlstedt markets the program by offering men leadership skills in addition to course credit.

USE OF THEATRE

Throughout history, playwrights and actors have used theatre as a method to bringing awareness of social issues in an artistic format that facilitates emotional engagement with the material. In other words, showing is often better than merely telling. Theatre is to be distinguished from mere entertainment. In the latter, the goal is to provide material that an audience will find interesting and perhaps pleasurable. Many Hollywood movies are entertaining but do not really constitute true theatre, which provides entertainment, but goes beyond mere diversion into a presentation of material in a mode that encourages audience members to change and develop in emotional ways.

Theatre can be a powerful tool in the effort to prevent gender-based violence in that it can provide awareness of the issues in a format that goes beyond the didactic. Following are several examples of theatrical presentations that speak to the issue at hand.

Reanae McNeal wrote and performs a one-woman show entitled *Don't Speak My Mother's Name in Vain*, which uses character sketches, dance, and song to illustrate gendered and racial violence across several generations of African American history. McNeal, who is a sexual assault survivor, expertly draws connections among slavery, sexual harassment, racism, incest, homophobia, drug abuse, sexism, and child molestation in a very moving presentation that focuses on victim/survivor issues. Susan Marine, then coordinator of Sexual Abuse Awareness Programs at Dartmouth College, responded to a 1999 performance by saying

> "In an hour and a half, Reanae made us laugh, cry, think, and feel. She is an amazingly astute performer with an eye for the universal in the human experience, and a gift for bringing the incredibly painful reality of violence against women home to everyone who "meets" the characters she portrays." (posted on Sexual Assault Program Coordinators listserv: sexualassault.virginia.edu/sapc–01–05–99).

Sex Signals is a two-person, mixed-sex play, written by Gail Stern and Christian Murphy, in which the performers blend improvisational comedy with education and audience participation. It begins in comedic format by illustrating gender expectations, fantasies, and the anxieties of dating and sex. The play then moves to a discussion of sexual assault and consent issues. *Sex Signals* is performed by several teams of actors and has toured to hundreds of college and university campuses. It is available from Catharsis Productions (www.catharsisproductions.com).

Gail Stern has also written a one-woman show, *Rant!* In this performance, the playwright/actor invites audiences to explore the use of language to dehumanize women as well as members of ethnic and racial groups. Like *Sex Signals*, *Rant!* is interactive and invites audience members to explore functions and effects of derogatory language. Stern addresses gender-based violence directly, but also puts it into the context of other hate crimes, as well as psychological violence. The performance takes advantage of the fact that most people think that racism is wrong, but many have trouble relating it to other forms of oppression, especially sexism. This show is expertly performed in an entertaining format that utilizes Gail

Stern's talents in improvisational comedy. It is also available from Catharsis Productions.

Many peer theatre groups have developed interactive programs for use within their high schools and colleges. The presentations of these groups are highly varied, but one typical approach is to portray a situation in which characters have committed gender-based violence or are at risk for doing so. The actors portraying the perpetrator, victim, and bystanders stay in character following the presentation and have discussions with the audience as a method for helping viewers to engage the issues for all who become involved in these situations.

Crimes Against Nature is a solo theatrical piece written and performed by Christopher Kilmartin. Although it addresses gender-based violence directly in one small segment of the performance, it is more focused on the masculine context of this violence and of other issues that affect men such as health problems, relationship difficulties, emotional constriction, and family-of-origin issues, especially with fathers. The title derives from the conception of mainstream masculinity as demanding unnatural things of men: risk of body, denial of feeling, hyper-independence, and separation from the "feminine." Using autobiographical material presented in a comedic format, *Crimes Against Nature* illustrates universal themes that audience members can apply to their own lives. Evidence indicates that, compared with control group members, viewers of this performance modified their view of "the ideal man" to incorporate more culturally defined feminine characteristics such as nurturing and emotional expression, although no data were collected on long-term effects (Galeone, Norbet, Kilmartin, & Altman, 1998). This show retired in 2004 after hundreds of performances but is available on videotape or DVD, along with a discussion guide, from the playwright/performer (ckilmart@umw.edu). Kilmartin's next play, tentatively entitled *Guy Fi: The Fictions that Rule Men's Lives,* is slated for debut by 2007. The basic premise of this work is that many men base their behaviors on a set of unarticulated fictions, and that exposing these fictions allows men to make more informed choices about their behaviors and thus live healthier and more fulfilled lives.

COMMUNITY EFFORTS

Recently, prevention programming has been making its way into communities. In September 2002, the Centers for Disease Control and Prevention (CDC) provided funding to nine states to participate in Domestic Violence Prevention Enhancement and Leadership through Alliances, or the DELTA project. The following year, the CDC extended funding to 79 communities in 14 states. A central goal of the project is to stimulate the development of prevention enhancements, population-based and/or system level services, policies, and actions that work to change the existing knowledge, attitudes, beliefs, and behaviors which provide the foundations for sexism and violence against women.

Because all communities are unique, DELTA directs each to assess its needs and goals and identify the prevention enhancement tools that community leaders believe will provide the best fit. Community action teams (CATs) undertake the actual work of violence prevention. It is DELTA's hope that the funding of these programs will eventually become (a) integrated within each community and (b) self-sustaining.

The prevention of gender-based violence is an enterprise that is still in its infancy. We have witnessed the creation and implementation of quite a few innovative approaches in recent years; however, research and program evaluation have often lagged behind in attempts to demonstrate the effectiveness of these programs, perhaps due to a number of factors. First, programming personnel may lack the expertise and/or the motivation to undertake solid assessment procedures. Second, human resources are often scarce, and so, for example, when a rape crisis center director is forced to choose between staffing a crisis hotline and doing outcome research, the more immediate need takes priority. Third, these human resources are inextricably tied to material resources, and agencies often survive on shoestring budgets. Finally, prevention entails causing something not to happen, and it is very difficult to produce evidence that violence would have occurred at higher levels if the particular program had not taken place. Hopefully, the future of prevention programming will include increased attention to outcome research.

SUMMARY

The past two decades have seen an increase in prevention programming, most undertaken on college and university campuses, more focused on sexual assault than on other forms of gender-based violence, and mainly addressing men as an under-addressed population. These efforts contain a wide variety of approaches from one-shot special programs and theatre performances to environmental interventions and the founding of local and national organizations. The future of effective prevention is the improvement of the theory-driven and evidenced-based characters of these varied efforts.

KEY TERMS

Bystander approach
Social norms approach

CRITICAL THINKING QUESTIONS

1. The social norms approach to violence prevention attempts to correct the misperception that most individuals are uncomfortable with both sexism and its concomitant violence. When individuals, especially men, come to understand that they are *not* in the minority, they feel more comfortable challenging sexist (or racist, etc.) behaviors. What steps could you take to help correct these misperceptions?
2. In his interview, Alan Berkowitz recalled the adage that "you're either part of the solution or part of the problem." What are your thoughts on this statement?
3. To become involved in violence prevention requires one to face his or her own prejudices and biases and their negative consequences for both the self and others. How is it possible to encourage such critical thinking without implying that having prejudices or biases is inherently negative, and hence, creating defensiveness?
4. Explain the concept of "both/and" thinking introduced by Alan Berkowitz. How is this unique from "either/or" thinking? What might be the implications of each type of thinking?
5. Jackson Katz has shared strategies for men to engage in that can help to prevent gender violence. Identify which of these strategies you would be willing to use in your own life. How would our society be different if the majority of individuals utilized these strategies?
6. Each of the violence prevention programs described in this chapter honor both positive masculinity and men. Given this positive approach, why do you think there exists an apparent reluctance for men to become involved in this work?
7. Encouraging men to become involved in violence prevention in no way precludes women from becoming involved in this work. In what ways could women play a critical role in violence prevention work?

Chapter 9

Developing Violence Prevention Programs

As we have stated in previous chapters, is it critical that men, in partnership with women, become involved in the prevention of gender-based violence. All citizens are stakeholders in the future of society, and violence prevention work involving men has become a popular concept across the nation. In spite of its intuitive appeal, the actual creation and implementation of men's violence prevention work is the exception in most communities.

Although there appears to be an increasing interest by both universities and community organizations to organize and implement violence prevention programs, there is limited research that identifies effective components of such programs (Berkowitz, 2004). Leaders interested in finding guidance for these programs must therefore rely on the proficiencies of those who have academic expertise on the issue and/or those who have experience in doing the work of violence prevention (see chapter 8 for examples of model programs.).

In a synthesis of the rather scant research and literature in the area, Alan Berkowitz (in Kilmartin & Berkowitz, 2005) identified a number of best practice characteristics in violence prevention. He concluded that the most effective prevention programs are comprehensive, intensive, relevant to the audience, and have positive messages.

Comprehensiveness. Comprehensive programs create connections among relevant entities in the community. In this sense, organizations that might otherwise be disconnected come together, communicate efficiently, and work together. State and national associations can serve as effective liaisons for programs interested in maintaining connections with other existing programs.

Intensive. Intensity occurs when programs provide learning opportunities that are both interactive and sustained over time. They allow for meaningful interactions and contact. The Fraternity Violence Education Project (FVEP) founded by Deborah Mahlstedt (see chapter 8) serves as an excellent example, as men are asked to commit one year of their time to violence prevention work.

Relevant to the audience. Effective programming is tailored to the demographics and culture of the community, and thus requires an understanding of the characteristics and needs of the target audience. A formal needs assessment may be useful in providing this critical information. Certainly programs in urban settings will be different both in content and process than programs developed in more rural settings. Private and public colleges would also be unique, as their student populations differ in important demographic characteristics (e.g, private colleges tend to attract students of greater privilege).

Positive. This element is critical to involving men in violence prevention. Programming efforts should characterize men as being a part of the solution instead of the problem. To honor the integrity of men interested in being involved in this work increases not only the integrity of the group, but the satisfaction of those engaged in violence prevention work.

These four elements provide excellent guidelines for anyone interested in forming a violence prevention program. Through our experiences, we have discovered that we can add a fifth: that the work is personally satisfying for the workers. Certainly, sometimes discussions over specific topics become uncomfortable, overwhelming, and discouraging; but while understanding this reality, one can also come to realize that, as an individual within an influential group, one can make a difference in the life of another person or help to changing the climate of a community culture creates an exciting possibility for many. The work can also be enjoyable, as activists and educators create satisfying relationships and connections with one another. It is also satisfying to most women and men who come together with sincerity in their attempts to gain a deeper understanding of each other. And it also raises people's self esteem when they develop new skills.

In much of the rest of this chapter, we will attempt to share the journey of a grassroots effort to build a violence response and prevention program at Pittsburg State University (Kansas), by one of the authors, Julie Allison. The process has included positive as well as difficult times, with many lessons learned that we can pass on to others in hopes of making their efforts effective and efficient.

Much of what will be shared here is anecdotal and is not intended to be the formula for all communities interested in developing their own programs, as cultures differ, sometimes to a great extent. We have data supporting the contention that educators and activists in these violence response and prevention programs find them educational, personally satisfying, and frequently life changing. We also have data indicating that the most audience members receive the educational presentations well; however, we are lacking data on the long-term effects of these programs. It is hoped that this chapter may serve to inspire others to develop programs in their own communities. Toward that end, readers interested in developing their own programs might pick and choose from the initiatives of the one described below, or perhaps even make advances on them.

Obtaining adequate financial resources is a common problem for many communities. The initiators of this effort began with a limited budget of $3,000 annually for the first 3 years. Although the program goals and operations continue to evolve as we learn more and strive to improve, its initial development was informed by learning about other programs and gaining advice from experts. In particular, the following consultants heavily influenced the process of founding and forming the program:

- Katie Koestner, a nationally known consultant and speaker on the issues of violence response on educational campuses. She is a consultant for Campus Outreach Services.
- Dr. Christopher Kilmartin (book coauthor), a college professor, author, consultant, stage performer, and professional psychologist, and a nationally recognized expert on sexual assault and sexual harassment prevention on college campuses.
- Donald McPherson, the Executive Director of the Sports Leadership Institute, and a former All-American athlete who played professional football for seven years. He is a nationally recognized expert in

violence prevention work, which he has been doing for nearly three decades. As a speaker, he also has instant credibility with male athletes.
- Dr. Alan Berkowitz, an independent consultant who helps agencies and communities design programs that address health and social justice issues, including substance abuse, sexual assault, gender, and diversity.
- Ben Atherton-Zeman, a spokesperson for the National Organization for Men Against Sexism (NOMAS) and the author and performer of a solo theatrical work, *Voices of Men*. He has worked as a prevention educator for over a decade.

Although the focus of this chapter is on developing men's prevention programs, it is critical to remember that the work that women do on this issue is of equal importance. Ultimately, we must all work together with the common goal of ending violence.

A BRIEF HISTORY

In the early 1990s, Pittsburg State University established a standing committee, the Sexual Assault and Safety Awareness (SASA) committee, to address the issues of sexual assault and rape, as well as general safety on the campus and in the community. This committee sought representation and leadership from diverse and relevant entities, including administration, faculty, students, student-athletes, military personnel, medical staff, and community-service representatives. The committee recommended the creation of two student organizations: (a) the Sexual Assault Response Team (SART) and (b) the Men against Violence Program (MVP).

The functions of SART include providing advocacy for survivors of sexual assault and rape, as well as awareness and education on the issues surrounding gender-based violence. The purpose of MVP is to involve men in the work of preventing violence by having its members serve as role models for other boys and men, and provide awareness and education on the same issues from a male perspective. Eventually, the organizers decided to create a third group to separate the advocacy work from the educational and awareness components. Students Against Violence through Education (SAVE) grew from the SART response program, which continues to provide advocacy for survivors and their supporters. SART members are selected from among those who have completed the SAVE or MVP training.

The work of the SART/SAVE/MVP programs was the impetus for the eventual creation of the Office of Violence Response and Prevention on the campus, which is staffed primarily by members of these programs. Since 2004, group membership has been maintained at approximately 50 women in SART/SAVE and 50 men in MVP. These programs are involved in both violence response and prevention work, both together and separately.

It was relatively easy to create the Sexual Assault Response Team in the Spring of 2001. In 2000, SASA sent representatives to the annual International Conference on Sexual Assault and Harassment on Campus, held in Orlando, Florida (currently, this conference is hosted by the Safe Society Zone; www.safesocietyzone.com.), where we received a plethora of information about how to develop an effective SART program. The programming developed by Steve Thompson at Central Michigan University (Sexual Assault Peer Advocates [SAPA]), served as an exceptional model for us as we developed both our structural and functional plans for SART. We also researched and collected information and gleaned ideas from other organizations across the United States. Once we had a plan and protocol in writing, we began recruiting students. The implementation of the Sexual Assault Response Team began in the Spring, 2001 semester, with 14 students: 12 women and 2 men.

Finding information on how to create a violence prevention program involving men was a more difficult endeavor, as there were fewer programs to serve as models. Additionally, efforts at recruiting a male from our campus to serve as leader of the organization were unsuccessful in the beginning. Hence, in the Spring, 2001 semester, we brought in Dr. Christopher Kilmartin to consult with us on how to operationalize our vision of creating a men's violence prevention program without a male leader. Based on his suggestions and ideas about how to work with men (now also available in Kilmartin & Berkowitz, 2005), we devised a plan and a structure for the program. (See Box 9.1 for a description of Kilmartin's "best advice" for this program.)

PROGRAM STRUCTURE

The work of both the violence response and prevention programs is guided by a constantly evolving member handbook and constitutions for each group. The handbook consists of six sections. The first gives a general introduction to the Office of Violence Response and Prevention and describes the specific programs. Importantly, it

> **BOX 9.1**
> **Start-Up Suggestions**
>
> Christopher Kilmartin visited the Pittsburg State Campus in 2001. Among the many suggestions offered, four were especially central to the guiding principles of the program: (a) provide incentives for participation, (b) seek out leaders across campus, (c) create diversity within the group, and (d) implement gender-aware programming (See also Kilmartin & Berkowitz, 2005).
>
> ***Provide Incentives for Participation***
>
> Without a doubt, participation in violence prevention would appeal to men with an orientation toward community service, however it is also important to recruit men into the program by appealing to their self-interests. From a psychological perspective, this approach makes sense. There are two routes to motivating behavior: (a) intrinsic and (b) extrinsic. Intrinsically motivated behaviors occur because they are personally satisfying. People will engage in other, less satisfying behavior because they are seeking an extrinsic reward such as money, social support, or recognition. At first glance, becoming involved in ending men's violence against women may not be intrinsically appealing to men. Hence, we first offered extrinsic rewards for participation. In exchange for participating in the required training, members receive three hours of academic credit that applies toward their bachelors' degrees. The class is experientially based and allows ample opportunity for both learning and academic success. Additionally, we created leadership positions within the organization, offering members the opportunity to develop highly marketable leadership skills. Finally, we encourage intrinsically motivated involvement by emphasizing that this work is important and needs men of strength, courage, and character, all of which are positively masculine. The participation of men who do this work seems to become more intrinsically motivating over time.
>
> ***Seek out Leaders From Across Campus***
>
> Leaders not only have the skills to guide others, they often have high status and visibility on the campus, as well as interpersonal connections and information about resources available outside of the organization. To find leaders that represent diverse

> **BOX 9.1** *(continued)*
>
> organizations also increases the diversity of the membership. We have found that challenging organizations across the college campus to identify a representative who would be willing to join has been a successful technique in recruiting leaders.
>
> ***Seek a Diverse Membership***
>
> This recommendation has been most significant to the program as an organization. The men of the program have represented a variety of men, including Hispanic American/Latino/ Americans; African Americans; European Americans; Native Americans; younger men and older men; gay, bisexual, and heterosexual men; fraternity and non-fraternity men; military and civilian men; single, cohabiting, married, and divorced men; and student athletes representing football, baseball, and track. Hence, when the group is at work, they are representing a heterogeneous population.
>
> ***Create Gender-Aware Programming***
>
> A gender-aware approach to violence prevention puts the various issues in the context of patriarchy and its concomitant views of men and of women. Basic to this type of programming is the assumption that the culture of masculinity can serve to place some men (e.g., those who subscribe to a hypermasculine ideology) at risk for perpetrating violence.

identifies members and leaders of each group. The second section provides information on the educational topics provided in the training. The third explains general policies and procedures and also includes legal statutes relevant to gender-based violent crimes. The fourth provides information about how members can provide support and help to survivors. (Some members have reported that once they join the program, friends, classmates, and/or acquaintances will reveal their victimization to them, some for the first time ever to anyone.) The fifth section is specific to policies and procedures for those on the Sexual Assault Response Team, and the last section includes organizational materials (e.g., forms, applications, presentation scripts).

The organizational structure of each program includes an executive committee and chairs for the following committees: (a) recruitment and selection, (b) public relations, (c) media and marketing, (d) research, (e) presentation, and (f) fundraising. Each group has a part-time, paid coordinator and an advisor from the university faculty. The advisors also serve as teachers of the class that students who want to be members take. Finally, all of this work is supported by the Director of the Office of Violence Response and Prevention.

THEORETICAL FOUNDATIONS

The core foundations of our men's program are based on social psychological theory and principles regarding gender and gender-based violence. These principles include

- Gender-based attitudes are learned.
- Gender-based violence against women is founded upon negative attitudes toward women.
- Negative attitudes towards women, and sexism against women, is supported by homophobia, specifically directed toward gay men.
- Gender-based violence is supported by a patriarchy that encourages male dominance and sexism against women, including both malevolent and benevolent sexism.
- Boys and men are more than their masculine stereotypes. Through MVP training, the men are encouraged to be themselves, and to support each other as they learn to step outside of the "box" of masculinity.
- Most boys and men are personally uncomfortable with sexism and gender-based violence.
- Boys and men have both the power and the responsibility to work to prevent gender-based violence.

The social psychological theoretical foundation also provides direction in the creation of goals for the group and its members. These goals include

- To listen to women.
- To discuss issues related to gender that serve to support the epidemic of violence against women.
- To encourage men to speak out against violence against women.
- To encourage men to examine their own attitudes about women and other men.
- To encourage men to examine their use of language and the consequences of such language.

- To learn to appropriately confront disrespect, sexism, homophobia, abuse, and/or violence.
- To honor men and positive masculinities.
- To promote good mental and physical health in men.

Hence, in the training of the members, men confront negative stereotypes of both females and males. They acknowledge that a system of hierarchical power (primarily patriarchy) exists in society and has powerful consequences for the lives of both males and females. They examine their own language and behavior, and identify ways that they may sometimes contribute to this system of patriarchy that creates vulnerability in some men to act in violent ways, and vulnerability in boys, girls, women, and gay men as targets of violence. Certainly, it takes a man of strength and courage to be willing to examine these issues. It is important to honor and acknowledge that this process of examination is difficult for many men, but that the outcome can be (and usually is) personally rewarding.

The process of examination can be highly beneficial on an individual level. In addition to gaining an understanding of the problems and dynamics of gender-based problems, members become aware that they are an important part of the solution to this problem in several ways. First, they acquire skills that serve to support survivors of gender-based crimes and learn the importance of such support. Second, they learn ways to appropriately confront examples of sexist or abusive behavior, serving as a voice for the silent majority of men who are offended by these actions. Third, they are provided a safe space to honestly discuss the pressures that they may feel to conform to the standards of masculinity, even when these pressures may be both personally and interpersonally toxic. Through this discussion, they are encouraged to grant each other permission to step outside of the false boundaries of masculinity, and to seek to discover and express the people whom they truly are.

OBTAINING EFFECTIVE MEMBERS

To join one of our teams, interested students must first apply for membership. In addition to asking about basic demographic information and references, the application requires that students write about (a) why they are interested in being a member of the program, (b) what experiences and/or abilities they have to offer the program, (c) how comfortable they are discussing sensitive topics such as rape, and (d) if there are any circumstance(s) in their past or present that could affect their performance and that would be important for the selection committee to know. The applicant is required to sign an oath that he or she has not ever been convicted of a crime involving violence or exploitation of others, and that he or she agrees to abide by all university policies, rules, and regulations regarding appropriate behavior and professional conduct. Finally, the applicant agrees in writing to allow the SASA committee to conduct a background check through governmental authorities. A selection committee reviews the applications and checks references. An interview may also be conducted. Accepted members are then granted permission to enroll in the class on gender-based violence.

After members are oriented to the mission and foundations of the class and the violence-prevention organization, they are asked to commit themselves to upholding the values of the group by pledging to support a model of nonviolence and integrity. (See Box 9.2 for examples of these pledges.).

The 16-week class that SAVE and MVP members complete is designed within a 5-hour per week time frame that includes 2 hours of class for the SAVE members alone, 1 hour of class for both SAVE and MVP members, and then 2 hours of class for MVP members alone. Hence, all members have time—both in single-sex and mixed-sex groups—to discuss the issues related to gender-based violence.

It is possible that the many requirements for interested members could inhibit them from joining the group; however, it seems more important to have measures of quality control in place. The harm that could result from involving a perpetrator in this work outweighs the risk of losing interested members. Paradoxically, it is also possible that having to be "accepted" into a program elevates its status in the eyes of both potential and actual members, as well as outside observers. Although recruitment strategies are utilized as both a means of obtaining effective members and raising awareness of the issue, in our experience, the most effective means of recruiting quality men to join the organization is simply to explain why you sincerely believe they would make great members and ask them if they would join.

EDUCATIONAL PROGRAMMING FOR MEN INTERESTED IN VIOLENCE PREVENTION

Training men who are interested in engaging in violence prevention work is critical. It is also important to identify where each individual member is with regard to their levels of awareness and

> **BOX 9.2**
> **Membership Commitment**
>
> The following pledges seek to impress upon the members the importance of their behavior as a representative of a men's violence prevention program. Additional, they seek to inspire men to honor positive masculinity.
>
> *Pledge of Non-Violence*
>
> **As an important member of the Men against Violence Program (MVP) and/or of Students Against Violence through Education (SAVE), I make the following pledge (please initial by each):**
>
> _____ I agree to respect myself physically, emotionally, and mentally by refusing to accept negative peer pressure, refusing to engage in self-destructive behaviors and to not allow only stereotypes to guide who I am or choose to become.
>
> _____ I agree to be respectful and supportive towards others. I will honor the individuality of individuals.
>
> _____ I agree to seek to engage in healthy communication with others by sharing my feelings honestly and respectfully. I will try to express my feelings and/or opinions in ways that will not hurt me or others. I will seek to resolve conflicts with others as peacefully as possible.
>
> _____ I agree to actively listen to others, even those with whom I disagree, and to take the feelings of others into consideration during such discussions.
>
> _____ I agree to forgive others and myself when deemed necessary, take time to apologize if I have hurt someone and avoid holding grudges.
>
> _____ I agree to avoid behaving in any way that might serve to objectify or dehumanize another or others. I understand that this includes refraining from using language that degrades others such as sexist statements, racial slurs, homophobic statements, name calling, etc.
>
> _____ I agree to appropriately and safely challenge sexist, racist, or homophobic comments or behavior.
>
> _____ I agree to appropriately confront abusive and violent behavior when I witness it or have reason to believe abusive or violent behavior has occurred. If for any reason, appropriate confrontation would put me or others in danger, I will intervene by contacting law enforcement.

BOX 9.2 *(continued)*

_____ I agree to practice non-violence in both my words and my actions.

_____   _____
Member Signature   Date

Integrity and Expectation Agreement

This agreement outlines the responsibilities and expectations of members of Students Against Violence through Education (SAVE) and Men against Violence Program (MVP).

As a SAVE / MVP member, I agree to:

Maintain confidentiality as stated in my signed confidentiality contract.

Uphold Pittsburg State University's Student Code of Conduct as well as SAVE and MVP Membership Code of Conduct.

Maintain a professional manner at all times when wearing SAVE or MVP identification, and when representing SAVE or MVP in any fashion.

Behave in a manner that is conducive with the philosophies of SAVE/MVP. I understand that as a SAVE/MVP member my actions reflect on the entire group and that any inappropriate actions, especially inappropriate physical or sexual behavior, compromise the integrity of SAVE/MVP.

I understand that failure to adhere to one or more of these expectations will lead to a meeting with the Executive Committee of SAVE or MVP and the Director of the Office of Violence Response and Prevention to discuss the issue in private. I understand that a breach of this agreement may jeopardize my status as a member of SAVE or MVP.

Name (Please Print): _____

Signature:_____ Date:_____

sensitivity of the issues. This assessment can be accomplished through both individual and group discussions, and through reflective writing. The course intersperses frank lectures on the realities and dynamics of gender-based violence with honest dialogue about gender issues, gender stereotypes and their consequences, and intimate relationships. The training is also designed to evolve from the negative to more positive—from problems to solutions—and addresses issues relevant to individuals, groups (including intimate relationships), and communities. Additionally, both new members and senior members are present at each training.

A structured curriculum based on the goals of the programs guides the format of the training; however, exercising flexibility within this structure has been important to group development, guided by members' varying levels of awareness and sensitivity towards gender-based violence, as well as by group dynamics. Additionally, the mode of presentation can take a variety of different forms. Traditional lecture presentations may be the most effective mode for providing information that is mainly factually based. Beyond that, learning about violence and violence prevention work can be achieved through active discourse, activities, the use of media, and through utilizing the expertise of those in the community. Suggested lecture topics may include (chapter coverage from this book is in parentheses)

- Facts about gender-based violence: Incidence and prevalence rates. (Chapter 1.)
- Myths about gender-based violence and their consequences. (Primarily in chapters 1 and 5.)
- The relationship between gender inequality and gender-based violence. (Primarily in chapter 1.)
- Power and control: The foundation of gender-based violence. (Primarily in chapter 1.)
- The cultural construction of gender-based violence. (Chapter 6.)
- Understanding the offenders. (Chapter 2.)
- The effects of offenders' violence on victims. (Chapter 3.)
- Supporting survivors of gender-based violence. (Chapter 4.)
- Responding to perpetrators. (Chapter 4.)
- The role of bystanders in the perpetuation of gender-based violence. (Primarily in chapter 7.)
- The relationship between homophobia and gender-based violence. (Chapter 1.)

DISCUSSIONS

Discussions between women and men, and among men, can be lively, intense, and extremely rewarding. It is helpful to remind members regularly of the ground rules (e.g., openness, honesty, sensitivity towards others, respect). Senior members can contribute to the quality of the discussion by demonstrating these attributes. A facilitator is critical in guiding discussions.

Ideas for Discussions/Activities between Women and Men

- The relationship between SAVE and MVP: support and accountability.
- Stereotypes of men and women: What are they? Are they accurate?
- Men, women, and power: How does it feel? What are the effects?
- Gender-based violence: Social perception vs. law.
- Consent vs. nonconsent: Where do you draw the line?
- The advantages of the disadvantages of feminine stereotypes for women.
- The disadvantages of the advantages of masculine stereotypes for men.
- Men, women, and sexuality.
- Communication about sexuality in relationships.
- Healthy relationships. What are they?

Discussion Topics among Men

- Social norms and men's attitudes toward gender-based violence.
- Masculinity and it's consequences for men and men's relationships.
- Going beyond stereotypes: being who you are.
- Men's power and responsibility to prevent violence.
- Appropriate confrontation of inappropriate behavior.
- Attitudes toward women: hostile vs. benevolent sexism.
- Chivalry vs. respect.
- Managing emotions.
- Redefining masculinity.
- Becoming an ally.

ACTIVITIES

Incorporating activities beyond group discussions has also been constructive to the training. For example, asking members to write down their thoughts, insights, questions, or concerns anonymously, and then sharing these with the group, can help to facilitate discussions.

The most common activity utilized in the training has been role-playing, which allows members to "witness" the demonstration of stereotypical and non-stereotypical behavior, as well as conversations between men and women. (e.g., demonstrations and perceptions of nonconsent). This activity can then lead to spirited discussions. Moreover, role-playing in the training is sometimes spontaneous and used to allow members to demonstrate their points of view.

Members also tend to enjoy the "fishbowl" activity. Here, a small group of members sit in a circle and share their feelings and opinions regarding a topic (e.g., the relationship between sex and love). The rest of the members are circled around the small group as they listen to the conversation (they are explicitly asked to be completely silent). After the conversation is over, members from the surrounding circle are invited to sit in the inside circle and share their thoughts and feelings on the issue. This activity has been particularly powerful when the men and women are together, as they take turns sharing and listening. After a particularly poignant fishbowl activity, one of the male members described his thoughts after the activity. He said, "I didn't know that I didn't know."

USING MEDIA

Film media can be a very powerful tool for broadening perspectives and conveying personal stories, usually leading to meaningful discussions. Some very powerful educational resources include

- ***The Undetected Rapist.*** This film is a reenactment of portions of an interview conducted by Dr. David Lisak with a college student who discusses his tactics for committing rape (©2000, National Judicial Education Program, njep@nowldef.org).
- ***Our Stories.*** This 21-minute documentary provides powerful and personal accounts of rape survivors, highlighting the nondiscriminatory nature of acquaintance rape (©2000, FotoKem).
- ***Rape is....*** A powerful 32-minute documentary that explores the dynamics of rape from a global and historical perspective (©Cambridge Documentary Films, Inc., www.cambridgedocumentaryfilms.org).
- ***Crimes Against Nature.*** This one-hour production is a humorous, one-man show that points out the absurdities and contradictions of masculinity (©2000, Christopher Kilmartin).
- ***Tough Guise.*** Available in both full and abridged versions, Jackson Katz exposes the relationship between popular culture and the social construction of masculinity (©2002, Media Education Foundation, www.mediaed.org).

- **Speak Up!** Through interviews with students, parents, teachers, administrators, and national activities, this production highlights ways in which gay, lesbian, bisexual, and transgendered (GLBT) students and their allies are working to create safer educational environments (30 minutes; ©2002, Media Education Foundation, www.mediaed. org).
- **Role Reversal.** During the course of a month, this documentary explores the extreme transformation of two men and two women who commit to switching genders (100 minutes; ©2001 A&E Television Networks).
- **Killing Us Softly 3.** Jean Kilbourne exhibits over 160 advertisements and commercials to highlight the social objectification of females and the effects of such objectification (34 minutes; ©2002, Media Education Foundation, www.mediaed.org).
- **Spin the Bottle: Sex, Lies, and Alcohol.** Jackson Katz and Jean Kilbourne illustrate how popular culture glamorizes alcohol consumption in gender specific ways (44 minutes; ©2004, Media Education Foundation, www.mediaed.org).
- **Searching for Angela Shelton.** Angela Shelton journeys across the United States to learn about the lives of 40 women who share her name, 23 of whom reveal personal experiences with gender-based violence (94 minutes; ©2004 *Searching for Angela Shelton*, www.searchingforangelashelton.com).
- **Wrestling with Manhood: Boys, Bullying and Battering.** Jackson Katz provides an inside look at professional wrestling, and its connection to current concepts of masculinity, homophobia, and gender-based violence (60 minutes; ©2003 Media Education Foundation, www. mediaed.org).

The use of popular cinema can also be an effective tool for conveying messages in a powerful and visual way. Movies such as *Brokeback Mountain, The Accused, Sandlot, The Tape,* and *Good Will Hunting* (and many others) can all serve to bolster an understanding of theoretical concepts and their implications. It is not necessary to show movies in their entirely. One or two scenes may be enough to illustrate a point.

Beyond filmed media, members may enjoy sharing scenes from television programs that they have watched recently, lyrics of songs that demonstrate the issues being highlighted in their training, or depictions of men and/or women in printed advertisements.

EXPERTS IN THE COMMUNITY

Inviting experts from the community to come and describe their work helps to create connections between our program and others. Additionally, these experts are able to share unique information and reinforce the importance of all programs that share the common goal of supporting survivors and ending violence, and the importance of working together. Experts who have presented in the trainings include the leaders of the local crisis center, Children's Advocacy Center, an Alternatives to Battering program, independent living service organizations (who work with people with disabilities), law enforcement, SART/SANE nursing, and prosecuting attorneys.

The very process of creating these programs constitutes violence prevention in action. All members are unique, and all begin at different levels of awareness and sensitivity about the issue. Similarly, individual members learn and develop heightened senses of awareness and sensitivity at their own paces. Because of this variation in process and the voluntary nature of the program, members will differ in their level of passion about violence prevention work, and hence, levels of participation in the work will also vary. Interestingly, many men who become involved express a sense of relief that they are not alone in their distress about violence and abuse perpetrated against women (and men), or disrespect in general, and that they can actually do something about it.

The actual work of the violence prevention program changes, as members and leadership change and new ideas emerge. Generally speaking, the work revolves around two themes: (a) providing education and (b) raising awareness. Of course, many times these are achieved simultaneously.

PROVIDING EDUCATION

Both the violence response and prevention programs provide educational presentations to other students on campus, local and regional middle schools, high schools, colleges, and professional organizations. The presentation itself was inspired by the work of Don McPherson (described earlier). Although the presentation begins and ends with males and females together, the groups break into single-sex groups for the bulk of the presentation. Since 2004, SAVE and MVP have presented to over 4,000 middle-school students, high-school students, college students, community citizens, and professionals.

After consulting with Dr. Alan Berkowitz, we also began incorporating social norms theory into our educational work. (See chapter 8 for more on this approach.). For interested schools, prior to our presentation, we collect social norms data on the students' attitudes towards violent or abusive behavior, and then incorporate data from that school into a poster prototype. For example, we marketed research that revealed that "96% of students at [the name of your school] are bothered when a guy tries to control a girl." The posters are put up prior to our arrival and can stay there indefinitely. We also share these data with the students during the presentation in order to encourage them to speak out against examples of sexist behavior by helping them to understand that their discomfort is shared by peers.

It is important to note that any time discussions on violence against women take place, there are likely to be both females and males who are either survivors or witnesses to such violence. It is not uncommon for survivors to reveal their victimization experiences with members following a presentation, and members must be prepared for this disclosure. Given the nature of the topic, it is also important that communication be clear regarding the specific content of the presentation or any needed modifications to it. Based on both our successes and our mistakes, we have developed a protocol for providing presentations that we regularly emphasize to members. (See Box 9.3 for an example of this ever-evolving protocol.)

RAISING AWARENESS

Efforts at raising awareness can take many forms. Additionally, it is important to think about not only what the group members would like to do, but the effects of such efforts on the community. Additionally, attempts to raise awareness can occur on local, regional, state, national, or international levels. For example, the White Ribbon Campaign (discussed in chapter 8) encourages men and boys to wear a white ribbon for one week as a personal pledge to never commit, condone, or remain silent about men's violence against

BOX 9.3
Protocol for Presenting to Schools

1. The school/organization should be contacted at least one week ahead of time to discuss the nature of the presentation and seek special guidelines for the school (e.g., language, discussion of alcohol or drugs). We want to ensure that the way we are defining "age appropriate" is the same as the way school administrators are defining "age appropriate."
2. If the school/organization is not local, we will compile a list of counseling resources available for students. We will also ask the school/organization if there are additional services placed on this list. This list will be distributed or made available to the students at the school.
3. The presentation chair of each team is responsible for finding presenters and communicating with them prior to the presentation what their roles will be. The presentation chair is responsible for making sure all necessary presentations materials are ready to go.
4. Prior to the presentation, a "disclaimer" will be provided stating that this material is a very sensitive issue, and may "push buttons" for some. Offer to speak to any individual that may have questions after the presentation. Let the audience members know prior to the presentation that they are free to leave, but that someone from our teams will be following them to make sure they are all right. In order to protect their privacy, the audience should also be told that you understand that some of you might need to leave for other reasons (e.g., going to the bathroom), so please do not get offended if we offer support and it turns out that it is not needed.
5. During the presentation, SART members should be available (when possible) and seated in a place where they can scan the audience members for potential trauma. When they can be inconspicuous, they should approach the individual to see if he/she is all right. ALL SART/SAVE/MVP MEMBERS SHOULD ASSUME SOME RESPONSIBILITY FOR WATCHING THE STUDENTS TO MAKE SURE THEY ARE ALL RIGHT.
6. If a student leaves the room during a presentation, a previously appointed member will follow them to ensure that they are okay and see if there is a way we can provide support to them.
7. Be aware of your language. At high schools, you may refer to students as girls or guys. At colleges or other adult audiences, refer to males and females as men and women, respectively. At no time is the "f-word" or the "c-word" to be used. Other "cuss" words may

> **BOX 9.3** (continued)
>
> be appropriate, if it is approved by the school and the judgment of the presenter that it makes the presentation more effective by its use.
> 8. SAVE/MVP members will demonstrate respect for each other at all times. No degrading racist, sexist, or homophobic comments or jokes should be used at any time.
> 9. Evaluation data will be collected following every presentation and given to respective research chairs.
> 10. A follow-up thank you note will be sent to the school by the coordinators.

women, and to talk about the problem of violence in their schools, workplaces, and faith communities. The White Ribbon office also provides specific instruction and advice on how to effectively conduct the campaign.

The potential activities that could be organized with the goal of raising awareness seem limitless, bounded only by the imaginations of those interested in participating. Additionally, there are many resources available for those wishing to organize an activity. For example, the Pennsylvania Coalition Against Rape (www.pcar.org) has phenomenal resources and ideas and will provide a "tool kit" on how to raise awareness during April, Sexual Assault Awareness Month.

Efforts to prevent violence through awareness raising can be as small as simply talking about it with a friend to month-long awareness campaigns that may take weeks to prepare. In addition to participating in national events like the White Ribbon Campaign, Domestic Violence Awareness Month (October), and Sexual Assault Awareness Month (April), the following events are some that have been coordinated by the response and prevention programs. They are included here because they were either fun, seemed to be effective, or both.

- Recruitment drive. This activity is held every semester prior to pre-enrollment. We have food (grilled hot dogs, or pizza donated by a local restaurant), drink, and lots of informational brochures. We also have applications and invite interested members to complete them on-site. To create a positive atmosphere, we play music and have a loudspeaker to talk about our message.
- Media campaigns. We have photo shoots using members of the groups and create posters that we distribute across campus.

- Clothesline displays and booth. We invite individuals across campus to share their thoughts about or experiences with violence by making a T-shirt that we display in the center of campus.
- Spot the Silence/Stop the Violence. Here, we ask those who are willing to resolve to remain silent for 12 hours (excluding professional/academic activities). Participants wear a sticker identifying themselves as a supporter of survivors. When someone attempts to talk with them, they give them a slip of paper explaining why they are not talking:

> *Please understand my reasons for not speaking today. It is to draw attention to those who have felt silenced due to sexual assault or rape. People who remain silent today are doing so in support of survivors of sexual assault and rape and speaking out; both about their experiences and against their aggressors. Please think about the voices you are not hearing today. What can you do to end the silence?* (See Box 9.4 for a personal reflection on committing to stay silent.).

- Participating in local parades.
- Participating in campus homecoming events.
- Sponsoring a "Why I Am against Violence" campaign for elementary school boys. Winners are rewarded with a bowling and pizza party with MVP leaders and captains from our football team. Local media are invited.
- Writing and taping public service announcements at local radio stations.

The violence response and prevention programs at Pittsburg State University continue to evolve, improve, and learn from mistakes. As more people have become aware of this work, more have become involved, including male faculty who now serve leadership roles. We have found that while this work can be amazingly difficult and frustration, it also provides moments of immense gratification and a contagious hope for a better future.

SUMMARY

Those who attempt to build prevention/intervention programs face a variety of challenges, including funding, recruitment, retention, program design, and evaluation. It is important to think developmentally about the program. Perhaps in the first year, one can invite a national or regional expert to give a speech and/or engage in the planning process. Perhaps later, a few interested people can organize an awareness effort like the White Ribbon Campaign.

> **BOX 9.4**
> **A Peer Educator Experience**
>
> The following story was written by MVP member Troy Bastion, shortly after his participation in "Spot the Silence/Stop the Violence."
>
> When I was a young boy I learned very early that self-assertion was a very important trait. My father was a salesman, my mother, a piano teacher. They were both consummate communicators, very succinct, and animated with the most eloquent diction. The type we seldom see today. "Express yourself" I remember hearing them say. "Always be clear and proper, always practice the joy of effective communication."
>
> I suppose I took that to heart. I became a piano player, and eventually, trumpet and banjo as well. I learned that I was also a pretty darn good salesman, too. No one could ever accuse me of being shy.
>
> When I heard about a day dedicated to spreading the message of the suffering in silence of many, many people in our society, I was game. However, when it was explained that I would not be raising my voice on behalf of the oppressed, or writing persuasive words for a "blow 'em away speech" I was somewhat taken aback. Silence. Silence? I was expected to spend an entire day "shutting up" This concept took some reflection. As a matter of fact, I elected to pass altogether. Then I attended the class. Just a class. A class like any other. We all met on Monday night, we all got together and spoke about victimization, about rape, violence, etc. We hashed out the topics, discussed the evil of it all. We all agreed there was a serious problem. Had it all stopped there, I think I would have been just fine. But that didn't happen. No, something quite amazing happened after that. Just a week ago Monday, I sat in a classroom and listened while some very brave young men broke silences that they had kept locked inside for years. One man spoke of the victimization of his sister. The other, of the many traumatic memories of his childhood. I sat in awe, listening to the pain in their trembling voices. I watched as the tears welled up, washing away the staunch facade of years of ever-enduring machismo. My heart pounded as inside I quietly begged: "Please stop, please don't say anything else, I'll cry with you." I realized, at that moment, how absolutely deafening the silence actually can be.

> **BOX 9.3** *(continued)*
>
> *I awoke on "Spot the Silence" day, dedicated to the cause. I went to my first class, and did rather well. I took no casual cell calls, though I did answer work-related calls. I didn't visit with my usual "talk buddies" after class. I simply walked to my car. Of course, I did function as a father that day, but explained to my children how much I truly love them, and their mother, and how they must never approve of, or tolerate violence. I was unable to attend the dinner that drew the day to a close, based upon professional obligations. However, I did explain to some friends and clients why I had chosen to pursue the cause.*
>
> *I am a vocal person. I LOVE to talk. However, I'll always remember that on one day of my life, I kept quiet on behalf of others. How truly difficult it was. I can only imagine how difficult it must be if one is terrified. I pray to God no one I love ever has to endure it.*

Afterwards, the program can become more elaborate and extensive, making its way into the very structure of the community. Peer educators and other program participants sometimes become frustrated at the limitations of their influence, and at these times, we have found it helpful to remind them that the full impact of their efforts may not be realized for years to come, and that they have contributed to the well-being of people whom they will never meet.

In closing, we hope that we have helped to educate the reader to the state of the art in violence prevention and intervention, from the big picture of macrosocietal considerations to the nuts-and-bolts of program development. We applaud the courage and commitment of all the women and men who undertake these efforts and look forward to a future when we can truly describe gender-based violence as a thing of the past.

CRITICAL THINKING QUESTION

1. This chapter offers ideas and suggestions, based on one program, on how to plan and implement other violence prevention programs. Given the unique characteristics of your own community, identify which of these or other strategies might be most effective in developing a violence prevention program in your community. What role are you willing to play in this effort?

Epilogue: Final Thoughts

We have explored the clinical, social, and cultural bases of gender-based violence. Since the modern feminist movement began in the 1970s, intense and fervent energy has led to significant social and legal changes in response to an awareness of the tragedy of gender-based violence. Some of these innovations include the establishment of centers aimed at supporting victims and survivors, the enactment of stricter laws, and the increase of accountability for convicted offenders. The people who pioneered these changes have played a critical role in raising social awareness about the issue. It is important that we acknowledge this work, which ultimately offers hope that the violence will end someday. The movement towards adding a prevention component that includes the work of men adds to this promise. Peaceful relationships and communities are real possibilities.

The path towards peace is a journey towards gender equality. The realization of this goal on both micro- and macro-societal levels would allow all individuals to be fully functioning human beings in a society free of behavioral and emotional constraints based on false stereotypes of males and females. Currently, feminists (mostly females) continue their efforts to combat the violence, and more recently, some men (mostly feminists) are joining these efforts. Those involved in this work recognize that gender equality will benefit both females and males.

In hindsight, our personal experiences in doing this work have revealed a surprising result: the process of working to improve the lives of others is personally beneficial to us as individuals and social beings. Accounts from others involved in this work corroborate our experiences. The following testimonies are from members of the violence response and prevention programs described in chapter 9.

TESTIMONIALS FROM WOMEN ACTIVISTS

The past four years have been the most empowering, encouraging, inspiring, and emotional experience of my life. I am eternally grateful to all the men and women who have touched my heart and given me the courage to take the risk to take a stand against interpersonal violence with the knowledge that I am not alone. I am personally touched by the commitment of both men and women who want to make a difference. Together we are able to unite and bond as women and men as well as create unforgettable friendships.

Through this work, I believe that the women are so empowered. I love that I can walk into a room, a party, wherever, see another person from the group, and know I have a friend. The men in the group mark the beginning of the end to violence. It's inspiring to see a man stand up for us and not just agree with the other guys.

While doing this work, I find myself surrounded by the most passionate and driven people I have ever had the pleasure of knowing. I wouldn't trade this experience for anything in the world.

This work is very challenging but very rewarding. I feel that because I have the skills and ability to help those in need, I have the responsibility to do so. The most important part is to believe the victim and listen.

I have learned that men care as much as we do about the violence against women. They can speak out to other men and they can prevent the violence.

Whether we like it or not, we can't change how we are treated by ourselves. It is very important that men and women work together.

I know that I can't change the world, but I have learned that I can change the lives of a few people. And they can change the lives of a few people, etc., etc. It seems so simple, and it wouldn't take long for the world to change.

Whether we like it or not, we can't change how we are treated by ourselves. It is very important that men and women work together.

TESTIMONIALS FROM MEN ACTIVISTS

I feel that this program has given my life more direction and meaning. I've been given the opportunity to meet very enthusiastic individuals that have been through similar situations as I have. It has made me feel like more of a man than ever.

Being in this program has been empowering, enlightening and real. I am better able to communicate with other men, and I have a deeper appreciation and understanding of women's views.

This organization forces a person to step out from behind anything they hide behind and to realize what they want to be and how to make the world feel more like home. We consider some dark places in which we live, but learn that there is plenty of light, if you learn how to see it.

To me, MVP is a brotherhood. SAVE and SART are our sisters, and together our family makes change. We grow closer, we form bonds. Never in front, never behind, always beside.

This program has given me courage and hope that one voice counts. To be a group of voices that represent a great movement to better our world is the best experience I have ever had. I am absolutely positive in my walk to be a better man for society and to serve as a role model that others can be.

If you think one person can't make a difference, you're wrong. If one person tells three people, and these three tell three more and so on, it adds up fast. Imagine if we all help.

This program for me has been an eye-opening experience. It has brought upon information that is sadly true. However, we've formed a coalition of men who are willing to take a stand against these statistics and move beyond a world of masculinity.

Being a member of MVP has been empowering, enlightening, and real. It has allowed me to better communicate with other men now, and I also feel more appreciative and understanding of women's views.

My participation and privilege in MVP is my duty as a friend, brother, son, nephew and young man. I am proud and honored to be in such a remarkable group of men.

The benefits to doing this work may begin on a personal level, but inevitably such changes will permeate one's relationships, community, social groups, and beyond. The work is challenging, honorable, and rewarding, and we invite you to join the thousands of women and men across the nation who are endeavoring to prevent and respond to men's violence against women.

Violence prevention work also reveals a prevailing paradox—people involved in this work discover that men or women who subscribe to the strict standards of their gender stereotypes are not very appealing. In a social psychology class, Julie Allison asked her students to identify characteristics of a "real man." Much like the box exercise demonstrated by Jackson Katz (see chapter 7), students quickly characterized the "real man" as stereotypical: strong, aggressive, competitive, athletic, dominating, etc. A second question created a pause. "Now, tell me about the man you look up to the most." This time, students generated characteristics largely unrelated to gender stereotypes: kind, loyal, honest, caring, hardworking, and supportive. Such qualities are also valued in women.

When it is successful, violence prevention work ultimately does more than simply remove a negative. The process of working to create a world free of violence supplants the toxic emotions of fear and hate, which serve as emotional foundations for violent behavior, with courage and love. It supports an acceptance of individual and group differences, and it allows individuals to be who they are.

We will close with words of inspiration from an extraordinary boy. Poet Mattie Stepanek, co-author with former President Jimmy Carter of *Just Peace: A Message of Hope* (2006), was only 13 years old when he died of a terminal illness. During his short but remarkable lifetime, he sought to spread his message of peace and hope. In a final interview with Larry King (aired April 26, 2006), he describes how peace is possible:

> *I believe that if we choose to make peace an attitude and want it, and we make it something that truly matters inside of our hearts and then if we choose to make peace a habit, not just think it but to live it, and share it. And if we choose to make peace a reality and spread it throughout the world and get involved and understand what's going on, we will have peace.*

Glossary

Affective component: A part of an attitude that predisposes a person to respond in a characteristic emotional way to an object, event, or idea.
Anger rapist: One who commits rape as an act of vengeance for perceived harm or injustice.
Antifemininity: The cultural definition of masculinity as the "not feminine," with accompanying avoidance of behaviors (e.g., cooperation, emotional expression) associated with girls and women, in males who conform to cultural masculinity.
Attitude: A predisposition to think, feel, and behave toward an object, idea, or event.
Automatic processing: The non-willful activation of a stereotype.
Availability heuristic: Judgment about the frequency of an event based on the ease of accessing information about the event.
Behavioral component: A part of an attitude that predisposes a person to respond with a characteristic action to an object, event, or idea.
Belief in a just world: The tendency for people to believe that the world is fair, and therefore that people get what they deserve.

Benevolent sexism: Disrespect of women expressed through an attitude that women are to be cherished, adored, and protected, with the underlying assumption that women are helpless and incompetent.

Bystander approach: An educational effort that highlights the role of observers of problematic behavior in helping to prevent gender-based violence.

Chivalry: A benevolent sexist attitude in the form of a set of "gentlemanly" behaviors that ostensibly convey respect for women, but actually reinforce the power differential between men and women.

Classically conditioned attitude: An emotional response to a previously neutral stimulus that develops from that stimulus being associated with an instinctual stimulus such as pain.

Coercive power: The ability to influence another through the use of threats or punishment.

Cognitive-behavioral therapy: A clinical approach to treating violence survivors that involves changing thought patterns that lead to negative emotional states and problematic behavior.

Cognitive component: A part of an attitude that predisposes a person to think about an object, event, or idea in a characteristic way.

Cognitive dissonance: An intrapersonal tension that results from the simultaneous awareness of two or more contradictory cognitions.

Cognitive processing therapy (CPT): A set of techniques for treating survivors that involves a psychological integration of the violent event.

Culpascope: A magnifying optical device, typically used to examine and photograph injuries in the genital region for victims of rape or sexual assault.

Cyberstalking: The use of electronic technology in the pursuit and harassment of a person.

Cycle of violence: A predictable pattern apparent in some cases of intimate partner violence in which the perpetrator alternates between the use of reinforcements and punishments in his/her quest for control.

Decision to act violently: A volitional moment in which there is a cognitive movement toward harming another person.

Depression: A mood disorder characterized by sadness, despair, feelings of worthlessness, and low self-esteem.

Diagnostic and Statistical Manual of Mental Disorders: The handbook used to diagnose mental disorders in the United States.

Diversion: A legal arrangement where a convicted criminal is allowed to avoid incarceration by successfully participating in an intervention program.

Economic abuse: A control tactic used by some perpetrators of intimate partner violence aimed at making the partner financially dependent upon the abuser.

Emotional abuse: A control tactic used by some perpetrators of intimate partner violence aimed at producing negative emotional states in their partners (e.g., fear, anxiety).

Empathy: A sympathetic awareness of another person's distress.

Empathy for the self: A sympathetic awareness of one's own distress.

Erotomanic stalker: A person who is delusional, wrongly believing that the victim of stalking is a romantic partner.

Expert power: The ability to influence another by purporting to have superior knowledge or skills.

Explicit Attitude: A conscious predisposition to respond in a characteristic way to an object, event, or idea.

Exploitive harasser: Someone who uses a position of power in the workplace to coerce subordinates into sexual behaviors.

Explosion phase: The third stage of the cycle of violence in which there is intense and acute violence.

Eye Movement Desensitization and Reprocessing (EMDR): A therapeutic technique used to treat survivors, which involves focusing on the traumatic event while engaging in a dual attention activity (following the therapist's finger across the visual field).

Femininity: Cultural beliefs about women's nature and place within the social order.

Femiphobia: The fear of women.

Feticide: The deliberate killing of a fetus.

Funnel effect: The tendency to transform negative and threatening emotions into anger, a process socially reinforced primarily in males.

Gender-based violence: An attack directed against a (usually female) person due, at least in part, to a disadvantaged position within male-dominated social systems.

Gender stereotypes: Beliefs about men's and women's nature and places within the social order.

Group treatment: A variety of techniques for treating survivors by having them interact with fellow survivors.

Hate crime: A violation of law motivated by feelings of hostility against a specific group of people in society.
Homophobia: Hostility, fear, and/or intolerance of homosexuality.
Honeymoon phase: The first phase of the cycle of violence, in which control tactics are subtle and reinforcing for the partner.
Hostile environment sexual harassment: Frequent and pervasive sexually oriented behaviors that occur in a workplace and are unwelcome and offensive to other employee(s).
Hostile sexism: Directly expressed antipathy toward women.
Hyperindependence: The eschewal of adaptive behaviors associated with connecting to and being influenced by another person.
Hyperfemininity: Extreme adherence to (often toxic) cultural beliefs about how women should behave and experience themselves.
Hypermasculinity: Extreme adherence to (often toxic) cultural beliefs about how men should behave and experience themselves.
Implicit attitude: An unconscious predisposition to respond in a characteristic way to an object, event, or idea.
Infanticide: The deliberate killing of an infant.
Intervention: Responding to incidents of violence after their occurrences to diminish the negative effects on victims/survivors and hold perpetrators accountable for their crimes.
Intimate partner piolence (IPV): Physical, sexual, and/or psychological/emotional harm committed by a current or former partner or spouse.
Intimidation: The use of implicit or explicit threats of violence to secure cooperation from another person.
Isolation: A control tactic used by some perpetrators of intimate partner violence aimed at separating one's partner from his/her support system.
Issuing threats: A control tactic used by some perpetrators of intimate partner violence aimed at invoking fear in the partner that they may harm themselves or others.
Learned helplessness: A sense of despair developed from repeated exposure to aversive and uncontrollable stimuli.
Legitimate power: The ability to influence another that stems from a position of authority, status, or power.
Limited confidentiality: A feature of intervention programs in which offenders are not guaranteed the kind of control over personal information that is customary in psychotherapy.

Love obsessional stalker: A person who pursues a celebrity in an attempt to initiate a romantic relationship.

Macrosocietal perspective: An analysis of a societal phenomenon as being embedded in large cultural forces such as economic circumstances and historical factors.

Masculinity: Cultural beliefs about men's nature and place within the social order.

Means to do harm: Weapons, physiological wherewithal, or other access to resources that enable a person to commit an act of violence.

Misogynistic harasser: A man who expresses animosity toward women through displays of sexist hostility in the workplace.

Misogyny: Hostility toward women.

Misperceiving harasser: A sexual harasser who misinterprets a coworker's dress and/or behavior as an invitation to a sexual relationship.

Modern sexism: Prejudicial gender attitudes that are expressed through a denial of sexist discrimination and/or a reluctance to support women's issues.

Negative reinforcement: The process by which behavior is rewarded by the removal of an undesired consequence (e.g., pain, fear), thus increasing the likelihood of that behavior occurring again in the future; also known as "escape conditioning."

Normative level of coercion: The level of sexual imposition behaviors for men that is endorsed by the culture.

Offender accountability: An intervention approach in which the offender acknowledges his criminal behavior and accepts responsibility for it.

Old-fashioned sexism: Overtly prejudicial attitudes toward women.

Operantly conditioned attitudes: Predispositions to respond to objects, events, or ideas in characteristic ways that are strengthened through reinforcement or weakened through punishment.

Out-group homogeneity bias: A belief that every member of a group is identical in some characteristic.

Pathology of the perpetrator: Unhealthy personality and personal-history aspects of men who commit gender-based violence, such as negative attitudes toward women, acceptance of rape myths, and history of childhood abuse. Pathology, in this sense, does not refer to diagnosable psychiatric disorders.

Patriarchy: A social condition whereby male members of a society tend to dominate females members of that society, particularly in positions of power.

Personality disorder: An enduring pattern of behavior and inner experience that results in interpersonal inflexibility and disturbed relationships.

Positive reinforcement: The process by which one's behavior is rewarded by the presentation of a desired consequence (e.g., money, intimacy), thus increasing the likelihood of that behavior's recurrence.

Power: The ability to impose one's will upon another person, regardless of the wishes of that person.

Power rapist: One who commits rape to compensate for feelings of inadequacy.

Prejudice: A hostile or negative attitude toward a distinguishable group of people, based solely on their membership in that group.

Primary prevention: Attempts to avoid problematic behaviors that are addressed to the entire population.

Privilege: Advantages granted to particular groups of society on the basis of arbitrary characteristics (e.g., gender, race, class).

Proactive batterer: A perpetrator of intimate partner violence who abuses the partner in order to maintain dominance and control.

Probable cause: The judgment by police that there is a reasonable likelihood that a crime has been committed and that law enforcement personnel should therefore seek criminal suspects.

Prolonged exposure (PE, or flooding): A technique for reducing a survivor's fear responses to a stimulus by having the person repeatedly experience that stimulus.

Punishment: The process by which a behavior is followed with undesired consequences (e.g., yelling), thus decreasing the likelihood of that behavior's recurrence.

Quid pro quo sexual harassment: An attempt by a person (usually of authority) in a workplace to coerce sexual cooperation through a proposed exchange.

Rape: A nonconsensual, coerced, or forced act of genital penetration or envelopment.

Rape kit: A guide for the collection of evidence from the body of a recent rape or sexual assault victim.

Rape myths: Beliefs that women secretly wish to be raped, that they often make false accusations, and/or that they cannot be raped against their will.

Rape Trauma Syndrome (RTS): A cluster of behavioral, somatic, and psychological reactions that sometimes develop following rape or attempted rape.

Reactive batterer: An emotionally volatile person who commits intimate partner violence when feelings threaten to overwhelm him/her.

Referent power: Power that stems from one's identification with, attraction to, or respect for another person.

Resistance awareness: A set of skills that potential victims can learn to attempt to thwart potential attackers.

Reward power: The ability to influence another through positive and/or negative reinforcement.

Risk reduction: A set of behaviors, mainly involving limiting of activities, undertaken by a potential victim to reduce the probability of being assaulted.

Sadistic rapist: One who commits rape to attain sexual arousal.

Secondary prevention: Attempts to influence at-risk individuals so that they do not engage in problem behaviors.

Self-blame: The tendency for a victim to erroneously assume some direct or indirect responsibility for his/her victimization.

Sexual abuse: A control tactic used by some perpetrators of intimate partner violence aimed at humiliating, degrading, or objectifying a partner in ways typically perceived as sexual.

Sexual assault: Any form of nonconsensual, coerced, or forced touching of the areas of the body that are typically associated with sexuality.

Sexual Assault Nurse Examiner (SANE/SART nurse): A nurse who has been specially trained to examine and treat rape victims.

Sexual bribery: A form of quid pro quo sexual harassment in which incentives are offered in exchange for sexual cooperation.

Sexual extortion: A form of quid pro quo sexual harassment in which punishments are threatened if sexual cooperation is refused.

Sexual harassment: Unwanted sexual attention in the workplace.

Shattered assumptions: Basic beliefs about one's world that are questioned after experiencing personal trauma. These include the assumptions that the world is fair, and that one is invulnerable and basically good.

Simple obsessional stalker: A person who has had a previous relationship with the victim and pursues and harasses to punish the victim as a means for obtaining perceived justice.

Skills training: An approach to treatment with the goal of eliminating behavioral deficits in offenders.

Social norms approach: A prevention effort that utilizes public information campaigns to undermine false but commonly held beliefs about a problem behavior.
Social psychology: The study of the effect of situational influences on behavior.
Social support for violence: Cultural acceptance of gender-based violence and/or the underlying attitudes that encourage violence.
Stalking: The willful and repeated pursuit and/or harassment of another person.
Stereotype: An overgeneralization about an individual based on that person's group membership.
Stress inoculation training (SIT): A set of techniques based on behavioral psychotherapy for helping a rape survivor deal with specific fears.
Survivor: One who has been harmed by another and is in process of recovering from the effects of that harm.
Survivor-centered approach: A feature of intervention programs in which the offender focuses on the effects of his crimes upon the victims.
Tension phase: A stage in the cycle of violence in which the perpetrator is beginning to replace reinforcement with punishment in order to control and dominate his/her partner.
Tertiary prevention: An attempt to keep a negative outcome from recurring; also known as "relapse prevention."
Toxic masculinity: Characteristics of masculinity that create vulnerabilities in males toward unhealthy behaviors, depression, and violence against themselves and/or others.
Using children: A tactic used by some perpetrators of intimate partner violence in which the perpetrator threatens to harm the victim/survivor through negative influence on her/his children.
Using male privilege: A tactic used by some male perpetrators of intimate partner violence in which the perpetrator asserts advantages in the relationship based on sex or gender.
Victim: One who is currently being harmed or has been very recently harmed by another.

References

Abbey, A., Clinton, A. M., McAuslan, P., Zawacki, T., & Buck, P. O. (2002). Alcohol-involved rapes: Are they more violent? *Psychology of Women Quarterly, 26,* 99–109.

Abrams, K. M., & Robinson, G. E. (2002). Occupational effects of stalking. *Canadian Journal of Psychiatry, 47*(5), 468–472.

Acierno, R., Resnick, H., Kilpatrick, D. G., Saunders, B., & Best, C. L. (1999). Risk factors for rape, physical assault, and posttraumatic stress disorder in women: Examination of differential multivariate relationships. *Journal of Anxiety Disorders, 13,* 541–563.

Aldarondo, E. (2002). Evaluating the efficacy of interventions with men who batter. In E. Aldarondo and F. Mederos (Eds.), *Programs for men who batter: Intervention and prevention strategies in a diverse society* (pp. 1–20). Kingston, NJ: Civic Research Institute.

Allison, J. A., & Wrightsman, L. S. (1993). *Rape: The misunderstood crime.* Newbury Park, CA: Sage.

Allport, G. W. (1954). *The nature of prejudice.* New York: Perseus.

American Psychiatric Association (1980). *Diagnostic and statistical manual of mental disorders* (3rd ed.) (DSM-III). Washington, DC: American Psychiatric Association.

American Psychiatric Association (2000). *Diagnostic and statistical manual of mental disorders* (4th ed., text revision). Washington, DC: American Psychiatric Association.

American Psychological Association (1998). *Hate crimes today: An age-old foe in modern dress.* www.apa.org/pubinfo/hate/. Retrieved on March 14, 2006.

Anonymous. (2004). Personal communication.
Arias, I., & Pope, K. T. (1999). Psychological abuse: Implications for adjustment and commitment to leave violent partners. *Victims and Violence, 14*(1).
Aronson, E. (2004). *The social animal* (9th ed.). New York, NY: Worth.
Aronson, E., Wilson, T. D., & Akert, R. M. (2005). *Social psychology* (5th ed.). Englewood Cliffs, NJ: Prentice Hall.
Asch, S. E. (1965). Effects of group pressure upon the modification and distortion of judgments. In H. Proshansky & B. Seidenberg (Eds.), *Basic studies in social psychology* (pp. 271–304). New York: Holt, Rinehart, & Winston.
Atkeson, B. M., Calhous, K. S., Resick, P. A., & Ellis, E. M. (1982). Victims of rape: Repeated assessment of depressive symptoms. *Journal of Consulting and Clinical Psychology, 50,* 96–102.
Avina, C., & O'Donohue, W. (2002). Sexual harassment and PTSD: Is sexual harassment diagnosable trauma? *Journal of Traumatic Stress, 15,* 69–75.
Babcock, J., Green, C., & Robie, C. (2004). Does batterers' treatment work?: A meta-analytic review of domestic violence treatment outcome research. *Clinical Psychology Review, 23*(8), 1023–1053.
Bachrach, P., & Baratz, M.S. (1963). Decisions and nondecisions: An analytical framework. *American Political Science Review, 57*(3), 632–642.
Baker, N., & McBride, B. (1991). *Clinical applications of EMDR in a law enforcement environment: Observations of the psychological.* Service Unit of the L.A. County Sheriff's Department Paper Presented at the American Psychological Association Annual Convention, San Francisco.
Ballenger, J. C., Davidson, J. R. T., Lecrubier, Y., & Nutt, D. J. (2000). Consensus statement on posttraumatic stress disorder from the International Consensus Group on Depression and Anxiety. *Journal of Clinical Psychiatry, 61,* 60–66.
Bard, M. & Sangrey, D. (1979). *The crime victim's book.* New York: Brunner/Mazel.
Baron, R. A., Byrne, D., & Branscome, N. R. (2006). *Social psychology* (11th ed.). Boston: Allyn & Bacon.
Bart, P. B., & O'Brien, P. H. (1985). *Stopping rape.* Exeter, England: A. Wheaton & Co.
Basile, K. C., & Saltzman, L. E. (2002). *Sexual violence surveillance: Uniform definitions and recommended data elements, Version 1.0* . Atlanta, GA: Centers for Disease Control and Prevention.
Basow, S. A. (1992). *Gender: Stereotypes and roles* (3rd ed.). Monterey, CA: Brooks/Cole.
Basow, S. A. (1995). Student evaluations of college professors: When gender matters. *Journal of Educational Psychology, 87*(4), 656–665.
Baumgartner, P. A. (1983). *My daddy might have loved me: Student perceptions of differences between being male and being female.* Denver: Institute for Equality in Education, University of Colorado at Denver.
Beach, S. H., Jouriles, E. N., & O'Leary, K. D. (1985). Extramarital sex: Impact on depression and communication in couples seeking marital therapy. *Journal of Sex & Marital Therapy, 11,* 99–108.
Becker, J. V., Skinner, L. J., Abel, G. G., Axelrod, R., & Treacy E. C. (1984). Depressive symptoms associated with sexual assault. *Journal of Sex and Marital Therapy, 10,* 185–192.
Bem, D. J. (1972). Self-perception theory. In L. Berkowitz (Ed.), *Advances in experimental social psychology* (Vol. 6, pp. 1–62). New York: Academic Press.

Bennett, L., & Williams, O. J. (2001). Intervention programs for men who batter. In C. M. Renzetti, J. L. Edleson, & R. K. Bergen (Eds.), *Sourcebook on violence against women*. Thousand Oaks, CA: Sage.

Berkowitz, A. D. (1994). *Men and rape: Theory, research, and prevention programs in higher education*. San Francisco: Jossey Bass.

Berkowitz, A. D. (2004). *Men's role in preventing violence against women*. Applied Research Forum of VAWNet. Alanberkowitz.com. Retrieved on March 2, 2006.

Berkowitz, A. D. (2005). An overview of the social norms approach. In L. C. Lederman & L. P. Stewart (Eds.), *Changing the culture of college drinking: A socially situated health communication campaign*. Cresskill, NJ: Hampton.

Bienen, L. (1983). Rape reform legislation in the United States: A look at some practical effects. *Victimology: An International Journal, 8*, 139–151.

Blumstein, P. & Schwartz, P. (1983). *American couples: money, work, sex*. New York: Morrow.

Bolton, F. G., Morris, L. A., & MacEachron, A. E. (1989). *Males at risk*. Newbury Park, CA: Sage.

Boswell, A. A., & Spade, J. Z. (1996). Fraternities and collegiate rape culture: Why are some fraternities more dangerous places for women? *Gender and Society, 10(2)*, 133–147.

Brannon, R. (1985). Dimensions of the male sex role in America. In A.G. Sargent, *Beyond sex roles* (2nd ed., pp. 296–316). New York: West.

Breslau, N., Chilcoat, H. D., Kessler, R. C., Peterson, E. L., & Lucia, V. C. (1999). Vulnerability to assaultive violence: Further specification of the sex difference in posttraumatic stress disorder. *Psychological Medicine, 29*, 813–821.

Brownmiller, S. (1975). *Against our will: Men, women, and rape*. New York: Simon & Schuster.

Bryant preliminary hearing contained graphic info, hints of what's to come. (2003, October 10). www.courttv.com/trials/bryant/101003_prelim_ap.html. Retrieved February 22, 2006.

Bryant prosecutors seek to delay trial as Accuser's father blasts judge in letter. (2004, August 12). www.courttv.com/trials/bryant/081204_letter_ap.html. Retrieved February 22, 2006.

Bryant's attorneys expected to put blame on accuser in trial. (2004, August 23). www.courttv.com/trials/bryant/082304_defense_ap.html. Retrieved February 22, 2006.

Bureau of Justice Statistics. (1997). Sex offenses and offenders. On line at http://www.ojp.usdoj.gov/bjs/pub/pdf/soo.pdf. Retrieved March 12, 2006.

Bureau of Justice Statistics. (2003). Criminal victimization, 2002. On line at http://www.ojp.usdoj.gov/bjs/pub/pdf/cv02.pdf. Retrieved March 12, 2006.

Burt, M. R. (1980). Cultural myths and supports for rape. *Journal of Personality and Social Psychology, 37*, 217–230.

Cable News Network (CNN). (2006, April 26). *Larry King Live: Interview with Mattie Stepanek* (television program).

Cacioppo, J. T., Marshall-Goodell, B. S., Tassinary, L. G., & Petty, R. E. (1992). Rudimentary determinants of attitudes: Classical conditioning is more effective when prior knowledge about the attitude stimulus is low than high. *Journal of Experimental Social Psychology, 28*, 207–233.

REFERENCES

Campbell, J. C., & Soeken, K. L. (1999). Forced sex and intimate partner violence: Effects on women's risk and women's health. *Violence Against Women, 3,* 271–293.

Campbell, R., & Martin, P. Y. (2001). Services for sexual assault survivors: The role of rape crisis centers. In C. Renzetti, J. Edleson, & R. Bergen (Eds.), *Sourcebook on violence against women.* Thousand Oaks, CA: Sage.

Campbell, R., Sullivan, C. M., & Davidson, W. S. (1995). Women who use domestic violence shelters: Changes in depression over time. *Psychology of Women Quarterly, 19,* 235–255.

Campbell, R., Wasco, S. M., Ahrens, C. E., Sefl, T., & Barnes, H. E. (2001). Preventing the "second rape:" Rape survivors' experiences with community service providers. *Journal of Interpersonal Violence, 16,* 1239–1259.

Center for Sex Offender Management (2000, January). *Community supervision of the sex offender: An overview of current and promising practices.* Washington, DC: U.S. Department of Justice Grant No. 97-WT-VX-KOO7.

Clinton-Sherrod, M., Gibbs, D., Vincus, A., Squire, S. Cignetti, C., Pettibone, K., et al. (2003). Report describing projects designed to prevent first-time male perpetration of sexual violence. www.nsvrc.org/resources/docs/rti_report.pdf. Retrieved on March 21, 2006.

Coltrane, S. (1998). Theorizing masculinities in contemporary social science. In D. L. Anselmi & A. L. Law (Eds.), *Questions of gender: perspectives and paradoxes* (pp. 76–88). Boston: McGraw-Hill.

Corcoran, C. B. (1992). From victim control to social change: A feminist perspective on campus rape prevention programs. In J. Chrisler & D. Howard (Eds.), *New directions in feminist psychology* (pp. 130–140). New York: Springer.

CourtTV.com (2004). Judge dismisses Kobe Bryant rape case. On line at http://www.courttv.com/trials/bryant/090104_ctv.html#continue. Retrieved January 24, 2007.

Crites, S. L., Fabrigar, L. R., & Petty, R. E. (1994). Measuring the affective and cognitive properties of attitudes: Conceptual and methodological issues. *Personality and Social Psychology Bulletin, 20,* 619–634.

Cromwell, N. A., & Burgess, A. W. (Eds) (1996). *Understanding violence against women.* Washington, DC: National Academy Press.

Crull, P. (1982). Stress effects of sexual harassment on the job. Implications for counselling. *American Journal of Orthopsychiatry, 52,* 539–544.

Curtin, J. J., Patrick, C. J., Lang, A. R., Cacioppo, J. T., & Birbaumer, N. (2001). Alcohol affects emotion through cognition. *Psychological Science, 12,* 527–531.

Dansky, B. S. & Kilpatrick, D. G. (1997). Effects of sexual harassment. In W. O'Donohue (Ed.), *Sexual Harassment: Theory, Research, and Treatment* (pp. 152–174).

DeAngelis, T. (1992, December). Hill-Thomas face-off brought harassment issues out in open. *APA Monitor, 23*(12), 32.

Deaux, K., Winton, W., Crowley, M., & Lewis, L. L. (1985). Level of categorization and content of gender stereotypes. *Social Cognition, 3,* 145–167.

DeCecco, J. (1984). *Homophobia: An overview.* New York: Haworth.

Deiner, E. (1980). De-individuation: the absence of self-awareness and self-regulation in group members. In P. Paulus (Ed.), *The psychology of group influence* (pp. 1160–71). Hillsdale, NJ: Lawrence Erlbaum.

Derlega, V. J., Metts, S., Petronio, S., & Margulis, S.T. (1993). *Self-disclosure*. Newbury Park, CA: Sage.
Devine, P. G. (1989). Stereotypes and prejudice: Their automatic and controlled components. *Journal of Personality and Social Psychology, 56*, 5–18.
Dickinson, L. M., Gruy, F. V., III, Dickinson, W. P., & Candib, L. M. (1999). Health-related quality of life and symptom profiles of female survivors of sexual abuse in primary care. *Archives of Family Medicine. 8*, 35–43.
Douglas, H. (1991). Assessing violent couples. *Families in Society, 71*, 525-535.
D'Ovidio, R., & Doyle, J. (2003, March). A study on cyberstalking: Understanding investigative hurdles. *FBI Law Enforcement Bulletin, 72*(3), 10–17.
Dovidio, J. F., Mann, J. A., & Gaertner, S. L. (1989). Resistance to affirmative action: The implication of aversive racism. In F. A. Blanchard & F. J. Crosby (Eds.),, *Affirmative action in perspective* (pp. 83–102). New York: Springer-Verlag.
Dutton, D. G., & Starzomsky, A. J. (1993). Borderline personality in perpetrators of psychological and physical abuse. *Violence and Victims, 2*(3), 145–156.
Dutton, D. G., & Golant, S. K. (1995). *The batterer: A psychological profile*. New York: Basic.
Eagly, A. H., & Chaiken, S. (1998). Attitude structure and function. In D. T. Gilbert, S. T. Fiske, & G. Lindzey (Eds.), *Handbook of social psychology* (4th ed., Vol. 1, pp. 269–322). New York: McGraw-Hill.
Earle, J. P. (1992). *Acquaintance rape workshops: Their effectiveness in changing the attitudes of first year college men*. Unpublished doctoral dissertation, University of Connecticut.
Epstein, A. (Director). (2003). *Until the violence stops* (documentary film). Aired on Lifetime Television Network, February 14, 2004.
Equal Employment Opportunity Commission (EEOC) (1980). Discrimination because of sex under Title VII of the Civil Rights Act 1964, as amended; adoption of interim interpretive guidelines. *Federal Register, 45*, 25024–25025.
Erickson, R. J., & Gecas, V. (1991). Social class and fatherhood. In F.W. Bozett and S.M. Hanson (Eds.), *Fatherhood and families in cultural context (*pp. 114–137). New York: Springer.
Erwin, P. A., & Vidales, G. (2001). Domestic violence, people of color and the criminal justice system: A case for prevention. *Domestic Violence Research for Racial Justice Report* (pp. 1–29). On line at www.endabuse.org. Retrieved February 21, 2006.
Estrich, S. (1987). *Real rape*. Cambridge, MA: Harvard University Press.
Ewing, C.P. (1987). *Battered women who kill*. New York: Lexington.
Fagan, J. (1996). *The criminalization of domestic violence: Promises and limits*. (NCJ 157641). Washington, DC: National Institute of Justice, U.S. Department of Justice.
Fals-Stewart, W. (2003). The occurrence of partner physical aggression on days of alcohol consumption: a longitudinal diary study. *Journal of Consulting Clinical Psychology, 71*(1), 41–52.
Falsetti, S. (1997). The decision-making process of choosing a treatment for patients with civilian trauma-related PTSD. *Cognitive and Behavioral Practice, 4*, 99–121.
Falsetti, S. A., & Bernat, J. A. (2000). Practice guidelines: Rape and sexual assault. http:www.vawprevention.org/advocacy/rape.shtml. Retrieved March 1, 2006.

Far, J. & Miller, J. (2003). The small group norms challenging model: social norms interventions with targeted high risk groups. In H. W. Perkins (Ed.), *The social norms approach to preventing school and college age substance abuse: A handbook for educators, counselors, clinicians.* San Francisco: Jossey-Bass.

Fazio, R. H., & Olson, M. A. (2003). Implicit measures in social cognition research: Their meaning and use. *Annual Review of Psychology, 54,* 297–327.

Federal Bureau of Investigation. (2002). Uniform Crime Reports: Crime in the United States, 2002. On line at http://www.fbi.gov/ucr/02cius.htm. Retrieved March 12, 2006.

Federal Bureau of Investigation. (2003). Uniform Crime Reports: Crime in the United States, 2003. On line at http://www.fbi.gov/ucr/03cius.htm. Retrieved March 12, 2006.

Federal Bureau of Investigation. (2004). Uniform Crime Reports: Crime in the United States, 2004. On line at http://www.fbi.gov/ucr/04cius.htm. Retrieved March 12, 2006.

Feild, H. S. (1978). Attitudes toward rape: A comparative analysis of police, rapists, crisis counselors, and citizens. *Journal of Personality and Social Psychology, 36,* 156–179.

Feild, H. S., & Barnett, N. J. (1978). Simulated jury trials: Students vs. "real" people as jurors. *Journal of Social Psychology, 104,* 287–293.

Feild, H. S., & Bienen, L. B. (1980). *Jurors and rape.* Lexington, MA: D.C. Health.

Fernandez-Lanier, Chard-Wierschem, D. J., & Hall, D. (2004). Comparison of domestic violence reporting and arrest rates in New York state: Analysis of the 1997 and 2000 domestic incident statistical databases. *Domestic violence: Research in Review* (Table 6A). http://criminaljustice.state.ny.us/crimnet/ojsa/domviol_ rinr/table6a.htm. Retrieved February 1, 2006.

Festinger, L. (1957). *A theory of cognitive dissonance.* Evanston, IL: Row, Peterson.

Fisher, B. S., Cullen, F. T., & Turner, M. G. (2000). *The sexual victimization of college women, research in brief.* (NCJ 182369). Washington, DC: National Institute of Justice, Department of Justice.

Fitzgerald, L. F. (1992). *Sexual harassment in higher education: Concepts and issues.* Washington, DC: National Education Association.

Fitzgerald, L. F. (1993). Sexual harassment: Violence against women in the workplace. *American Psychologist, 48*(10), 1070–1076.

Fletcher, G. J. O., Fincham, F. D., Cramer, L., & Heron, N. (1987). The role of attributions in the development of dating relationships. *Journal of Personality and Social Psychology, 53,* 510–517.

Foa, E. B., Hearst-Ikeda, D. E., & Perry, K. (1995). Evaluation of a brief cognitive behavioral program for the prevention of chronic PTSD in recent assault victims. *Journal of Consulting and Clinical Psychology, 63,* 948–955.

Foa, E. B., Rothbaum, B. O., Riggs, D. S., & Murdock, T. (1991). Treatment of posttraumatic stress disorder in rape victims: A comparison between cognitive behavioral procedures and counseling. *Journal of Consulting and Clinical Psychology, 59,* 715–723.

Follette, V. M., Polusny, M. A., Bechtle, A. E., Naugle, A. E. (1996). Cumulative trauma: The impact of child sexual abuse, adult sexual assault, and spouse abuse. *Journal of Traumatic Stress, 9*(1), 25–35.

Fontana, A., & Rosenheck, R. (1998). Duty-related and sexual stress in the etiology of PTSD among women veterans who seek treatment. *Psychiatric Services, 49,* 658–662.

Foote, W. E. & Goodman-Delahunty, J. (2004). *Evaluating sexual harassment: Psychological, social, and legal considerations in forensic examinations.* Washington, DC: American Psychological Association.

Forsythe, D. R. (1999). *Group Dynamics* (3rd ed.). Belmont, CA: Wadsworth.

Foubert, J. D. (2005). *The Men's Program: A peer education guide to rape prevention* (3rd ed.). New York: Taylor & Francis.

Frank, E., & Stewart, B. D. (1984). Depressive symptoms in rape victims: A revisit. *Journal of Affective Disorders, 1,* 269–277.

Freeman-Longo, R. E. (1996). Prevention or problem? *Sexual Abuse: A Journal of Research and Treatment, 8(2),* 91–100.

French, J. R. P., & Raven, B. H. (1959). The bases of social power. In D. Cartwright (Ed.), *Studies in social power* (pp. 150–167). Ann Arbor: University of Michigan.

Frieze, I. H., & Browne, A. (1989). Violence in marriage. In L. Ohlin & M. Tonry (Eds.), *Family violence* (pp. 163–218). Chicago: University of Chicago Press.

Funk, R. E. (1997). Men who are raped: A profeminist perspective. In M. Scarce, *Male on male rape: The hidden toll of stigma and shame* (pp. 221–231). New York: Plenum.

Gaertner, S. L., & Dovidio, J. F. (1986). The aversive form of racism. In J. F. Dovidio & S. L. Gaertner (Eds.), *Prejudice, discrimination, and racism* (pp. 61–89). Orlando, FL: Academic Press.

Galeone, M., Norbet, T., Kilmartin, C. T., & Altman, J. (1998). *The use of theatre for education and attitude change.* Paper presented at the Spring Convention of the Virginia Psychological Association.

Gelles, R. J., Straus, M. A., & Steinmetz, S. K. (1980). *Behind closed doors: Violence in American Families.* New York: Doubleday.

Gelles, R. J., Straus, M. A., & Steinmetz, S. K. (1988) *Intimate violence: The causes and consequences of abuse in the American family.* New York: Touchstone.

Gidycz, C. A., Coble, C. N., Lathan, L., & Layman, M. J. (1993). Sexual assault experience in adulthood and prior victimization experiences: A prospective analysis, *Psychology of Women Quarterly, 7,* 151–168.

Gidycz, C. A., Hanson, K., & Layman, M. J. (1995). A prospective analysis of the relationships among sexual assault experiences: An extension of previous findings. *Psychology of Women Quarterly, 19,* 5–29.

Gidycz, C. A., & Koss, M. P. (1991). The effects of acquaintance rape on the female victim. In A. Parrot & L. Bechhofer (Eds.), *Acquaintance rape: The hidden crime* (pp. 270–283). New York: Wiley.

Gilmore, D. (1990). *Manhood in the making: Cultural concepts of masculinity.* New Haven, CT: Yale University Press.

Glick, P., & Fiske, S. T. (1996). The ambivalent sexism inventory: Differentiating hostile and benevolent sexism. *Journal of Personality and Social Psychology, 70,* 491–512.

Glick, P. & Fiske, S. T. (2001a). An ambivalent alliance: Hostile and benevolent sexism as complementary justifications for gender inequality. *American Psychologist. 56*(2), 109–118.

Glick, P., & Fiske, S. T. (2001b). Ambivalent sexism. In M. P. Zanna (Ed.), *Advances in experimental social psychology* (Vol. 33, pp. 115–188). Thousand Oaks, CA: Academic Press.

Golding, J. M. (1999). Intimate partner violence as a risk factor for mental disorders: A meta-analysis. *Journal of Family Violence, 14*(2), 99.

Gondolf, E. W. (1988). Who are those guys? Toward a behavioral typology of batterers. *Violence and Victims, 3,* 187–203.

Gondolf, E. W. (1995). Characteristics of batterers in a multi-site evaluation of batterer intervention systems: A preliminary report. www.mincava.umn.edu. Retrieved February 1, 2006.

Gondolf, E. W. (2002). *Batterer intervention systems: Issues, outcomes, and recommendations.* Thousand Oaks, CA: Sage.

Gondolf, E. W., & Jones, A. S. (2001). The program effect of batterer programs in three cities. *Violence and Victims, 16*(6), 693–704.

Gordon, M. T., & Riger, S. (1989). *The female fear.* New York: Free Press.

Greenfield, L. A., & Rand, M. R. (1998). *Violence by intimates.* (NCJ 167237). Washington, DC: U.S. National Institute of Justice, Department of Justice.

Groth, A. N. (1979). *Men who rape.* New York: Plenum.

Grusznski, R., & Bankovics, G. (1990). Treating men who batter: A group approach. In D. Moore & F. Leafgren (Eds.), *Men in conflict* (pp. 201–212). Alexandria, VA: American Association for Counseling and Development.

Haines, M. P. (1997). *A social norms approach to preventing binge drinking at colleges and universities.* Newton, MA: Higher Education Center for Alcohol and Other Drug Prevention.

Hall, G. C. N. (1996). *Theory-based assessment, treatment, and prevention of sexual aggression.* New York: Oxford University Press.

Halligan, S. L., & Yehuda, R. (2000). Risk factors for PTSD. *PTSD Research Quarterly, 11(2),* 1–8.

Hamby, S. L., & Sugarman, D. B. (1996). *Power and partner violence.* Paper presented at the 104th annual meeting of the American Psychological Association, Toronto, Canada.

Hammock, G., & O'Hearn, R. (2002). Psychological aggression in dating relationships: Predictive models for males and females. *Violence and Victims, 17,* 525–540.

Hanson, R. K., & Bussiere, M. T. (1998). Predicting relapse: A meta-analysis of sexual offender recidivism studies. *Journal of Consulting and Clinical Psychology, 66,* 348–362.

Hanson, R. K., Gordon, A., Harris, A. J. R., Marques, J. K., Murphy, W., Quinsey, V. L., & Seto, M. C. (2002). First report of the collaborative outcome data project on the effectiveness of treatment of sex offenders. *Sexual Abuse: A Journal of Research & Treatment, 14*(2), 169–194.

Hanson Frieze, I. (2005). *Hurting the one you love: Violence in relationships.* Belmont, CA: Thomson Wadsworth.

Hart, H. L. A. (1968). *Punishment and responsibility: Essays in the philosophy of law.* New York: Oxford University Press.

Harvey, M. R., & Herman, J. L. (1992). The trauma of sexual victimization: Feminist contributions to theory, research, and practice. *PTSD Research Quarterly, 3(3),* 1–3.

Hatfield, E., Traupmann, J., Sprecher, S., Utne, M., & Hay, M. (1985). Equity in close relationships. In W. Ickes (Ed.), *Compatible and incompatible relationships* (pp. 91–117). New York: Springer-Verlag.

Hawkins, S. (2006). Evaluation findings: Men can stop rape men of strength club, 2004–2005. Washington, DC: Men Can Stop Rape.

Heider, F. (1958). *The psychology of interpersonal relations.* New York: Wiley.

Heise, L., Ellsberg, M., & Gottemoeller, M. (1999, December). Ending violence against women. *Population Reports,* Series L, No. 11.

Herek, G. M., Cogan, J., & Gillis, R. J. (1997, November). *The impact of hate crime victimization.* Paper presented at a congressional briefing co-sponsored by the American Psychological Association and the Society for the Psychological Study of Social Issues, Washington, DC.

Holley, J. & Sweezey, C. (2006, March 30). Rape accusation against lacrosse players roils Duke. *The Washington Post,* p. E1.

Holtzworth-Munroe, A. (2000). A typology of men who are violent toward their female partners: Making sense of the heterogeneity in husband violence. *Current Directions in Psychological Science, 9,* 140–143.

Holtzworth-Munroe, A., Meehan, J. C., Herron, K., Rehman, U., & Stuart, G. L. (2001). Testing the Holtzworth-Munroe and Stuart (1994) batterer typology. *Journal of Consulting Clinical Psychology, 68*(6), 1000–1019.

Holtzworth-Munroe, A. & Stuart, G.L. (1994). Typologies of male batterers: Three subtypes and the differences among them. *Psychology-Bulletin, 116*(3), 476–497.

hooks, b. (1992). *Black looks: Race and representation.* Boston: South End Press.

Hyer, L. (1995). Use of EMDR in a "dementing" PTSD survivor. *Clinical Gerontologist, 16,* 70–73.

Jacobson, N. (1993). *Domestic violence: What are the marriages like?* [Videotape]. (Available from Audio Visual Education Network, Inc., 16052 28th Avenue NE, Seatlle, WA 98155)

Jackson, S., Feder, L., Forde, D. R., Davis, R. C., Maxwell, C. D., & Taylor, B.G. (2003). *Batterer intervention programs: Where do we go from here?* (NCJ 195079). Washington, DC: National Institute of Justice, U.S. Department of Justice.

Jacupak, M., Lisak, D., & Roemer, L. (2002). The role of masculine ideology and masculine gender role stress in men's perpetration of relationship violence. *Psychology of Men and Masculinity, 3,* 97–106.

Janoff-Bulman, R. (1979). Characterological versus behavioral self-blame: Inquiries into depression and blame. *Journal of Personality and Social Psychology, 37,* 1798–1809.

Janoff-Bulman, R. (1985a). The aftermath of victimization: Rebuilding shattered assumptions. In C. R. Figley (Ed.), *Trauma and its wake:* The *study and treatment of posttraumatic stress disorder* (pp. 15–35). New York: Brunner/Mazel.

Janoff-Bulman, R. (1985b). Criminal vs. non-criminal victimization: Victims' reactions. *Victimology: An International Journal, 10,* 498–511.

Janoff-Bulman, R. (1992). *Shattered assumptions: Towards a new psychology of trauma.* New York: Free Press.

Janoff-Bulman, R. (1998). From terror to appreciation: Confronting chance after extreme misfortune. *Psychological Inquiry, 9*(2), 99–101.

Janoff-Bulman, R.,,& Frieze, I. H. (1983). A theoretical perspective for understanding reactions to victimization. *Journal of Social Issues, 39*(2), 1–17.

Jaschik-Herman, M.L., & Fisk, A. (1995). Women's perceptions and labeling of sexual harassment in academia before and after the Hill-Thomas hearings. *Sex Roles, 33* (5–6), 439–446.

Johnson, M. P. (1995). Patriarchal terrorism and common couple violence: Two forms of violence against women. *Journal of Marriage and the Family, 57,* 283–295.

Kanin, E. J., (1957). Male aggression in dating-courtship relations. *American Journal of Sociology, 63,* 197–204.

Kanin, E. J., & Parcell, S. R. (1977). Sexual aggression: A second look at the offended female. *Archives of Sexual Behavior, 6,* 67–76.

Katz, B. L. (1991). The psychological impact of stranger versus nonstranger rape on victims' recovery. In A. Parrot & L. Bechhofer (Eds.), *Acquaintance rape: The hidden crime* (pp. 251–269). New York: John Wiley.

Katz, J. (2002). Building a "big tent" approach to ending men's violence. http://www.endabuse.org/bpi/discussion1/Discussion1-short.pdf

Katz, J. (2003). *MVP playbook for male college students.* Boston: Self.

Kawakami, K., Dovidio, J. F., Moll, J., Hermsen, S., & Russin, A. (2000). Just say no to stereotyping: effects of training in the negation of language use in intergroup contexts: The linguistic intergroup bias. *Journal of Personality and Social Psychology, 57,* 981–983.

Kersting, K. (2003). New hope for sex offender treatment. *Monitor on psychology, 34*(7), 52.

Kilmartin, C., & Funk, R. E. (2004). A frank and open discussion for men in the movement against violence. Professional Workshop, Tennessee Coalition Against Domestic and Sexual Violence, 2nd Annual Conference.

Kilmartin, C. T., & Berkowitz, A .D. (2005). *Sexual assault in context: Teaching men about gender.* Mahwah, NJ: Lawrence Erlbaum Associates.

Kilmartin, C. T., Chirico, B., & Leemann, M. (1997). *The White Ribbon Campaign: Evidence for social change on a college campus.* Paper presented at the Spring Convention of the Virginia Psychological Association.

Kilmartin, C. T., Conway, A., Friedberg, A., McQuoid, T., Tschan, T., & Norbet, T. (1999, April). *Using the social norms model to encourage male college students to challenge rape-supportive attitudes in male peers.* Paper presented at the Virginia Psychological Association Spring Conference, Virginia Beach, VA.

Kilmartin, C. T., & Funk, R. E. (2004). *A frank and open discussion on men in the movement against violence.* Professional workshop, Tennessee Coalition Against Domestic and Sexual Violence Annual Conference.

Kilmartin, C., Green, A., Heinzen, H., Kuchler, M., & Smith, T. (2004). *Sexual assault in context: Teaching college men about gender.* Poster presentation at the Annual Convention of the American Psychological Association, Honolulu, HI.

Kilmartin, C. T. (2005). *Sexual assault in context: Teaching college men about gender.* Mahwah, NJ: Erlbaum.

Kilmartin, C. T. (2007). *The masculine self* (3rd ed.). Cornwall-on-Hudson, NY: Sloan.

Kilmartin, C. T., Conway, A., Friedbert, A., McQuoid, T., & Tschan, T. (1999, April). *Social conformity and sexism in all male peer groups.* Paper presented at the annual meeting of the Virginia Psychological Association, Virginia Beach, VA.

Kilpatrick, D. G., Edmunds, C., & Seymour, A. (1992). *Rape in America: A report to the nation*. Charleston, SC: National Victims Center & the Crime Victims Research and Treatment Center, Medical University of South Carolina.

Kilpatrick, D. G., Resick, P., & Veronen, L. (1981). Effects of a rape experience: A longitudinal study. *Journal of Social Issues, 37*(4), 105–112.

Kilpatrick, D. G., Saunders, B. E., Amick-McMullan, A., Best, C. L., Veronen, L. J. & Resnick, H. S. (1989). Victim and crime factors associated with the development of crime related posttraumatic stress disorder. *Behavior Therapy, 20*, 199–214.

Kilpatrick, D. G., Veronen, L. J., & Resick, P. A. (1982). Psychological sequelae to rape: Assessment and treatment strategies. In D.M. Doleys, R. I. Meredity, & A. R. Ciminero (Eds.), *Behavioral medicine: Assessment and treatment strategies* (pp. 214–231). New York: Plenum

Kimmel, M. S. (2002). 'Gender symmetry' in domestic violence: A substantive and methodological research review. Women's use of violence in intimate relationships, part 1. *Violence Against Women* [Special Issue], *8*(11), 1332–1363.

Kimmel, M. S. (2006). *Manhood in America* (2nd. ed.). New York: Oxford University Press.

Kimmel, M. S., & Mahler, M. (2003). Adolescent masculinity, homophobia, and violence: Random school shootings, 1982–2001. *American Behavioral Scientist, 46*(10), 1439–1458.

Kleinknecht, R. A., & Morgan, M. P. (1992). Treatment of posttraumatic stress disorder with eye movement desensitization. *Journal of Behavioral Therapy and Experimental Psychiatry, 23*(1), 43–49.

Knoll, J. (2004). *Psychiatric aspects of stalking*. Symposium conducted at the meeting of the Enhanced Advocacy Conference, Waterville Valley, NH.

Koss, M. P. (1988). Hidden rape: Incidence, prevalence, and descriptive characteristics of sexual aggression and victimization in a national sample of college students. In A. W. Burgess (Ed.), *Sexual assault* (Vol. 2, pp. 3–25). New York: Garland.

Koss, M. P. (2000). Blame, shame, and community: Justice responses to violence against women. *American Psychologist, 55*, 1332–1343.

Koss, M. P., Bailey, J. A., Yuan, N. P., Hererra, V. M., & Lichter, E. L. (2003). Depression and PTSD in survivors of male violence: Research and training initiatives to facilitate recovery. *Psychology of Women Quarterly, 27*, 130–142.

Koss, M. P., & Burkhart, B. R. (1989). A conceptual analysis of rape victimization: Long-term effects and implications for treatment. *Psychology of Women Quarterly, 13*, 27–40.

Koss, M. P., Gidycz, C. A., & Wisniewski, N. (1987). The scope of rape: Incidence and prevalence of sexual aggression and victimization in a national sample of higher education students. *Journal of Consulting and Clinical Psychology, 55*, 162–170.

Koss, M. P. & Harvey, M. R. (1989). *The rape victim: Clinical and community interventions* (2nd ed.). Newbury Park, CA: Sage.

Koss, M. P., Heise, L., and Russo, N. F. (1994). The global health burden of rape. *Psychology of Women Quarterly, 18*, 509–530.

Koss, M. P. & Oros, C. J. (1982). Sexual experiences survey: A research instrument investigating sexual aggression and victimization. *Journal of Consulting and Clinical Psychology, 50(1)*, 455–457.

Krantz, D. L. (1998). Taming chance: Social science and everyday narratives. *Psychological Inquiry*, 9(2), 87–94.
Landes, A. B., Squyres, S. & Quiram, J. (Eds.) (1997). *Violent relationships: Battering and abuse among adults*. Wylie, TX: Information Plus.
Lane Council of Governments (2003). *Managing sex offenders in the community: A national overview*. Eugene, OR: Author.
Lang, J. (2002). Introduction. In *Partners in change: Working with men to end gender-based violence* (pp. 1–12). Santo Domingo, Dominican Republic: INSTRAW.
Largen, M. A. (1988). Rape-law reform: An analysis. In A. W. Burgess (Ed.), *Rape and sexual assault II* (pp. 271–292). New York: Garland.
Larimer, M. E., Lydum, A. R., Anderson, B. K., & Turner, A. P. (1999). Male and female recipients of unwanted sexual contact in a college student sample: Prevalence rates, alcohol use, and depression symptoms. *Sex Roles: A Journal of Research*, 40(3–4), 295–308.
Ledray, L. E. (1999). *Sexual assault nurse examiner, SANE: Development & operation guide*. Washington, DC: U.S. Department of Justice, Office of Justice Programs..
Lefkowitz, B. (1997). *Our guys: The Glen Ridge rape and the secret life of the perfect suburb*. Berkley: University of California Press.
Lepowsky, M. (1999). Women, men, and aggression in an egalitarian society. In L. A. Peplau, S. C. DeBro, R. C. Veniegas, & P. L. Taylor, (Eds.), *Gender, culture, and ethnicity: Current research about women and men.* (pp. 284–290). Mountain View, CA: Mayfield.
Lerner, G. (1986). *The creation of patriarchy*. New York: Oxford University Press.
Lerner, M. (1986). *Surplus powerlessness: The psychodynamics of everyday life— and the psychology of individual and social transformation.* Oakland, CA: Institute for Labor & Mental Health.
Lerner, M. J. (1970) The desire for justice and reactions to victims. In J. Macaulay & L. Berkowitz (Eds.), *Altruism and helping behavior* (pp. 205–229). Orlando, FL: Academic Press.
Lerner, J. J., & Miller, D. T. (1978). Just world research and the attribution process: Looking back and ahead. *Psychological Bulletin, 85,* 1030–1051.
Linville, P. W., Fischer, G. W., & Salovey, P. (1989). Perceived distributions of characteristics of in-group and out-group members: Empirical evidence and a computer simulation. *Journal of Personality and Social Psychology*, 57, 165–188.
Lipman, M. (Producer). (1982). *To have and to hold: A film about men who batter women.* Franklin Lakes, NJ: New Day Films.
Lisak, D. (1991). Sexual aggression, masculinity, and fathers. *Signs: Journal of Women in Culture and Society, 16,* 238–262.
Lisak, D. (1993). Men as victims: Challenging cultural myths. *Journal of Traumatic Stress,* 6(4), 577–580.
Lisak, D. & Miller, P. M. (2002). Repeat rape and multiple offending among undetected rapists. *Violence and Victims, 17*(1), 73–84.
Lisak, D., & Roth, S. (1988). Motivational factors in nonincarcerated sexually aggressive men. *Journal of Personality and Social Psychology,* 55, 795–802.

Lombardi, J. (2004, August 16). Defending Joel Steinberg. *New York Magazine*. On line at nymag.com/nymetro/news/people/features/9607/. Retrieved on January 19, 2006.

Lonsway, K. A. (2000). *Successfully investigating acquaintance sexual assault: A national training manual for law enforcement*. Washington, DC: National Center for Women and Policing.

Lonsway, K. A. (2000). *Hiring and retaining more women: The advantages to law enforcement agencies*. Los Angeles: National Center for Women and Policing.

Lonsway, K. A., & Fitzgerald, L. F. (1994). Rape myths: In review. *Psychology of Women Quarterly, 18*, 133–164.

Lynch, J., & Kilmartin, C. T. (1999). *The pain behind the mask: Overcoming masculine depression*. Binghamton, NY: Haworth.

Magley, V. J., Waldo, C. R., Drasgow, F., & Fitzgerald, L. F. (1999). The impact of sexual harassment on military personnel: Is it the same for men and women? *Military Psychology, 11*, 283–302.

Mahoney, E. R., Shively, M. D., & Traw, M. (1986). Sexual coercion and assault: Male socialization and female risk. *Sexual Coercion and Assault, 1*, 2–8.

McAdams, D. P., Lester, R. M., Brand, P. A., McNamara, W. J., & Lensky, D. B. (1988). Sex and the TAT: Are women more intimate than men? Do men fear intimacy? *Journal of Personality Assessment, 52*, 397–409.

McCauley, J., Kern, D. E., Kolodner, K., Dill, L., Schroeder, A. F., DeChant, H. K., et al. (1995). The "battering syndrome": Prevalence and clinical characteristics of domestic violence in primary care internal medicine practices. *Annals of Internal Medicine, 123*, 737–746.

McConahay, J. B. (1986). Modern racism, ambivalence, and the modern racism scale. In J. F. Dovidio & S. L. Gaertner (Eds.), *Prejudice, discrimination, and racism* (pp. 91–125). Orlando, FL: Academic Press.

McPherson, D. G. (2001). Personal communication. October 14.

Mechanic, M. B. (2003). Responding to the psychological impact of stalking victimization. In M. P. Brewster (Ed.), *Stalking: Psychology, risk factors, interventions, and law* (pp. 114–131). Kingston, NJ: Civic Research Institute.

Mechanic, M. B., Uhlmansiek, M. H., Weaver, T. L., & Resick, P. A. (2000). The impact of severe stalking experienced by acutely battered women: An examination of violence, psychological symptoms and strategic responding. *Violence and victims, 15*(4), 443–458.

Mechanic, M. B., Uhlmansiek, M. H., Weaver, T. L., & Resick, P. A. (2002). The impact of severe stalking experienced by acutely battered women: An examination of violence, psychological symptoms and strategic responding. In I. H. Frieze & K. E. Davis (Eds), *Stalking: Perspectives on victims and perpetrators*. (pp. 89–111). New York: Springer.

Meichenbaum, D. (1977). *Cognitive-behavior modification: An integrative approach*. New York: Plenum.

Melani, L. & Fodaski, L. (1974). The psychology of the rapist and his victim. In N. Connell & C. Wilson (Eds.), *Rape: The first sourcebook for women*. New York: Plume.

Meloy, J. R. (1995). The antisocial personality disorder. In G. Gabbard (Ed.) *Treatment of Psychiatric Disorders: The DSM-IV Edition*. Washington, DC: American Psychiatric Press.

Meloy, J. R. (1998). *The psychology of stalking: Clinical and forensic perspectives*. New York: Academic Press.

Mezey, G.C., & King, M. B. (Eds.). (1992). *Male victims of sexual assault*. London: Oxford University Press.

Miller, T. R., Cohen, M. A., & Wiersema, B. (1996). Victim costs and consequences: A new look. Washington, DC: U.S. Department of Justice.

Moffeit, M., & Herdy, A. (2003, November 16). Betrayal in the Ranks: For crime victims, punishment. *The Denver Post*, p. B6.

Morgan, M. (1986). Conflict and confusion: What rape prevention reports are telling women. *Sexual Coercion and Assault, 1*, 160–168.

Mosher, D. L., & Anderson, R. D. (1986). Macho personality, sexual aggression, and reactions to guided imagery of realistic rape. *Journal of Research in Personality, 20*, 77–94.

Mosher, D. L., & Sirkin, M. (1984). Measuring a macho personality constellation. *Journal of Research in Personality, 18*, 150–163.

Mullen, P. E., Pathe, M., Purcell, R., & Stuart, G. W. (1999). A study of stalkers. *American Journal of Psychiatry, 156*, 1244–1249.

Murnen, S. K. (1998). The hyperfemininity scale. In C. M. Davis, W. L. Yarber, R. Bauserman, G. Scheer, & S. L. David (Eds.), *Handbook of sexuality-related measures* (pp. 258–261). Thousand Oaks, CA: Sage.

Murnen, S. K., & Byrne, D. (1991). Hyperfemininity: Measurement and initial validation of the construct. *Journal of Sex Research, 28*(3), 479–489.

Murnen, S. K., Wright, S. K., & Kaluzny, G. (2002). If "boys will be boys," then girls will be victims? A meta-analytic review of the research that relates masculine ideology to sexual aggression. *Sex Roles: A Journal of Research 46*, 359–375.

Myers, D. G. (2005). *Social psychology*. Boston: McGraw-Hill.

National Center for Policy Analysis. (1999). *Crime and punishment in America: 1999*. (No. 229) Washington, DC: Author.

National Center for Policy Analysis (1999). Crime and punishment in America, 1999 (NCPA policy report #229). On line at http://www.ncpa.org/studies/s229/s229.html. Retrieved March 17, 2006.

National Institute of Justice and the Bureau of Justice Statistics. (1998). *National Stalking Resource Center*. ncve.org/src/main.aspx. Retrieved January 31, 2006.

Neidig, P. H., & Friedman, D. H. (1984). *Spouse abuse: A treatment program for couples*. Champaign, IL: Research Press.

Neville, H. A., & Heppner, M. J. (1999). Contextualizing rape: Reviewing sequelae and proposing a culturally inclusive ecological model of sexual assault recovery. *Applied & Preventive Psychology, 8*, 41–62.

Nicholas, P. (2004, July 18). Schwarzenegger deems opponents "girlie-men"—twice, Governor's rhetoric incites mall crowd, infuriates others. *Los Angeles Times*, p. A7.

Nishith, P., Mechanic, M. B., & Resick, P. A. (2000). Prior interpersonal trauma: The contributions to current PTSD symptoms in female rape victims. *Journal of Abnormal Psychology, 109*, 20–25.

Norris, J., & Cubbins, L. A. (1992). Dating, drinking, and rape: Effects of victim's and assailant's alcohol consumption on judgments. *Psychology of Women Quarterly, 16*(2), 179–191.

Olson, M. A. & Fazio, R. H. (2001). Implicit attitude formation through classical conditioning. *Psychological Science, 12,* 413–417.

Orth, U. (2002). Secondary victimization of crime victims by criminal proceedings. *Social Justice Research, 15*(4), 313–325.

O'Sullivan, C. (1991). Acquaintance gang rape on campus. In A. Parrot & L. Bechhofer (Eds.), *Acquaintance rape: The hidden crime* (pp. 140–156). New York: Wiley.

Page, A. C., & Crino, R. D. (1993). Eye-movement desensitization: A simple treatment for posttraumatic stress disorder? *Journal of Psychiatry, 27*(2), 288–293.

Pandya, V., & Gingerich, W. J. (2002). Group therapy intervention for male batterers. *Health and Social Work, 27*(1), 47–56.

Parrot, A., & Bechofer, L. (Eds.) (1991). *Acquaintance rape: The hidden crime.* New York: Wiley.

Pavlov, I. I. (1927). *Conditioned Reflexes* (G.V. Anrep, Trans.). London: Oxford University Press.

Pence, E., & Paymar, M. (1993). *Education groups for men who batter: The Duluth Model.* New York: Springer.

Perkins, D., Hammond, S., Coles, D., & Bishop, D. (1998). *Review of Sex Offender Treatment Programmes.* Report prepared for High Security Psychiatric Services Commissioning Board. Liverpool, UK.

Petty, R. E., & Wegener, D. T. (1998). Attitude change: Multiple roles for persuasion variables. In D. Gilbert, S. Fiske, & G. Lindzey (Eds.), *The handbook of social psychology* (4th ed., pp. 323–390). New York: McGraw-Hill.

Pollack, W. (1998). *Real boys: Rescuing our sons from the myths of boyhood.* New York: Random House.

Pino, N. W., & Meier, R. F (1999). Gender differences in rape reporting: Statistical data included. *Sex Roles: A Journal of Research, 40,* 979–985.

Pryor, J. B. (1987). Sexual harassment proclivities in men. *Sex Roles: A Journal of Research, 17*(5–6), 269–290.

Pyszczynski, T., Greenberg, J., Solomon, S., Arndt, J., & Schimel, J. (2004). Why do people need self-esteem? A theoretical and empirical review. *Psychological Bulletin, 130*(3), 435–468.

Pyszczynski, T., Greenberg, J., Solomon, S., & Hamilton, J. (1990). A terror management analysis of self-awareness and anxiety: The hierarchy of terror. *Anxiety Research, 2,* 177–195.

Quattrone, G. A. (1986). On the perception of a group's variability. In S. Worchel and W. G. Austin (Eds.), *Psychology of intergroup relations* (2nd ed.). Chicago: Nelson-Hall.

Quigley, B. M., Corbett, A. B., & Tedeschi, J. T. (2002). Desired image of power, alcohol expectancies, and alcohol-related aggression. *Psychology of Addictive Behaviors, 16,* 318–324.

Ramsland, Katherine. *Stalkers: The psychological terrorist.* On line at www.crimelibrary.com/criminal_mind/psychology/stalkers/1.html. Retrieved: February 25, 2005.

Rape attempts drop 46% over 14 years. (1991, January 14). *Kansas City Star,* p. A3.

Reiss, I. L. (1986). *Journey into sexuality: An exploratory voyage.* Englewood Cliffs, NJ: Prentice-Hall.
Rennison, M. (2000). Intimate partner violence. 1993–2001 (NCJ 178247), pp. 1–2. Washington, DC: National Institute of Justice, Department of Justice.
Rennison, M., & Rand, M. R. (2003). *Criminal victimization, 2002.* (NCJ 199994), pp. 1–12. Washington, DC: National Institute of Justice, Department of Justice.
Resick, P. A. (1987). Psychological effects of victimization: Implications for the criminal justice system. *Crime and Delinquency, 33,* 468–478.
Resick, P. A., Jordan, C. G., Girelli, S. A., Hutter, C. K., & Marhoefer-Dvorak, S. (1988). A comparative outcome study of behavioral group therapy for sexual assault victims. *Behavior Therapy, 19,* 385–401.
Resick, P. A., & Schnicke, M. (1993). *Cognitive processing therapy for rape victims.* Newbury Park, CA: Sage.
Resnick, H. S., & Kilpatrick, D. G. (1994). Crime-related PTSD: Emphasis on adult general population samples. *PTSD Research Quarterly, 5*(3), 1–5.
Resnick, H. S., Kilpatrick, D. G., Dansky, B. S., Saunders, B. E., & Best, C. L. (1993). Prevalence of civilian trauma and posttraumatic stress disorder in a representative national sample of women. *Journal of Consulting and Clinical Psychology, 61,* 984–991.
Resnick, H. S., Yehuda, R., Pitman, R. K., & Foy, D. W. (1995). Effect of previous trauma on acute plasma cortisol level following rape. *American Journal of Psychiatry, 152,* 1675–1677.
Richman, J. A., Rospenda, K. M., Flaherty, J. A., & Freels, S. (2001). Work place harassment, active coping, and alcohol-related outcomes. *Journal of Substance Abuse, 13,* 347–366.
Rodriguez, E., Lasch, K. E., Chandra, P., & Lee, J. (2001). Family violence, employment status, welfare benefits, and alcohol drinking in the United States: What is the relation? *Journal of Epidemiology of Community Health, 55*(3), 172–178.
Rosenblatt, A., Greenberg, J., Solomon, S., & Pyszczynski, T. (1989) Evidence for terror management theory I: The effects of morality salience on reactions to those who violate or uphold cultural values. *Journal of Personality and Social Psychology, 57*(4), 681–690.
Rothenberg, B. (2003). We don't have time for social change: Cultural compromise and the battered woman. *Gender and Society, 17*(5), 771–787.
Rothbaum, B. O., Foa, E. B., Riggs, D. S., Murdock, T., & Walsh, W. (1992). A prospective examination of posttraumatic stress disorder in rape victims. *Journal of Traumatic Stress, 5,* 455–475.
Routbort, J. C. (1998). What happens when you tell: Disclosure, attributions, and recovery from sexual assault. *Dissertation Abstracts International: Section B: The Sciences and Engineering, 58*(10-B) 5655.
Rozee, P.D., & Koss, M. P. (2001). Rape: A century of resistance. *Psychology of Women Quarterly, 25*(4), 295–311.
Rubin, L. (1985). *Just friends: The role of friendship in our lives.* New York, Harper.
Rutherford, J. & Chapman, R. (1988). Male order: unwrapping masculinity. London: Lawrence and Wishart.
Sanday, P. R. (1981). The socio-cultural context of rape: A cross-cultural study. *Journal of Social Issues, 37,* 5–27.

Sanday, P. R. (1990). *Fraternity gang rape: Sex, brotherhood, and privilege on campus*. New York: New York University Press.
Sanday, P. R. (1996). *A woman scorned: Acquaintance rape on trial*. New York: Doubleday.
Sandler, B. R., & Shoop, R. J. (Eds.). (1997). *Sexual harassment on campus: A guide for administrators, faculty, and students*. Boston: Allyn and Bacon.
Sapadin, L. A. (1988). Friendship and gender: Perspectives of professional men and women. *Journal of Social and Personal Relationships, 5,* 387–403.
Saunders, D. G. (1984). Helping husbands who batter. *Social Casework, 65*(6), 347–353.
Saunders, D. G. (1996). Interventions for men who batter: Do we know what works? *In Session: Psychotherapy in Practice, 2/3,* 81–94.
Saunders, D. G., & Hamill, R. M. (2003). *Violence against women: Synthesis of research on offender interventions*. (NCJ 201222). Washington, DC: National Institute of Justice, Department of Justice.
Scarborough, R. (2006, January 9). Military academies see less harassment. *The Washington Times,* A2.
Schram, D., & Milloy, C. D. (1995). *Community notification: A study of offender characteristics and recidivism*. Olympia, WA: Washington Institute for Public Policy.
Schwartz, J. P., Waldo, M., & Daniel, D. (2005). Gender-role conflict and self-esteem: Factors associated with partner abuse in court-referred men. *Psychology of Men and Masculinity, 6,* 109–113.
Scott, K. L., & Wolfe, D. A. (2000). Change among batterers: Examining men's success stories. *Journal of Interpersonal Violence, 15,* 827–842.
Sears, D. O. (1988). Review of Communication and persuasion: Central and peripheral routes to attitude change. *Public Opinion Quarterly, 52,* 262–265.
Segal, D. L., Stewart, S. E., Peck, D. T., & Coolidge, F. L. (2000). Personality profiles of men who abuse their partners. Paper presented at the Annual Convention of the American Psychological Association, Washington, DC.
Seligman, M. E. (1990). *Learned Optimism*. New York: Knopf.
Sex offender murder suspect kills self. (2006, April 17). CBS News. www.cbsnews.com/stories/2006/04/17/national/main1501271. Retrieved May 15, 2006.
Shapiro, B. (1991). *Sexual harassment: managing ambiguity and conflict*. Oakland, CA: Barry M. Shapiro & Associates.
Shapiro, B. (2000). *Sexual harassment prevention*. Symposium conducted at the 25th Annual Conference on Men and Masculinity, Colorado Springs, CO.
Shapiro, F. (1989). Eye movement desensitization procedure: A new treatment for posttraumatic stress disorder. *Journal of Behavior Therapy and Experimental Psychiatry, 20,* 211–217.
Shapiro, F. (1999). Eye movement desensitization and reprocessing (EMDR) and anxiety disorders: Clinical and research implications of an integrated psychotherapy treatment. *Journal of Anxiety Disorders, 13,* 35–68.
Shapiro, F. & Solomon, R. (1995). Eye movement desensitization and reprocessing: Neurocognitive information processing. In G. Everley (Ed.), *Innovations in disaster and trauma psychology*. Ellicott City, MD: Chevron.
Shaver, K. G. (1985). *The attribution of blame: Causality, responsibility, and blameworthiness*. New York: Springer-Verlag.

Shaver, K. G., & Drown, D. (1986). On causality, responsibility, and self-blame: A theoretical note. *Journal of Personality and Social Psychology, 4*, 697–702.

Shaw, M. (1981). *Group dynamics: The psychology of small group behavior.* New York: McGraw-Hill.

Skinner, B. F. (1938). *The behavior of organisms.* New York: Appleton-Century-Crofts.

Smiler, A. P. (2004). Thirty years after the discovery of gender: psychological concepts and measures of masculinity. *Sex Roles: A Journal of Research, 50*, 15–26.

Smith, K. (1971). Homophobia: A tentative personality profile. *Psychological Reports, 29*, 1091–1094.

Spohn, C., & Horney, J. (1992). *Rape law reform: A grassroots revolution and its impact.* New York: Plenum.

Stockdale, M. S., Visio, L., & Batra, L. (1999). The sexual harassment of men: Evidence for a broader theory of sexual. *Psychology, Public Policy, and Law, 5*, 630–664.

Street, A. E., Stafford, J., & Bruce, T. A. (2003, Winter). Sexual harassment. *PTSD Research Quarterly, 14*(4), 1–3.

Stucky Halley, D. A. (2004) Understanding battering behavior: The influence of human development. Unpublished manuscript.

Sullivan, C., & Gillum, T. (2001). Shelters and other community based-services for battered women and their children. In C. Renzetti, J. Edleson, & R. Bergen (Eds.), *Sourcebook on violence against women* (pp. 247–260). Thousand Oaks, CA: Sage.

Sullivan, C. M., & Bybee, D. I. (1999). Reducing violence using community-based advocacy for women with abusive partners. *Journal of Consulting and Clinical Psychology, 67*, 43–53.

Sullivan, J. P., & Mosher, D.L. (1990). Acceptance of guided imagery of marital rape as a function of macho personality. *Violence and Victims, 5*, 275–286.

Swim, J. K., Aiken, K. J., Hall, W. S., & Hunter, B. A. (1995). Sexism and racism: Old-fashioned and modern prejudices. *Journal of Personality and Social Psychology, 68*, 199–214.

Testimony before the United States Senate Judiciary Panel. (1990, August 29) (testimony of M. P. Koss).

Thompson, J. (1984, February 2). Case thrusts Wichita into national debate over drug for rapists. *Kansas City Times,* pp. A1, A14.

Tjaden, P., & Thoennes, N. (1998). *Stalking in America: Findings from the national violence against women survey.* Denver, CO: Center for Policy Research.

Tjaden, P., & Thoennes, N. (2000). *Extent, nature, and consequences of intimate partner violence: Findings from the National Violence Against Women Survey.* Publication No. NCJ181867. Washington, DC: Department of Justice. On line at www.ojp.usdoj.gov/nij/pubsum/181867.html. Retrieved March 21, 2006.

UNIFEM (n.d.). *UNIFEM fact sheet no. 5: Masculinity and gender-based violence.* www.unifem-eseasia.org/resources/factsheets/UNIFEMSheet5.doc. Retrieved August 12, 2005.

Van Yperen, N. W., & Buunk, B. P. (1990). A longitudinal study of equity and satisfaction in intimate relationships. *European Journal of Social Psychology, 20*, 287–309.

Veinot, T. (December 1999). *Violence prevention programming: A summary of recent evaluation research.* Toronto, ON: Education Wife Assault.

Veronen, L. J., & Kilpatrick, D. G. (1982). Stress inoculation training for victim of rape: Efficacy and differential findings. Symposium conducted at the16th Annual Convention of the Association for the Advancement of Behavior Therapy, Los Angeles, CA.

Veronen, L. J., Kilpatrick, D. G., & Resick, P. A. (1979). Treatment of fear and anxiety in rape victims: Implications for the criminal justice system. In W. H. Parsonage (Ed.), *Perspectives on Victimology* (pp. 148–159). Beverly Hills, CA: Sage.

Vobejda, B. (1995, August 17). Survey finds familiar face on sex crime: Four out of five victims report they knew assailant. *The Washington Post,* p. A6.

Wagner, E. J. (1992). *Sexual harassment in the workplace: How to prevent, investigate, and resolve problems in your organization.* New York: AMACOM.

Wakefield, H., & Underwager, R. (1991). Sex offender treatment. *IPT Journal, 3.* http://www.ipt-forensics.com/journal/volume3/j3_1_2.htm. Retrieved May 2, 2006.

Walker, L. (1979). *The battered woman.* New York: Harper & Row.

Warshaw, R. (1988). *I Never Called it Rape.* New York: Harper & Row.

Watts, C., & Zimmerman, C. (2002). Violence against women: Global scope and magnitude. *Lancet, 239*(9313), 1232–1237.

Weber, M. (1947). *The theory of social and economic organization.* A. M. Henderson & T. Parsons (trans.). New York: Free Press.

Westlander, E. (2004, September 17). *Judge faces recall effort: Rape victim's mother mobilizes against Martin..* www.ljworld.com/news/2004/sep/17/judge_faces_recall. Retrieved December 2004.

Whealin, J. M. (2004). Men and sexual trauma: a National Center for PTSD fact sheet. In C. Turner & S. Frayne (Eds), *Veterans health initiative: Military sexual trauma* (pp. 7–8). Birmingham, Ala.: Employee Education System, Department of Veterans Affairs.

Whiting, B. (1965). Sex identity conflict and physical violence: A comparative study. *American Anthropologist, 67*(2) 123–140.

Wilson, A. M. (personal communication, 2004)

Wolfe, D. A., & Jaffe, P. G. (2003). *Prevention of domestic violence and sexual assault*: Applied Research Forum, VAWNet. Violence Against Women Online Resources. University of Minnesota. www.vawnet.org.domesticviolence/research/vawnetdoc:war_prevention.php. Retrieved February 14, 2006.

Wrightsman, L. S., & Fulero, S. M. (2004). *Forensic psychology* (2nd ed.). Belmont, CA: Wadsworth.

Wrightsman, L. S., Greene, E., Nietzel, M. T., & Fortune, W. H. (2002). *Psychology and the Legal System.* Belmont, CA: Wadsworth.

Zanna, M. P., & Rempel, J. K. (1988). Attitudes: A new look at an old concept. In D. Bar-Tal, & A. W. Kruglanski (Eds.), *The social psychology of knowledge* (pp. 315–334). Cambridge, UK: Cambridge University Press.

Zawacki, T., Abbey, A. Buck, P. O., McAuslan, P. & Clinton-Sherrod, A. M. (2003). Perpetrators of alcohol-induced sexual assaults: How do they differ from other sexual assault perpetrators and nonperpetrators? *Aggressive Behavior, 4,* 366–380.

Zona, M. A., Sharma, K. K., & Lane, J. C. (1993). A comparative study of erotomanic and obsessional subjects in a forensic sample. *Journal of Forensic Sciences, 38*(4), 894–903.

Zuwerink, J. R., Monteith, M. J., Devine, P. G., & Cook, D. (1996). Prejudice toward blacks: With and without compunction? *Basic and Applied Social Psychology, 18,* 131–150.

Author Index

A

Abbey, A., 42–43
Abrams, K. M., 75
Abel, G. G., 74
Acierno, R., 78
Adams, G., 176
Ahrens, C. E., 130
Aiken, K. J., 96
Akert, R. M., 96–97
Aldarondo, E., 154, 157
Allison, J. A., 11, 34, 43, 101, 124, 137, 163, 213
Allport, G. W., 97, 104
Altman, J., 207
Amick-McMullan, A., 71
Anderson, B. K., 42
Anderson, R. D., 102
Arias, I., 74
Aronson, E., 96–97, 109, 170
Asch, S. E., 59–60
Atherton-Zeman, B., 214
Atkeson, B. M., 82
Avina, C., 75
Axelrod, R., 74

B

Babcock, J., 154
Bachrach, P., 6
Bailey, J. A., 75, 79–82, 130
Baker, N., 134
Ballenger, J. C., 79
Bankovics, G., 50
Baratz, M. S., 6
Bard, M., 71
Barnes, H. E., 130
Baron, R. A., 44
Bart, P. B., 138
Basow, S. A., 100, 116
Bastion, T., 232
Batra, L., 26
Baumgartner, P. A., 117
Beach, S. H., 80
Bechhofer, L., 10, 43
Bechtle, A. E., 80
Becker, J. V., 74
Bem, D. J., 94
Bem, S. L., 120
Bennett, L., 157

Berkowitz, A. D., 33, 164, 171, 173–175, 197, 199, 203, 209, 211, 214, 216, 228
Bernat, J. A., 131–133
Best, C. L., 71, 78
Birbaumer, N., 43
Bishopp, P., 152
Blumstein, P., 181
Boswell, A. A., 22
Brand, P. A., 181
Brannon, R., 98
Branscombe, N. R., 44
Breslau, N., 79
Browne, A., 20
Brownmiller, S., 39, 106, 116
Bruce, T. A., 26, 75
Buck, P. O., 42–43
Burgess, A. W., 15, 17, 50
Burkhart, B. R., 82
Burt, M. R., 107, 189
Buunk, 180
Bussiere, M. T., 151
Bybee, D. I., 83
Byrne, D., 44, 103

C

Cacioppo, J. T., 43, 95
Campbell, J. C., 81, 136
Campbell, R., 80, 130
Candib, L. N., 80
Chaiken, S., 92
Chandra, P., 42
Chapman, R., 113
Chard-Wierschem, D. J., 145
Chilcoat, H. D., 79
Chirico, B., 203
Cignetti, C., 173
Clinton-Sherrod, M., 42–43, 173–174, 188
Cogan, J., 32
Cohen, M. A., 69
Coles, D., 152
Coltrane, S., 61, 117
Conway, A., 164, 189
Cook, D., 97
Coolidge, F. L., 50
Corbett, A. B., 43
Corcoran, C. B., 33, 163
Cray, A., 93
Crino, R. D., 134
Crites, S. L., 92
Cromwell, N. A., 15, 17, 50
Crowley, M., 100, 102

Crull, P., 26
Cubbins, L. A., 42
Cullen, F. T., 29
Curtin, J. J., 42

D

Dalton, T. 176
Daniel, D., 46
Dansky, B. S., 77
Davidson, J. R. T., 79
Davidson, W. S., 79–80
Davis, R. C., 154
DeAngelis, T., 23
Deaux, K., 100, 102
DeCecco, J., 31
DeChant, H. K., 80
Derlega, V. J., 181
Devine, P.G., 97
Dickinson, L. M., 80
Dickinson, W. P., 80
Diener, E., 121
Dill, L., 80
Douglas, H., 20
Dovidio, J. F., 96, 98
D'Ovidio, R., 29–30
Doyle, J., 29–30
Drawgow, F., 25
Dutton, D. G., 21, 51
Dworkin, A., 40

E

Eagly, A. H., 92
Earle, J. P., 174
Edmunds, C., 11, 77–78
Ellis, E. M., 82
Ellsberg, M., 16
Erickson, R. J., 178
Erwin, P. A., 136
Estrich, S., 9
Ewing, C. P., 101

F

Fabrigar, L. R., 92
Fagan, J., 136, 145
Fals-Stewart, W., 42
Falsetti, S., 131–133
Far, J., 198
Fazio, R. H., 94–95

Feder, L., 154
Feldman-Summers, S., 74
Fernandez-Lanier, A., 145
Festinger, L., 109
Fincham, F. D., 180
Fischer, G. W., 97
Fisher, B. S., 29
Fisk, A., 23
Fiske, S. T., 103–105, 189
Fitzgerald, L. F., 25–26, 107–108
Flaherty, J. A., 77
Fletcher, G. J. O., 180
Foa, E. B., 77–78, 133
Follette, V. M., 80
Fontana, A., 77
Foote, W. E., 55–56
Forde, D. R., 154
Forsythe, D. R., 6
Fortune, W. H., 152
Foubert, J. D., 203–204
Foy, D. W., 80
Frank, E., 80
Freels, S., 77
Freeman-Longo, R. E., 149
French, J. R. P., 6–7
Friedberg, A., 164, 189
Friedman, D. H., 156
Frieze, I. H., 20, 42, 70
Funk, R. E., 37, 67

G

Gaertner, S. L., 96
Galeone, M., 207
Gecas, V., 178
Gelles, R. J., 12
Gibbs, D., 173
Gidycz, C. A., 10, 73, 78–79, 143, 203
Gillis, R. J., 32
Gillum, T., 130
Gilmore, D., 118–119
Gingerich, W. J., 154
Girelli, S. A., 132
Glick, P., 103–106, 189
Golant, S. K., 51
Golding, J. M., 80
Gondolf, E. W., 16, 46, 50, 154
Goodman-Delahunty, J., 55–56
Gordon, A., 148
Gordon, P. E., 74
Gottemoeller, M., 16
Green, A., 59–60, 164, 189

Green, C., 154
Greene, E., 152
Greenfield, L. A., 141
Groth, A. N., 44–46, 141
Grusnski, R., 46
Gruy, F. V., 80

H

Haines, M. P., 188
Hall, D., 145
Hall, G. C. N., 151
Hall, W. S., 96
Halligan, S. L., 78
Hamby, S. L., 21
Hamill, R. M., 153
Hammock, G., 42
Hammond, S., 152
Hanson, K., 79, 148
Hanson, R. K., 151
Harris, A. J. R., 148
Hart, H. L. A., 161
Harvey, M. R., 71, 78, 163
Hatfield, E., 180
Hawkins, S., 202
Hay, 180 AU: Initial?
Healy, D. R., 190
Hearst-Ikeda, D. E., 133
Heider, F., 161
Heinzen, H., 59–60, 164, 189
Heise, L., 16, 130
Heppner, M. J., 82
Herdy, A., 3
Herek, G. M., 32
Herman, J. L., 71, 78, 98
Heron, N., 180
Hermsen, S., 98
Herrera, V. M., 75, 79–82, 130
Herron, K., 50
Holley, J., 122
Holtzworth-Munroe, A., 16, 50
hooks, b. 16
Horney, J., 9
Hunter, B. A., 96
Hutter, C. K., 132
Hyer, L., 134

J

Jacobson, N., 51
Jackson, S., 154
Jacupak, M., 46

270 • AUTHOR INDEX

Jaffe, 162
Janoff-Bulman, R., 70–71, 82
Jaschik-Herman, M. L., 23
Johnson, M. P., 20
Jones, A. S., 154
Jordan, C. G., 132
Jouriles, E. N., 80

K

Kaluzny, G., 103
Kanin, E. J., 10–11
Katz, B. L., 78
Katz, J., 162, 164, 177, 200, 225–226
Kawakami, K., 98
Kern, D. E., 80
Kersting, K., 148, 151
Kessler, R. C., 79
Kilmartin, C. T., 20, 25–26, 31, 34, 51, 59–60, 81, 103, 143, 164, 171, 173–175, 178, 199, 203, 207, 211, 214, 216, 228
Kilpatrick, D. G., 11, 71–73, 75, 77–80, 131–132
Kimmel, M. S., 8, 15, 31, 101, 118, 182
King, L., 176
King, M. B., 32
Kleinknecht, R. A., 134
Knoll, J., 58
Kolodner, K., 80
Koss, M. P., 10–11, 40, 43, 45, 71, 73, 75, 79–82, 130, 141, 163, 203
Krantz, D. L., 70
Kuchler, M., 59–60, 164, 189

L

Lafond, J. Q., 148
Landes, A. B., 120
Lane, J. C., 54
Lang, J., 42
Largen, M. A., 137
Larimer, M. E., 42
Lasch, K. E., 42
Layman, M. J., 79
Lecrubier, Y., 79
Ledray, L. E., 130, 135
Lee, J., 42
Lefkowitz, B., 122
Lensky, D. B., 181
Lepowsky, M., 121
Lerner, G., 58, 114

Lerner, J. J., 71
Lester, R. M., 181
Lewis, L. L., 100, 102
Lichter, E. L., 75, 79–82, 130
Linville, P. W., 97
Lisak, D., 11, 44–46, 49, 145, 151, 178–179, 225
Lombardi, J., 14
Lonsway, K. A., 107–108, 135
Lucia, V. C., 79
Lydum, A. R., 42
Lynch, J. R., 51, 81

M

Magley, V. J., 25
Mahler, M., 31
Mahlstedt, D., 204, 212
Mahoney, E. R., 102
Mann, J. A., 96
Margulis, S. T., 181
Marhoefer-Dvorak, S., 132
Marques, J. K., 148
Marshall-Goodell, B. S., 95
Martin, P. Y., 130
Maxwell, C. D., 154
McAdams, D. P., 181
McAuslan, P., 42–43
McBride, B., 134
McCauley, J., 80
McConahay, J. B., 96
McNamara, W. J., 181
McQuoid, T., 164, 189
Meagher, J. R., 74
Mechanic, M. B., 75, 79
Meehan, J. C., 50
Meichenbaum, D., 131
Meier, R. F., 143
Meloy, J. R., 54
Meloy, R., 28
Metts, S., 181
Mezey, G. C., 32
Miller, D. T., 71
Miller, J., 198
Miller, P. M., 11, 44, 145
Miller, T. R., 69
Milloy, C. D., 149
Moffeit, M., 3
Moll, J., 98
Monteith, M. J., 97
Morgan, M., 138, 163
Mosher, D. L., 100, 102

Mullen, P. E., 54
Murdock, T., 77–78, 133
Murnen, S. K., 103
Murphy, W., 148
Myers, D. G., 92, 107, 178

N

Neidig, P. H., 156
Neville, H. A., 81
Nicholas, P., 99
Nietzel, M. T., 152
Nishith, P., 79
Norbet, T., 164, 189, 207
Norris, J., 42
Nutt, D. J., 79

O

O'Brien, P. H., 138
O'Dickinson, L. M., 80
O'Donohue, W., 75
O'Hearn, R., 42
O'Leary, K. D., 80
Olson, M. A., 94–95
O'Sullivan, C., 121
Oros, C. J., 45
Orth, U., 141

P

Page, A. C., 134
Pandya, V., 154
Parcell, S. R., 10
Parrot, A., 10, 43
Pathe, M., 54
Patrick, C. J., 43
Pavlov, I. I., 94
Paymar, M., 155
Peck, D. T., 50
Pence, E., 155
Perkins, D., 152
Perry, K., 133
Peterson, E. L., 79
Petronio, S., 181
Pettibone, K., 173
Petty, R. E., 92, 95
Pino, N. W., 143

Pitman, R. K., 80
Pollack, W., 178
Polusny, M. A., 80
Pope, K. T., 74
Purcell, R., 54

Q

Quattrone, G. A., 97
Quigley, B. M., 43
Quinsey, V. L., 148
Quiram, J., 120

R

Ramsland, K., 27
Rand, M. R., 67–68, 141, 143
Raven, B. H., 6–7
Reiss, I. L., 103
Rempel, J. K., 92
Rennison, M., 67–68, 143–144
Resick, P. A, 72–73, 75, 79, 82, 131–132
Resnick, H. S., 71, 78–80
Richman, J. A., 50, 77
Riggs, D. S., 77–78, 133
Robie, C., 154
Robinson, G. E., 4–5, 75
Rodriguez, E., 42
Roemer, L., 46
Rosenheck, R., 77
Rospenda, K. M., 77
Roth, S., 46
Rothbaum, B. O., 77, 133
Rothenberg, B., 76
Routbort, J. C., 82
Rozee, P. D., 11
Rubin, L. 179
Rutherford, J., 113
Russin, A., 98
Russo, N. F., 130

S

Salovey, P., 97
Saltzman, L. E., 12
Sanday, P. R., 39, 60, 116, 123–124
Sangrey, D., 71
Sandler, B. R., 25
Sapadin, L. A., 179
Saunders, B., 79

Saunders, B. E., 71
Saunders, D. G., 153
Schnicke, M., 133
Schram, D., 149
Schroeder, A. F., 80
Schwartz, J. P., 46, 180
Scott, K. L., 154
Sears, D. O., 96
Sefl, T., 130
Segal, D. L., 50
Seligman, M. E. P., 21
Seto, M. C., 148
Seymour, A., 11, 77–78
Shapiro, B., 134
Shapiro, B., 57
Shapiro, F., 133–134
Sharma, K. K., 54
Shaver, K. G., 160
Shaw, M., 6
Shelton, A., 226
Shively, M. D., 102
Shoop, R. J., 25
Sirkin, M., 100
Skinner, B. F., 95
Skinner, L. J., 74
Smiler, A. P., 176
Smith, T., 59–60, 164, 189
Soeken, K. L., 82, 136
Solomon, S., 134
Spade, J. Z., 122
Spohn, C., 9
Sprecher, S., 180
Squire, S., 173
Squyres, S., 120
Starzomski, A. J., 21
Stafford, J., 26, 75
Street, A. E., 26
Steinmetz, S. K., 12
Stewart, B. D., 50, 80
Stockdale, M. S., 26
Straus, M. A., 12
Street, A. E., 75
Stuart, G. W., 16, 50, 54
Stucky Halley, D. A., 15, 148
Sugarman, D. B., 21
Sullivan, C. M., 80, 83
Sullivan, J. P., 102
Sweezey, C., 122
Swim, J. K., 96

T

Tassinary, L. G., 95
Taylor, B. G., 154

Tedeschi, J. T., 43
Thompson, J., 152
Thoennes, N., 11, 15, 29, 54–55, 144
Tjaden, P., 11, 15, 29, 54–55, 144
Traupmann, J., 180
Traw, M., 102
Treacy E. C., 74
Tschan, T., 164, 189
Turner, A. P., 42
Turner, M. G., 29

U

Uhmansiek, M. H., 75
Underwager, R., 148, 150
Utne, M., 180

V

Van Yperen, N. W., 180
Veinot, T., 163
Veronen, L. J., 71–73, 75, 131–132
Vidales, G., 136
Vincus, A, 173
Visio, L., 26
Vobejda, B., 10–11, 43

W

Wagner, E. J., 26
Waldo, C. R., 25, 46
Walker, L., 15–16, 21, 76
Walsh, W., 77–78
Warshaw, R., 71–72
Wasco, S. M., 130
Watts, C., 5–6
Weaver, T. L., 75
Weber, M., 6
Wegener, D. T., 92
Westlander, E., 142
Whealin, J. M., 67, 131
White, 106
Whiting, B., 123
Wiersema, B., 69
Williams, O. J., 157
Wilson, A. M., 96, 142
Wilson, T. D., 96
Winton, W., 100, 102
Wisniewski, N., 10, 78, 143, 203
Wolfe, D. A., 154, 162
Wright, S. K., 103

Wrightsman, L. S., 11, 43, 96, 124–125, 137, 152, 163

Y

Yehuda, R., 78, 80
Yuan, M. P., 75, 79–82, 130

Z

Zanna, M. P., 92
Zawicki, T., 42–43
Zimmerman, C., 5–6
Zona, M. A., 54
Zuwerink, J. R., 97

Subject Index

A

Alcohol, role in violence, 42–46
Anger rapist, 44
Antifemininity, 53, 98–99
Arrest to conviction of perpetrators charged with violent crimes against women, 141–148
Assumptions of victims, 70–81
  of invulnerability, 70
  world is fair, 71
Attitudes, 92
  ABC model, 92
    affective component, 92, 94
    behavioral component, 92, 94
    cognitive component, 92–94
  Classically conditioned, 94
  Explicit, 95
  Implicit, 95
  Operantly conditioned, 94–95
Audience relevant programs, 212
Automatic processing of stereotypes, 97–98
Availability heuristic, 43

B

Battered woman syndrome, 76–77
Belief in a just world, 71
Blame and responsibility of gendered violence, 160–161
Box of masculinity, 177
Bystander approach, 199–201

C

Cognitive dissonance theory, 108–110
Collaboration among agencies for intervention, 147
Community efforts in prevention, 207–208
Comprehensive programs, 212
Conformity, 59–60
Consequences of victimization, 69–81
  psychological, 70–72
  of sexual assault and rape, 72
  of intimate partner violence, 74–75
  of stalking, 75
  of sexual harassment, 75

SUBJECT INDEX

Costs of victimizing, 68–69
  tangible, 68
  intangible, 69
Criminal justice intervention for perpetrators of violent crimes against women, 139–142
Culpascope, 135
Culture and violence, 120–124

D

Decision to act violently, components of a violent incident, 38, 56–57
Depression, 80–81
Discussions among men, 223–224
Discussions between women and men, 223–224

E

Educational programming for men, 220–223
Effectiveness of intimate partner violence programs, 154, 157
Empathy for the self, 179
Exploitive harasser, 55

F

Femininity, 100
Femiphobia, 176
Feticide, 67
Fraternity Violence Education Project, 204–205

G

Gang rape, 121–122
Gender, 98–102, 114–120
  Gender and labor, 114–120
  historical foundations of gender inequality, 114
Gender-based violence-prevention programs, 173–174
  curriculum-based, 174
  discussion groups, 173
  environmental change strategies, 174
  one-time awareness, 173
Goals of violence-prevention programming for men, 175–183

H

Healthy relationships, 181
History of developing programs, 214–215
Hyperindependence, 53
Hypermasculinity, 41, 103

I

Infanticide, 67
Intensive programs, 212
Intervention for survivors, 130–137
  personal intervention, 130–136
    application phase, 132
    behavior therapy, 131
    cognitive processing therapy, 133
    cognitive-behavioral therapy, 132
    educational phase, 131
    eye movement desensitization and reprocessing, 133–134
    group treatment, 134–135
    legal intervention, 135–136
    medical intervention, 135
    prolonged exposure, 132–133
    psychological and emotional intervention, 130
    psychotherapy, 130–131
    Skill-building phase, 131–132
  public intervention, 136–137
    advocacy, 136–137
    education, 137
Intervention with perpetrators, 137, 139
Intimate partner violence, 46–53
Involving experts in the community in programs, 227

L

Laws on gender based violence, 124–125
  intimate partner violence, 124–125
  rape, 124
  violence Against Women Act, 125

M

Macrosocietal perspective, 114
Masculinity, 98–101
Means to do harm, components of a violent incident, 38, 57–58
Men Can Stop Rape, 201–202

SUBJECT INDEX • 277

Men's primary prevention efforts to end men's violence against women, 162–173
Men's violence-prevention programs, 171–173
Mentors in Violence Prevention, 199–201
Misogynistic harasser, 56
Misogyny, 176
Misperceiving harasser, 55
Modern sexism, 95–96

O

Obtaining effective program members, 219–220
One in Four, 203–204
Out-group homogeneity bias, 97

P

Pathology of the perpetrator, 37–38, 41, 56
Peer educator experience, 232–233
Personality disorder, 50
Police Response Advocacy intervention, 146–147
Positive message programs, 212–214
Posttraumatic Stress Disorder, 72, 74–75, 77–80
  criterion for Posttraumatic Stress Disorder, 72, 74–75
  factors related to Posttraumatic Stress Disorder symptomology or diagnosis, 77–80
Power asymmetry, 123–124
Power rapist, 44
Prejudice, 96–97
Primary prevention of gender-based violence, 162
Privilege, 182–183
Proactive batters, 50
Program activities, 224–225
Program membership commitment, 221–222
Program structure, 215–218
Protocol for school presentations, 229
Providing educational presentations to communities, 227–228

R

Raising awareness about gender violence, 228–231

Rape, 41–49, 56, 60, 73–74, 106–110, 135
  rape kit, 135
  rape myths, 106–110
  rape Trauma Syndrome, 73–74
Reactive batters, 51
Recidivism rates among sex offenders, 151
Recovering from gendered violence, 81–82
Reporting gender-based violence, 141, 143
Resistance awareness, 163
Revictimization, 79–80
Risk reduction of rape and sexual assault, 138–139

S

Sadistic rapist, 45
Safe dates, 172
SANE/SART nurse, 135
Secondary prevention of gender-based violence, 162
Self-blame, 71
Self-perceptions, 71–72
Sex offender community notification, 149–150
Sexism, 58–59, 103–108
  hostile, 104
  benevolent, 104–106
Sexual assault prevention, 189–199, 203–204
Sexual assault, 41, 56–57
Sexual harassment, 55–56
Sexual objectification, 58
Sexual script, 37–38
Shattered assumptions of victims, 70
Social cognitions of survivors, 82
Social norms approach to prevention, 188–199
Social psychology, 92
Social support for violence, 38, 58–61
Social support for victims, 82–83
Solutions of gender violence, 124
Stalkers, 53–55, 57
  erotomanic, 54
  love obsessional, 54–55
  simple obsessional, 54
Starting violence prevention and response programs, 216–217
Stereotypes, 97, 102
Stress inoculation training, 131
Survivor, 67
Survivor-centered approach to intervention, 147–148, 153

T

Ten things men can do to prevent gender violence, 200–201
Tertiary prevention of gender-based violence, 162
Theoretical foundations of programs, 218–219
Treatment for perpetrators, 148–153
  cognitive-behavioral approach, 150–151
  limited confidentiality of offenders, 153
  offender accountability, 152–153
  pharmacological approach, 152
  psychoeducational approach, 152
Treatment of offenders of intimate partner violence, 153–154
  cognitive approach, 154–157
  skills training, 153

U

Use of theatre in prevention, 205–207
Using media in programs, 225–226

V

Victim, 67–68
  race, 68
  age and sex, 68
  household income, 68
  region, 68
  residence, 68

W

White Ribbon Campaign, 202–203
Women's prevention work, 174–175